THE BLESSING OF GOD

THE BLESSING OF GOD

PREVIOUSLY UNPUBLISHED SERMONS OF
JONATHAN EDWARDS

MICHAEL D. McMULLEN

EDITOR

BROADMAN
&HOLMAN
PUBLISHERS

NASHVILLE, TENNESSEE

0–8054–2617–5

Published by Broadman & Holman Publishers,
Nashville, Tennessee

Dewey Decimal Classification: 252
Subject Heading: SERMONS \ JONATHAN EDWARDS

1 2 3 4 5 6 7 8 9 10 08 07 06 05 04 03

I dedicate this volume to EAB,
who trusted me with her life.

Contents

Acknowledgments

I would like to acknowledge my great debt to Dr. Kenneth Minkema, of the Edwards project at Yale University, who has been a good friend for many years, and a source of much valuable help in my deciphering of Edwards; Leonard Goss of Broadman & Holman, for his enthusiasm for this volume and for giving so much encouragement as the work took shape; Tom Purkaple for his valuable expertise and encouragement on the more technical side of trying to get the microfilms of Edwards's sermons into a manageable form to work on; Mindy Rose, my valuable secretary; and my many good friends among the faculty, administration, staff, and students at Midwestern Baptist Theological Seminary, for all their encouragement in Christ.

I have encouraged my students at Midwestern Seminary to interact as much as possible with primary documents, and many have taken the challenge to become involved in the very difficult work of transcription. Three students made particular contributions to three sermons which appear in this volume. They are Daniel Dorr, Jack Jacob, and Daniel Ruiz.

Introduction
to Jonathan Edwards
the Preacher

The following twenty-two sermons were preached by Jonathan Edwards (1703–1758), the minister of the Congregational Church of Northampton, and later missionary to the Housatonic Indians in Stockbridge, Massachusetts. Edwards became sole pastor of the Northampton church on the death of his grandfather, Solomon Stoddard, in 1729. These sermons have never, to my knowledge, appeared in print before now. They appear here as part of my ongoing interest in the writings and influence of Jonathan Edwards, after having successfully pursued doctoral studies on Edwards, at both the University of Aberdeen, Scotland, and at Yale University.

The manuscripts that these transcriptions are taken from are part of the wonderful manuscript collection of Edwards Papers, housed at the Beinecke Rare Book and Manuscript Library of Yale University. They have been transcribed as a labor of love and are published here by Broadman & Holman as a valuable contribution to the three hundredth anniversary of Edwards' birth. There has been no principle of selection involved in which sermons appear here from the many I am currently working on, except the intention to give a broad range of examples of sermons Edwards preached. So there are examples from both the Old and New Testament; there are brief sermons, together with examples of longer manuscripts; and there are examples of evangelistic, as well as more doctrinal sermons.

Anyone who has ever worked on Edwards's manuscripts—including me—has discovered what a daunting task it is. The condition of the manuscripts, Edwards's shorthand, and even the lack of constructive punctuation, are nothing in comparison with what Thomas Schafer has rightly identified Edwards's handwriting as being, namely, exasperatingly formless. In this edition, Edwards's spelling has been modernized and his shorthand changed into full words. Where he clearly reads a biblical passage, that has been inserted from the King James Version.

Edwards very rarely completely or accurately punctuated his sermons. What punctuation they have is erratic and inconsistent. I am responsible for most of the punctuation that appears in his work. Edwards would often delete words, sentences, and entire paragraphs. Where he has done that, they have not been included in this volume. He would sometimes be reworking the sense of a paragraph and reproducing what he had himself deleted. To have included them could have led to much repetition and an inaccurate sense of his message.

There has never been any lack of material on Jonathan Edwards, but in the twentieth century that stream became a flood, and there seems to be no sign of decline in this interest. Jonathan Edwards was unique in several ways. One of those is the sheer volume of material that has appeared, portraying Edwards as so much more than an eighteenth-century colonial minister who was possessed of an amazing mind. Edwards has been depicted among other things as a bogeyman, philosopher, man of letters, theologian, natural scientist, supporter of missions, and tragedy.

An excellent illustration of the degree of continuing interest in, and the importance of, Jonathan Edwards is to be seen in the range and quantity of scholarly periodicals that have published articles on Jonathan Edwards and his thought; the result reads like a comprehensive index of theological, philosophical, and historical periodicals. I have included a representative sample of periodical titles, together with the dates that an article on Edwards appeared. What must be kept in mind is that there were often several articles in that one volume, and also, that this list is by no means exhaustive:

Accent (1948); *American Literature* (1930); *American Quarterly* (1951); *American Theological Review* (1861); *Andover Newton Quarterly* (1975); *Andrews University Seminary Studies* (1977); *Anglican Theological Review* (1990); *Bibliotheca Sacra* (1976); *British and Foreign Evangelical Review* (1860); *Calvin Theological Journal* (1996); *Center Journal* (1982); *Christian Century* (1993); *Christian Education Journal* (1990); *Christianity and Literature* (1998); *Christianity Today* (1958); *Church History* (1965); *Church Quarterly Review* (1966); *Cithara* (1987); *Concordia Theological Quarterly* (1984); *Congregationalist and Christian World* (1903); *Continental Monthly* (1862); *Crane Review* (1959); *Criticism* (1973); *Crux* (1988);

Dialog: A Journal of Theology (1976); *Duke Divinity School Review* (1966); *Early American Literature* (1970); *Epworth Review* (1998); *Evangelical Quarterly* (1990); *Expository Times* (1994); *Faith and Philosophy* (1990); *Fides et Historia* (1989); *Fides Reformata* (1998); *Forum* (1926); *Foundations* (1978); *Fundamentalist Journal* (1985); *Great Thoughts* (1900); *Hartford Seminary Record* (1903); *Harvard Theological Review* (1988); *Historical Magazine* (1868); *History of European Ideas* (1990); *Hudson Review* (1950); *International Bulletin of Missionary Research* (1997); *Interpretation* (1985); *ISIS* (1951);

Journal for the Scientific Study of Religion (1966); *Journal of American History* (1983); *Journal of American Studies* (1980); *Journal of Ecumenical Studies* (1973); *Journal of Presbyterian History* (1967); *Journal of Psychology and Theology* (1978); *Journal of Religion* (1989); *Journal of Religious Ethics* (1991); *Journal of the American Academy of Religion* (1972); *Journal of the Evangelical Theological Society* (1995); *Journal of the History of Ideas* (1972); *Journal of the History of Philosophy* (1969); *Journal of the Presbyterian Historical Society* (1961); *Lucas* (1993);

Midwestern Journal of Theology (2003); *Munsey's Magazine* (1906); *Nassau Review* (1976); *New England Quarterly* (1949); *New Englander* 1884); *Ohio Journal of Religious Studies* (1976); *Open Court* (1908); *Philosophical Review* (1948); *Preaching* (1992); *Presbyterian* (1998); *Pro Ecclesia* (1995); *Publications of the Colonial Society of Massachusetts* (1931); *Publications of the Massachusetts Historical Society* (1902); *Princeton Seminary Bulletin* (1999); *Princeton University Library Chronicle* (1953); *Reformation and Revival* (1995); *Reformed Review* (1965); *Religion and American Culture* (1993); *Religion in Life* (1958); *Religious Studies Review* (1998); *Review of Metaphysics* (1976); *Revue d'Histoire et de Philosophie Religieuses* (1996);

Scientific Monthly (1949); *Scottish Bulletin of Evangelical Theology* (1997); *Scottish Journal of Theology* (1961); *Soundings* (1969); *Southern Baptist Journal of Theology* (1999); *Southern Quarterly* (1977); *Southern Review* (1875); *St Luke's Journal of Theology* (1990); *Studia Mystica* (1985); *Theological Studies* (1981); *Theologische Zeitschrift* (1978); *Theology Today* (1953); *This World* (1989); *Trinity Journal* (1982); *Union Seminary Quarterly Review* (1975); *Wesleyan Theological Journal* (1984); *Westminster Theological Journal* (1984); *Urban Mission* (1994); *William and Mary Quarterly* (1949); *Word and World* (1984); and *Worldview* (1975).

Who was Jonathan Edwards, and why such interest? Tradition has often represented Jonathan Edwards as a sort of bloodless specter, with pale drawn face, whereas recent scrutiny has found a mind more congruous with the beaming eye and sensitive mouth of the portrait.[1] Puritanism, said T. Schafer,[2] was the skeleton of skeletons in the national closet, until studies in the mid-twentieth century by men like S. E. Morison, H. W. Schneider, R. B. Perry, and especially Perry Miller, seemed to show that the Puritans, in spite of their quaint ideas, were intellectually respectable and, occasionally, even good company.

The similar argument then is also made that Edwards too needs to be "freed from the dust of the past,"[3] for, argues Ola Winslow, "he is one of the few men of the far past who still have something to say to men of the present hour."[4] The present writer also agrees with Bogue's view that the unfortunate plight of Edwards since his own day is that most people have an opinion about him, but apart from the serious student of Edwards few of them have ever read his writings. Bogue is further correct that regrettably it is still true that the image of Edwards hangs suspended by the single thread of one sermon over the pit of popular condemnation.[5] Those who have set aside the stereotype of Edwards the hellfire preacher, and "encountered Edwards' penetrating mind and breathtaking power of literary expression find he exerts a fascination that belies all expectation."[6]

This is not to say that all can or actually will do this. Edwards has always had and probably always will have his detractors. C. Darrow denounced Edwards the hellfire preacher: "Nothing but a distorted or diseased mind could have produced his 'Sinners in the Hands of an Angry God.'"[7] For Darrow as for many others, Edwards' "main business in the world was scaring silly women and little children; and blaspheming the God he professed to adore."[8]

However, it should also be noted that the genius or otherwise of Edwards as displayed in his writings has not been the only way he has

been viewed as being of great value and influence. In the early literature on Edwards, one finds, for example, that Edwards was adopted
by a generation of eugenists who discoursed at seemingly interminable length on the worthiness of his "germ plasm." Both E. A. and
A. E. Winship argued with vigor that Edwards' most important contribution to the world was not the written product of his mind but his
genetic structure. In 1900, A. E. Winship contrasted fourteen hundred
descendants of Jonathan Edwards with twelve hundred descendants
of the pseudonymous "Max Jukes," in a study of intelligence, morality,
and character.[9]

Three years later, E. A. Winship presented a representative array
of Edwards' illustrious descendants.[10] In this article Winship argued
that Edwards's teachings excited no more than a passing interest, and
that his writings were read only by students of literary history.
However, the writer, in common with the other eugenists, considered
his influence as being paralleled by very few men. Winship argued that
what Edwards bequeathed to his lineal descendants is shown by the
striking story of what they have done.

The writer then proceeded to prove the argument by listing the
achievements of Edwards's offspring. Direct descendants became
presidents of Princeton, Hamilton, Union, Amherst, Johns Hopkins,
Litchfield Law School, Andover Theological Seminary, the University
of Tennessee, and the University of California. Also, missionaries in
Asia Minor, Africa, India, China, Hawaii, and the South Sea Islands.
Also numbered among his descendants were sixty eminent physicians;
more than one hundred lawyers; thirty judges; city attorneys of New
York, Philadelphia, and Chicago; mayors of Cleveland, Troy, and New
Haven; governors of Connecticut, South Carolina, and Ohio; several
U.S. representatives; U.S. senators; and U.S. ambassadors. This was a
very detailed work, and it was illustrated with many such examples of

the amazing achievements of the Edwards family, of which the above are only examples of many more.

Three years later D. Lowell produced a similar contribution to this line of argument.[11] Lowell's argument, however, is more specific. There passed between Edwards and his offspring a heredity gene, he says, whose main result was the production of college presidents! Of the five generations that followed Jonathan Edwards, argues Lowell, never was a college president lacking among his direct descendants. Moreover, many of the direct descendants who were disqualified through accident of sex, have, in Lowell's terminology, made college presidents of their husbands!

Not to be outdone, Lowell adds to his list Rutgers, Yale (3), Columbia, and the Carnegie Institution. He then turns from colleges and universities to there being a president of the Association of American Anatomists, a president of the Boston Society of Natural History, one bank president, and a president of three railroads. He then tops the list off with the inclusion of one vice president and one president of the United States.

What is one to say of these studies? One marvels at the time spent on the collecting of the data and respects the utter seriousness with which the material is presented. Is it something that has been outgrown? The answer appears to be no, for similar pieces have continued to appear, drawing the family line even as far as Winston Churchill as a descendant.

On January 18, 1758, Jonathan Edwards paid a last visit to his friend Samuel Hopkins. Edwards had taken several of his own manuscripts with him, and he left them with Hopkins for safekeeping. On January 19, Edwards left, promising to return in the spring. It is said that Hopkins felt a chill of foreboding and that same day wrote to Joseph Bellamy, saying that Mr. Edwards "expects not to return 'til next May," but he grimly added, "Alas, his mantle has gone with him."[12] The spring came, but Edwards never returned.

It would be Samuel Hopkins who would write the first full biography of Jonathan Edwards in 1765. The fact that the record of received subscriptions for Hopkins's planned *Life* of Edwards was very poor could be used to argue that the lack of interest in Edwards that would be displayed later had in fact already begun. Hopkins was not deterred, however, and began to edit several of Edwards's writings for publication. But he soon recorded that "they would not be sold and . . . turned his mind to other projects."[13]

The Boston publishers seemed to have met the local demand for Edwards's writings, but the evidence suggests Edwards became better known throughout Europe. That this is true is proven by the great number of editions of his works that were published in London, Glasgow, and Edinburgh, and the frequent translation of his works into Dutch, French, and German. In fact, ten of his works were soon translated into French, German, Arabic, Gaelic, Dutch, Welsh, and even Choctaw![14]

The lack of American interest may account for the fact that the first collected edition of Edwards' works would not appear for another forty years after Hopkins's *Life*. Even then they would not appear from American presses but British presses. The first American edition was printed two years later, in 1808 at Worcester, Massachusetts. However, by the end of the nineteenth century, Edwards's works had been more widely printed than those of any other American except Benjamin Franklin.[15] Murray argues that the lack of American interest was due directly to the lack of spirituality in America at that time.[16]

Since the "rehabilitation" of Edwards and the Puritans in the twentieth century, Jonathan Edwards has become a man to be reckoned with. Yale University has named one of its colleges after him.

Princeton has had exhibitions in his honor. Wheaton has held confer-
ences on him, as have Yale and Fairleigh Dickinson Universities.
Doctoral dissertations appear at ever-increasing rates. It has been cal-
culated that numbers are doubling every decade, and dissertations
completed twenty or thirty years ago are being revised for publication,
as Edwards becomes increasingly topical and marketable. Scarcely a
work now appears in the fields of American theology, the history of
American philosophy, psychology, religion, literature, or culture, that
does not have something to say about Jonathan Edwards.

The problem is that all this material on Jonathan Edwards exhibits
the great differences of opinion that are held concerning him. This
makes for good scholarship, but it seems that Edwards can almost be
anything to everyone. How can this be? Are they all talking and writing about the same man and the same writings? It probably all goes
back to the outlook and stance of the writers themselves.

The Yale edition of the works of Jonathan Edwards, which produced its first offering in 1957 with *The Will*, has as one of its primary
aims that of letting Edwards speak for himself in a way never before
allowed. The Yale editors promise "a full and complete exposure of his
ideas in a manner never before possible."[17] The need for such an edition had long been felt. Over one hundred years had passed, says
Morris,[18] since the first suggestion for its publication was made. In
fact, there has been no new collected edition of Edwards's works
since the Dwight edition of 1830!

It is not ironic that the president of Yale in 1787 assigned Edwards'
writings to the rubbish of libraries, and now that very same university
is entrusted with the task of publishing the completely new edition of
those writings. Surely the new edition will mean that we will be
obliged to reexamine long-held assumptions about Jonathan Edwards
and his thought. This can only be for the good, for my ongoing
research on Edwards confirms what he has always suspected:

Edwards has been much maligned, often quoted, unfairly caricatured, highly misrepresented, heavily criticized, but hardly ever read. If there is any single aim in my labor of love on the unpublished writings of Edwards, it is to counter that problem. Edwards deserves to be read even—and especially—by those who believe they are opposed to his viewpoints.

NOTES

1. I. W. Riley, "The Real Jonathan Edwards," *Open Court*, 22 (1908), 705.

2. T. Schafer, "MS. Problems in the Yale Edition of Jonathan Edwards," *Early American Literature*, 3 (1968–69), 159.

3. I. W. Riley, 705.

4. O. Winslow, *Jonathan Edwards: Basic Writings* (New York, 1960), xvii.

5. C. W. Bogue, *Jonathan Edwards and the Covenant of Grace* (Cherry Hill, N.J., 1975), 3.

6. D. E. Laurence, "The Foolishness of Edwards," *Worldview*, 18 (1975), 49.

7. C. Darrow, "The Edwardses and the Jukeses," *American Mercury*, 6 (1925), 153.

8. Ibid.

9. A. E. Winship, *Jukes-Edwards: A Study in Education and Heredity* (1900).

10. E. A. Winship, "The Human Legacy of Jonathan Edwards," *World's Work*, 6 (1903), 3,981–84.

11. D. Lowell, "The Descendants of Jonathan Edwards," *Munsey's Magazine*, 35:3 (1906), 263–273.

12. S. Hopkins to J. Bellamy, 19 January 1758 in "Bellamy Papers" as quoted in C. Dennison and R. Gamble, *Pressing Toward the Mark* (1986), 1.

13. E. A. Park, "Memoir of S. Hopkins" in *The Works of S. Hopkins* (Boston, 1854) Vol. 1, 219.

14. T. Johnson, *The Printed Writings of Jonathan Edwards* (New York, 1940), vii.

15. T. H. Johnson, "Jonathan Edwards' Background of Reading," *Publications of the Colonial Society of Massachusetts*, 28 (1931), 196.

16. I. H. Murray, *Jonathan Edwards: A New Biography* (Edinburgh, 1987), 454.

17. S. J. Stein, ed., *Apocalyptic Writings* by Jonathan Edwards (New Haven, 1977), x.

18. W. S. Morris, "The Reappraisal of Edwards," *New England Quarterly*, 30 (1957), 515.

1

The Way to Obtain the Blessing of God Is Not to Let Him Go Except He Bless Us

And he said, Let me go, for the day breaketh. And he said, I will not let thee go, except thou bless me. And he said unto him, What is thy name? And he said, Jacob. And he said, Thy name shall be called no more Jacob, but Israel: for as a prince hast thou power with God and with men, and hast prevailed. And Jacob asked him, and said, Tell me, I pray thee, thy name. And he said, Wherefore is it that thou dost ask after my name? And he blessed him there.

GENESIS 32:26–29

The evidence that we have from the Edwards sermon manuscripts is that he did not begin dating his sermons before January 1733. But scholars connected with the Edwards corpus have done much work on assigning dates to the undated manuscripts, and one of the leading names on this project would be Thomas A. Schafer. The work of deduction and investigation is painstakingly undertaken by analyzing the ink types Edwards used, the various watermarks present in the paper Edwards wrote on, and even the spacing of the chain lines in that paper.

This sermon, which is an example of one of those undated pieces, is an examination of Jacob's wrestling with God. Edwards uses this as an example of one of Christ's several theophanies in the Old Testament and believes that this account was added to typify and represent what he refers to as the wonderful power and prevalency of the faithful and fervent prayers of the saints. Edwards has a simple doctrine. He believes the way to obtain God's blessing is not to let him go until his blessing is given.

To show what it is, Edwards describes what it is not. First, it is not ours by right. Nor will it be received if we are not serious about it, either in our words, actions, or constancy in seeking it. We must also be sure that we acknowledge it as God given and not something worked up of ourselves.

This sermon is an example of a very pointed, direct, and challenging plea from Edwards to believers not to be weary or weak in their prayer lives. In his application he challenges his hearers to seek out for themselves why—if they have not been recipients of God's blessings—that should be the case. He proposes several possible reasons, many of which would have been very hard-hitting.

The sermon manuscript is a typical duodecimal booklet, consisting of twenty leaves with little or no evidence of damage. In the body of the sermon, there is some evidence of deletions, additions, and corrections in Edwards's own hand, but nothing on the scale of a major rework of the sermon as a whole.

We have here that remarkable account of Jacob's wrestling with God. It was at a time when Jacob was expecting to meet his brother Esau, who was now coming out with four hundred armed men upon a hostile design against him. Jacob had divided his company and put them into that order in which he would have them meet Esau and sent them away over the break in the night, but he himself stayed behind alone. Probably it was that he might have the better opportunity to pour out his supplication to God and seek his favor and mercy at that instance when they were so threatened with destruction from Esau and his company. And while he was there alone, there came a man to him as one in a human form and with a human body. It seems to have been the second person in the Trinity that appeared to him.

The Son of God, who had undertaken to be man's mediator and surety and was to take on him the human nature, was wont frequently under the Old Testament to appear in human shape. He probably sometimes occasionally assumed a human body before his proper incarnation as he did when he ate and drank with Abraham in the plains of Mamre and as he did now when he wrestled with Jacob. Whenever God appeared in the Old Testament, it is probable it was the second person of the Godhead by what is said in John 1:18, "No man hath seen God at any time; the only begotten Son, which is in the bosom of the Father, he hath declared him."

We have an account that he came to Jacob and wrestled with him all the remainder of the night. It seems that Jacob did not know that it was God 'til the last. But he doubtless immediately perceived by his appearance, though it was in the night, and also by his conversation that he was some extraordinary person, eminently wise and holy and not a mere man and might think him to be an angel. For Jacob had not been altogether unused to such a thing as angels appearing to him, for he had had a vision of angels at Bethel and the angel of God met him again at Manahaim before this.

Jacob did not only wrestle with him in a figurative sense as the saints may be said to wrestle with God in prayer, but he wrestled with him literally, though he did not know then that it was God.

I will not presume to determine what was the occasion of Jacob's wrestling with him or how they came to be engaged in such exercise.

But I will venture to inform you what appears to me to be probable—that the man who came to Jacob, who appeared to him as a man, had been conversing with Jacob. He appeared to Jacob in his conversation with him so excellent and amiable a person, conversed with him in so condescending and friendly a manner, that Jacob was greatly delighted with his company. And upon his making as though he would go away, Jacob—because he could not bear to part with him—laid hold of him to stay, that he might have more of his company. And the person striving as though he would get away and Jacob to hold him back, hence followed a wrestling between them. Jacob might be emboldened to such freedom by the extraordinary meekness, goodness, and friendliness of his conversation with him. And so it is said, they wrestled 'til break of day.

The person then appears more resolute to depart and says to Jacob, "Let me go, for the day breaketh." Jacob replies, "I will not let thee go, except thou bless me." Jacob was resolved upon this, that if he would depart and he could have no more of his company, yet he would, if possible, obtain his blessing before he went. That extraordinary excellency and word and holiness that appeared in him made Jacob want his blessing. He still did not know that it was God. Upon this, the person asked Jacob what his name was and told him that his name would be no longer *Jacob* but *Israel*. As a prince Jacob had power with God and had prevailed. And upon his saying, "Hast thou power with God?" Jacob began to suspect that it was God. Upon that, Jacob asks him to tell him his name. God did not tell Jacob his name. "Wherefore is it," says he, "that thou dost ask after my name?" But before he departed, he blessed him according to Jacob's desire.

Then Jacob was sensible that it was God and was, as it were, astonished what conversation be his with God himself. Therefore, it is said that "Jacob called the name of the place Peniel: for I have seen God face to face, and my life is preserved." It was a most wonderful fascination, a marvelous manifestation of the infinite grace and con-descension of God to his people. It seems to have been added on pur-pose to typify and represent the wonderful power and prevalency of the faithful and fervent prayers of the saints with God.

DOCTRINE

The way to obtain the blessing of God is not to let God go except he bless us. Under this doctrine I would first explain what is implied in this duty here expressed by not letting go until God blesses. Second, I will show that this is the way to obtain the blessing of God.

1. I would explain the duty here expressed by not letting God go except he bless us, and I will explain it negatively by showing what it is not, by which it will sufficiently appear what it is.

It is not demanding the blessing of God as a mere debt, with a dis-position to contend with him if he doesn't bestow it. Not to let God go in the sense of the doctrine doesn't intend not to let him go as a cred-itor who won't forgive his debtor. He may be said not to let him go, as he in the parable who took his creditor by the throat saying, "Pay me what thou owest."

There are some who won't let God go in this sense. They won't express themselves so in their prayers. "Thy blessing is my due," they say. "I have merited it by what I have done. I have behaved myself so well and have taken so much pain for a blessing that it will be very unreasonable to deny it me. Thou hast bestowed a blessing upon others that did a great deal more to deserve thy curse than ever I did and that none took half so much pain for a blessing. And if thou deny it me, it will be very unfair. I cannot see the reasonableness of it. And therefore I won't let thee go; I'll hold thee to thy obligation. If I am denied I shall look upon myself wronged and think that I have just cause to complain."

I say they won't say so to God. It may be they will express themselves counterwise, but if they should express themselves so, they would express the very thoughts of their hearts. But not letting God go in this sense is far enough from being the way to obtain the blessing of God. 'Tis the way to stir up his fearful indignation to pronounce his curse and to be pursued with his wrath.

The duty expressed in the doctrine is not merely an importuning God for a blessing in words without seeking of it in deeds at the same time. Some people joy in God often for a blessing and in earnestness and in suitable expressions and content themselves with that. They don't at the same time use other proper means but neglect attending of those institutions which God hath appointed as means for the obtaining a blessing and in which he directs them to wait for it. Or if they pray and seem to beg God's blessing but at the same time indulge their lusts and live in some known sin, those are not some of those intended in the doctrine that won't let God go except he bless them nor are they in the way to obtain a blessing. For they know themselves not to be in earnest when they ask God to give them, a blessing and make as if they were constantly desirous of it. Their practice contradicts their words and shows that—let them say what they will—they are not very desirous of it.

Such persons coming importuning to God for a blessing is nothing but a mere mockery. They speak as though they have a right for God to bless them, but they ask as though they designed to provoke God to curse them.

'Tis not asking the blessing of God and at the same time expecting it for ourselves. There is such a thing, and it is common among men. They will beg that God would bestow the blessing upon them and seem to be importunate, but at the same time they expect to have it of themselves. They hope to get it by their own strength. They beg of God to give them his grace and sanctify them. But they are hoping to make themselves holy, to work up their own hearts to a gracious frame, to a disposition to love God and trust in Christ. They who won't let God go except he bless them, they only make a show as though they expected the blessing of him. But they are sensible that it must be he who must bestow the blessing upon them. They can never get it of themselves, and no other can bestow it upon them but God only.

The duty spoken of in the doctrine is not a being constant and fervency in seeking a blessing in a careless and unresolved manner. There are some who seek the blessing after a fast, and they seem to be really constant at it. They keep doing something, and so it may be they continue as long as they live. But yet these be not some of those who are like Jacob who won't let God go except he bless them. They who would imitate him must do something to answer his wrestling. There must be an earnest spirit for a blessing. Jacob was exceeding loathe to let God go. He could not bear the thoughts of parting with him.

So those who do the duty mentioned in the doctrine have a great and very earnest desire for a blessing. They can't bear to think to go without it. They are engaged in their spirits to obtain a blessing and resolved that if it be possible by anything they can do they can obtain a blessing, they will obtain it.

They are so engaged that they seek a blessing with their might. They are vigorous in it and lay out their thoughts. Jacob laid out his strength in wrestling with the angel.

The duty spoken of in the doctrine is opposite to being remiss and dull and lacking, whether it be for want of earnest duties of a blessing or from discouragement. He who will not let God go except he blesses him is sensible of his necessity of a blessing and of the great worth of it and is also encouraged with hopes that it won't be altogether a vain thing to seek a blessing of God. And if God seems to deny him for the present, it doesn't discourage and disventure him so, but that he will still be very earnest for it. A man, when he seeks an earnest of another and be denied it, thinks that asking and pleading is in vain. He will leave off or will have no heart to plead with him.

He who won't let God go except he bless him, he encourages himself by thinking that it may be God will bestow a blessing though he has not yet, yet who can tell but that he will turn and repent and leave a blessing behind him, as in Joel 2:12–14?

'Tis not a being earnest for a blessing in an inconstant way. Some at some times seem to be very earnest and much engaged in their spirits for a blessing. But it doesn't hold they are unsteady in it. They are one while seemingly very earnest. Another while they are cold and remiss, and it may be are as earnest for the world as they were before for a blessing. Or one while they are all for holiness and another while they are for their pleasures and vanities and have their minds taken up about the vanities of youth. These are not some of those who won't let God go except he bless them.

'Tis not being both earnest and constant for a limited or set time. A man takes up a resolution with himself: "I'll seek so long for a blessing, and during that time I'll make a business of it. I'll do all that I can and obtain a blessing in that time. Well if not, I'll leave off and won't trouble myself about it and bereave myself of the comfort of my life any longer."

They who resolve that they will seek a blessing of God for a year or for two years or three years or any other limited time—short of the limits of their—can't be said to resolve that they won't let God go except he bless them. Waiting upon God for his blessing in that way of seeking of that which his Word directs us to is one thing implied in not letting God go except he bless us.

2. Not to let God go except he bless us is the way for us to obtain the blessing. This is the way God hath taught us to seek a blessing. 'Tis the way that Christ has taught. Christ compares it to the wearing out of a person with perpetual importunity. He encourages us to follow

God with incessant prayer for a blessing by representing to us evil men who are very backward and unwilling of themselves to do what another seeks of them, yet may be tired out and overcome with unceasing importunity, as in the parable of the unjust judge and the importunate widow in the beginning of the eighteenth chapter of Luke. There was a widow who besought a judge who feared not God nor regarded man in order to avenge her of her adversary. Now she being a widow and poor, the judge thought he should get nothing by it, and he refused. But she followed him with her importunity so that he was tired out and did what she asked to get rid of the trouble of her importunity. From this example of an unjust judge, Christ encourages us not to let God go, not to let him alone, who is far from being unjust or unmerciful, 'til he blesses us.

Christ teaches us the same thing again in the eleventh chapter of Luke beginning at the fifth verse, in the parable of the man who went to his friend's house at midnight for bread for his guest. The man was loathe to get out of bed to give him what he asked and refused at first. But he continuing his importunity 'til he see the trouble would be greater than of getting up, he finally arose and gave him what he desired.

There is again great encouragement to take this method from the influence of the woman of Canaan, whom we have an account of in the fifteenth chapter of Matthew, beginning with the twenty-first verse. She came and begged Christ to have mercy on her daughter and told him how much she needed his pity, since she was grievously tormented with a devil. First, Christ gave her no answer at all, but she continued still. Then he gave her a repulse and such a repulse that she must be very resolute indeed, not to be repelled by it. But this did not discourage her but only made her the more importunate—and then she obtained the blessing she sought. And the experience of God's people all through the world will confirm that this is the way to obtain the blessing.

I will say a few words respecting the reasons of it. 'Tis not that God needs it to make him willing to bestow the blessing. Or that the will of God is properly overcome by men's importunity. God did not need Jacob's wrestling with him in order to make him willing to bless him. God was willing before and came to him with that design to bless him. God is willing to bless his people, and this is the reason he stirs them up to wrestle with him for a blessing. When God seems to delay and to give repulses to what they seek, 'tis not that he is unwilling, 'tis not because he is backward. He is all the while exceeding ready, for God delights to bestow his blessing as much and more than man delights to have him. And therefore they don't tire him out, though the part be much the same as 'tis with men when they are tired out with importunity and so are represented by it in Christ's parables.

But there are four reasons we shall give why God will bestow his blessing in this way.

1. 'Tis very suitable and becoming that before men have the blessing they should this way show their sense of their need of it and of the value of it. 'Tis very suitable that before God bestows his blessing upon them, persons should be sensible they need it. And 'tis by their importunity and earnest seeking of it—their not letting God go except he bestows it—that they show their sense of their need of it.

'Tis very suitable that before God bestows his blessing, persons should be sensible of the great value of the blessing and the advantage it will be to them. They show also a sense of this by their not letting God go except he bestows it.

2. God's seeming to deny persons the blessing for a while when they seek tends to lead persons to reflect on their unworthiness of the blessing. They have that seeming denial to put them upon thinking what they have done to provoke God to withhold a blessing from

them. While Christ seemed to deny the woman of Canaan what she sought, she was put in mind of her unworthiness. Jesus said, "It is not meet to take the children's bread, and cast it to dogs" (Matt. 15:26). This leads them to seek it in a more humble manner.

3. 'Tis suitable before God bestows the blessing upon a person that he should this way acknowledge him to be the author of the blessing. This earnestly seeking of it of God so as not to let him go 'til he bestows it is a becoming acknowledgment that God is the fountain of blessing and that no other can bestow it but he. This earnestness and resolvedness in seeking it of God shows a person to be in earnest in such an acknowledgment.

4. The person by such a seeking of the blessing is prepared for it. He is put into a suitable disposition to receive it, to entertain it joyfully and thankfully, and to make much of it when it is obtained and to give God the glory of it.

APPLICATION

The application may be in a use of direction. This doctrine may be to direct those who would have the blessing what method to take in order to the obtaining of it. There are many who have some method to have the blessing, but yet how few have obtained it. Most men do to all eternity live under the wrath and curse of God. The greatest blessing that here is bestowed is that which God bestows on men when they are converted. This may be called the blessing. Many seek this blessing but few obtain it. We may conclude the reason is that they don't seek this blessing in the method that we have spoken of. 'Tis not because the blessing is not a thing attainable. All of us have a happy and blessed opportunity to obtain it if we will but take this method in order to it. Here I would particularly apply myself to two sorts of persons.

First, to those who for a long time have been doing something for a blessing and have had no success. You maybe are ready to wonder why God hasn't blessed you who have been seeking of it so long. But haven't you reason to reflect upon yourself and consider whether or not you have ever taken this method? Have you wrestled and reflected that you would not let God go except he blessed you? You who have been seeking a long time have been so many years in the wilderness. But has your heart been earnestly engaged all the while as for the most part for a blessing? Or has it been so in any steady way for one-half the time? You think it may be you have done a great deal, have taken what pains you can. You don't see how you can do any more. But if God should give you a truly earnest engaged spirit, you would soon see how you could do more. By the little opportunity I have had to observe, I think I may judge that when once God gives persons a truly engaged spirit for a blessing, to wrestle and resolve that they will not let God go except he bless them, ordinarily they don't hold on in that way, but a little while before they obtain the blessing.

You are ready, it may be, to be discouraged and think it is in vain for you to seek any longer. You have sought so long and not obtained. But you have no reason to be discouraged, for you have no reason to think it will be in vain for you to seek for anything you have found as yet. For you never have made trial yet of the right way of seeking, whether it will be in vain or no. You never have made trial of this way that you have had on in the text and doctrine. It is not time for you to talk of being discouraged 'til you have made trial.

If you mean that you have reason to be discouraged with the way that you have been seeking in hitherto, that very likely may be true. It may be high time for you to be discouraged with that and to draw up that conclusion that it is like to be in vain to seek as you have done in such a fleshly, dull, irresolute manner any longer, and that it's high time for you to begin in a new method.

It may be you attribute your want of success to God. You say God won't hear you. You fear God has given you up. But you lay it quite wrong. You lay it to God but 'tis all the while to be laid to yourself, to your own coldness and sloth and unresolvedness. God is ready enough to bestow the blessing upon you if you would but seek it with suitable earnestness and resolution. 'Tis no wonder at all God doesn't hear you and give you the blessing in the way that you have sought it hitherto. Here I would purpose two or three things to you more particularly.

1. Haven't you found that when at any time you have been stirred up and thought you would be more earnest than ever that your resolutions have been short-lived? You have been doing something a long time for the blessing and very probably at one time and another when you have heard sermons upon some particular subjects or have seen awful providences, you have for the present been stirred up and thought that you would turn over a new leaf, that you would for time to come seek more earnestly and make more of a business out than ever you had done. But haven't you found that in a little time all this has vanished away and you have been no more earnest than you used to be? And in all this while you have never come to it, both in resolution and deed, not to let God go except he blessed you. And so if your heart abide, you may keep along in such a way 'til you die. You may take up good resolutions from time to time, but soon lose them and never come to be thoroughly engaged as long as you live.

2. Have you reason to think that the world has been one great cause of hindering the business of your seeking a blessing? You have a long time sought salvation and the grace of God but have not yourself been awakened about many things. Have the cares of the world very much taken up your mind and possessed your thoughts? When you have received awakening impressions the word providences, have not the cares of the world soon wore them off and crowded out the thoughts of it? Cannot worldly concerns seem what have in a great measure kept down your concern about your soul all this while and prevented your fasting and wrestling for a blessing as is needful?

Is it not therefore needful that you should now disengage your heart of worldly cares and that you should watch yourself more carefully, that the world be not your attending and that your heart may be taken up about the concern of your souls?

3. Do you not find that there arise more difficulties in this affair of seeking your salvation as you grow older? Don't you find that your heart grows harder? Don't you find that you are not so apt to have impressions made upon you by anything you heard the in Word or by awful providences as once you were? Do you not find that you can hear dreadful things now and be less moved and afflicted than formerly? Don't you find that the older you grow, the less apt you are to be moved with anything? And don't you find it more difficult to engage your thoughts on the things of religion, more difficult to have an engaged spirit in prayer? And are you not more apt to be discouraged than once you were? If it be thus, surely it is judgment enough that it is high time for you to awake out of sleep and alter your soul and now to begin to make more thorough work of seeking salvation.

Second, I would direct myself to those who are but newly setting out in seeking a blessing, if any such are here present. See that you set out in a right method. Take that method that you directed to in the doctrine. It is pity but that you should be well directed now at your first setting out. A person who is setting out on a journey should be sure to take care that he sets out in a right road at his beginning. Otherwise he may travel all day in vain and get nothing in the end but to be lost and it may perish in the woods in the night. Therefore, see to it that you seek in such a manner as you have now been told of, for this is the very way to obtain a blessing.

Here I will briefly forewarn you of two true things you will be in danger of.

1. You will be in danger of looking upon yourself as more in earnest than you be. You will be in danger of judging by your

affections—the affections, your prayers, and the tears you shed, and the like. Those who are very young are commonly very full of such kinds of affections when under some awakening. And yet it may be you have not so seriously resolved as some others, who have so deep a sense of their danger and misery and less things would turn them aside than some who be not half so affectionate. The most affection-ate persons be not always the steadiest. Tears are very deceitful things and are much less to be regarded than some other things.

If you think you are more engaged than you are, it will be a great disadvantage to you, for then you will think you are more likely to obtain than you are and will rest as you be and won't endeavor to be more earnest because you will think you are earnest enough already. And then you won't be aware how little a thing would divert you, and being not sensible of your danger won't be so caring as otherwise you would.

2. You will be in danger of flattering yourself in your beginning and then afterwards falling into discouragement. 'Tis common for persons when they first set out in seeking salvation to flatter themselves that they shall soon get through. Then when they keep along a while and don't find it as they expected, they run into the other extreme and are discouraged.

It may be now in the heat of your affection you think you are resolved, that you will seek 'til you die though it should be fifty years. But it may be you have a secret expectation at the same time that it won't be above one year before you shall obtain. When you come to be disappointed of your expectation, you won't hold your resolution of seeking as long as you live and never would have made such a prom-ise to yourself of seeking as long as you lived, but only you promised yourself at the same time that you should never have occasion to seek half so long. It is this that makes you so sure of your promises you never expect to have occasion to perform.

3. You will be in danger of having carelessness about your soul flood upon you insensibly. You will be in danger of lacking concern and convictions. Probably for a good while after you have begun to lose them, flatter yourself that you hope you have not left your convictions but are as much concerned as ever in the general.

Like a person in a consumption or under some other lingering distemper, the distemper steals on them insensibly and often flatters them. The patient flatters himself that he doesn't grow worse, and sometimes he hopes he grows better. And so often they will flatter themselves 'til they see their strength and life is almost gone and death again approaching.

2

That Such Persons Are Very Imprudent and Foolish Who Don't Consider Their Latter End

O that they were wise, that they understood this, that they
would consider their latter end!
DEUTERONOMY 32:29

This sermon was preached by Edwards in the winter of 1728 while he was still assistant to Solomon Stoddard, who was not only Edwards's grandfather but was held in such high regard that he was known as the "pope" of New England.

This is a very clear sermon on the folly of living only for the present and of not giving serious consideration to the important issue of one's latter end. Edwards's argument is simple—that just as a person in the natural state should give careful thought to the end of the paths he chooses in life, how much more should this apply in the spiritual and eternal realm.

Edwards reminds his hearers of the inevitability and certainty of death for everyone. Then he makes clear that death is only a passage into another state that there is no end to. One finds in many of Edwards's sermons the fact of the uncertainty and unpredictability of life in his day. This is a theme that he used often and to great effect. Edwards speaks, for example, of the high mortality rate, of the ever-present danger of serious sicknesses, of the danger of losing one's reason, and the imprudence of not considering seriously these truths. If one looked for a brief summary of all Edwards says here, it would be, "Get ready for death; be prepared."

The sermon manuscript is an example of an oversize original. But it is slightly different from most of Edwards's other large-format sermons, in that pages have been used from a variety of sources, some of which made the sermon too wide even to be placed in Yale's oversize file. Of the total twenty leaves, several leaves seem to have the typical semicircle cuts reminiscent of fan paper, and several pages also show signs of water damage.

Prophets foretold. The children of Israel put these warnings far away either out of their minds by unbelief or inconsideration. This is part of Moses' song, which he wrote and left among the children before he died. He warned them of their future perverseness and of that great inclination they had to wander and to forsake the God who chose them for his peculiar people and of the judgment and anger of God that they will from time to time expose themselves to by their folly and stiff-neckedness. He leaves it with them that it might be as a glass wherein they might at all times behold their own hearts to be a continued sign to them suited to their case in future ages.

God was well aware of the dreadful perverseness of that nation. He told them all along that he did not choose them because they were better than other people, for they were a stiff-necked people. He knew how often they would grieve him and forsake him and fall off to the worship of other gods. In this song he prophetically represents it to them how it will be. He tells them in verse 22 and the following verses what judgments and vengeance they must expect when they thus corrupt themselves: "For a fire is kindled in mine anger, and shall burn unto the lowest hell, and shall consume the earth with her increase, and set on fire the foundations of the mountains. I will heap mischiefs upon them; I will spend mine arrows upon them." In the twenty-eighth verse, he complains of their ignorance and folly that they will run themselves into such misery when they might, if they pleased, live quietly and happily in the care and charge of the true God. "They are a nation void of counsel, neither is there any understanding in them."

In our text God manifests himself as grieved for their great folly in thus undoing themselves and lightheartedly wishing that it was otherwise and that they were wise so that they could understand this and that they would consider their latter end.

Here observe:

1. What is that so desirable thing that God wishes for in his people—that is their being wise. So merciful and so compassionate is he toward them that he laments that imprudence whereby they undo and ruin themselves.

2. What is that great point of wisdom which God more especially wishes for in them—and that is that they would consider their latter end. Those words that they understood this from probably relate to what is said in the following verses or that they understand this. How should one chase a thousand and two put ten thousand to flight, except their Rock had sold them, and the Lord had shut them up?

DOCTRINE

It shows great folly and sottishness of men to mind only what is present and not consider what is future. That such persons are very imprudent and foolish who don't consider their latter end. They are as the expression is in the twenty-eighth verse, "Void of counsel, neither is there any understanding in them."

The following things are included in considering our latter end.

1. A considering what will be the issue and event of our actions and manner of life. The latter end of anything is frequently put in Scripture for the issue of a thing. It is every man's prudence to consider where he is going and what he is doing, to ponder the paths of his feet and consider where it will land him. If a man is traveling, if he has common understanding and prudence, he will consider where the path that he is going in will lead and whether it will lead him home or to his desired place, or whether it would lead him where he is lost or to an enemy's country, where he is likely to be lost and ruined.

So in whatever business a man sets himself about, it is reckoned as a point of prudence to consider what will be the issue to consider, what benefit he is like to keep of his labors. In the scales with the pain and loss he sustains, he needs to see whether he is likely to get anything by it or whether he will run himself to ruin.

So it above all things becomes a man of prudence to consider what is likely to be the issue of the cause and manner of life that he is engaged in. Men take every affluent course, and some live after a manner exceeding different from others. Some choose a sober and religious life, a life of self-denial and conscientious obedience to God's commands. Some live a vicious and sinful life, live in a way of gratifying their lusts. Some live a worldly life. All their thoughts and all their desires and all their endeavors pursue after riches and worldly profits. Some live a sensual life. Their main pursuit is the pleasure of sense. Some live a life of intemperance and hard drinking. Some live a luxurious life, spend their time very wastefully in much bad company in extravagant, determined talk and lascivious conversation.

Now it is every man's prudence to consider what his manner of life is likely to bring him to. It won't be always as it is now. It won't be always with godly men as it is now, nor will it be always with the ungodly as it is now. Their state will be changed—that we all very well know. The state of some will be changed one way and of others another according to their different manner of life. The paths that some go in lead quite contrary ways from the paths that others go in, and they lead to very different places and conditions. It becomes those who live a godly life, a life of obedience to God, to consider what will be the end of that life. They need to consider all the difficulties that it is likely to bring them into, all the advantages they are likely to obtain, and compare them together.

It becomes those who choose worldly things to consider what they are likely to get by it, and what they are likely to cause, and what the end of all will be a great while hence, and to compare the worldly profit they hope to get with those spiritual and eternal profits they are likely to cause and with the worth of their own souls, which they are likely to lose. So it becomes them who give themselves up to a sensual life with a neglect and disregard of the concerns of their soul and another world to consider what their manner of life is likely to bring them to, what benefit they are likely to get by it in this world, and what they are likely to get by it in another world.

2. To consider our latter end is also to consider the end of our lives. The life of every man will have an end. It is appointed to all men once to die. There are many things that men are told of about another world, but they don't very much regard because they never saw them. But this truth is what everyone sees. The world has found it true through all successive ages that all men must die. Nor is death a thing that is so far off that one can scarcely think of it or hardly comprehend the intermediate time, but at furthest it is near to every man. Forty or fifty or sixty or seventy years will appear but a very short time if we consider how quick those revelations are repeated so many times. It concerns every man therefore to consider that this is so certain, and that this is so near, and that this is so great a thing. Death is not a light matter, not worth a regarding and thinking much about. But if

33

anything in this world is of such concern and importance, and to be worth regarding, death is—for it is an end to all the things of this world. Indeed, if that were an utter end to our beings—let us consider what we would and do what we would—it would not alter the case.

Then indeed it would be hardly worth the while to think much about it to no other purpose but only to make our lives so much the more uncomfortable. But the best way then would be to direct ourselves from the thoughts of death as much as we could. It would be a kindness to us if we might die suddenly in a moment, before we had time to think of it, but it is not so. When men are dead, they be not done with; there is not an end of them. But death is only a passage into another state that there is no end to.

Therefore it is great folly and argues that men are void of prudence if they do not consider and provide against death. If men are going on a journey or a voyage, they are careful to provide beforehand for it— to get all matters ready. Men know that winter will come, and they are careful to lay up food for themselves and their children and cattle against that time. Men who don't take care against such times are careless as slothful, imprudent men. How much more imprudent are they who don't consider that death is coming and make ready against it.

Particularly there are these following things that 'tis our prudence often to consider of relating to the end of our lives.

1. The uncertainty of the time of it. It is strange that the world should so delude themselves with such sort of imaginations that there is no great danger that they shall die, when reason and experience and the Word of God teach the great uncertainty of life. Indeed this is a thing that all will own and seem to be sensible of in others. They dare not trust their estates in a dependence upon another man's life. But yet most men do secretly flatter themselves as if there were no great danger of their own dying very soon.

Sinners are very often disappointed with regard to these promises they make themselves; the greater part of them die. They are surprised by death. It comes upon them and answers contrary to their expectation, and then they will own their folly and imprudence that they did not duly consider how uncertain their lives were. They are very full of it and much in warning others not to put off, but yet the living won't take warning by it. They think though it did happen that such a person died suddenly and died in youth that they may live 'til they are old for all that. And it may be by and by, some of them also are taken sick and die. Then they regret their folly, yet others who live will still flatter themselves. Such madness is in men's hearts while they live, and afterwards they go to the dead.

If we consider how many more people die before they are old than after they arrive to old age, then no particular person has any peculiar reason to think that he shall live 'til he is old when others have not. We shall find that such an expectation of living long is groundless and unreasonable because if everyone entertains such an expectation, we know that according to the ordinary course of things, it will fall out more often contrary to such an expectation, than according to it.

2. It concerns men to consider what death would be to them if it should find them unprepared. Thus multitudes of men, the greatest part, are hitherto unprepared for death. As death shoots his arrows among mankind and hits one and another without distinction, so the greater part of them who are smitten are unprepared. For if the greater part of them who live are unprepared, undoubtedly the greater part of those who die are also unprepared. Death does not distinguish but falls upon all sorts alike.

It therefore especially concerns those who are not prepared for death to consider how it would be to die unprepared. What would it be to hear the cry made, "Behold, the bridegroom cometh; go ye out to meet him"(Matt. 25:6), and to have no oil in their vessels. When persons die of sickness, if they have the exercise of their reason, they generally have notice of approaching death. Before it comes they have opportunity to see that they are going, that nature is dissolving, and when the distemper prevails so far that it gives notice that death is certainly coming, then is the midnight cry. When that cry is made and they are sensible that they are unprepared, it must needs put them into a dreadful amazement. There is a fearful expectation when they see they must go, and the medicines of physicians signify nothing. They are given over by them, and their friends give them over and start weeping over them, as those whom they are going forever to part with. The sinner sees that he must certainly go and appear before God, and he expects an hour when his soul shall be swallowed up in the pit—in the pit of everlasting darkness. They see that their breath fails more and more, and their extreme parts begin to grow cold. They feel death creeping on them, and the shadows of death are drawing over their eyes.

It concerns sinners to consider this their latter end, to consider how it would be with them at such a time. Men who don't act brutishly will consider these things, for there is no sinner who knows that it will not be his own case. What judgment they should make of many things, they now plead for and say there is no heart in. What judgment they should make of a holy life and serious godliness, whether they should not think that those who made their spiritual concern their main concern be not the wisest, most prudent men, and whether they should not have made this their great concern.

They should also consider how another world would look to them at such a time. What they should think of judgment and hell and the wrath of God which they make such a light matter of now and seem to be unconcerned about they should care. How it would be with them with regard to those things, for it may be in a little while they will have the trial.

We don't know indeed that we shall have notice beforehand of approaching death. Some are soon deprived of the use of their reason and are so far the most part 'til they go out of the world, and some are suddenly killed by accidents. But we had so much the more need to consider of death beforehand, far off though it should be. We should have no time of consideration then for as it concerns them to consider how it would be so by going out of the world to be in immediate expectation of death, so also how it would be to them actually to die and to have the union broken between soul and body. After they have been in a fearful expectation of it and have seen it gradually coming upon them irresistibly, notwithstanding all that they can do, or their friends can do, or physicians can do, at last actually to have their souls fired on by devils and so harried down into hell to enter that horrid company and that dreadful place of torment. God being inexorably and shutting them forever out of his presence and pouring his wrath upon them.

3. They should consider what an exceeding different thing death would be to them if they were prepared for it. Death is awful in itself, terrible in nature, and there is that in death which is awful even to most godly persons. This is true not only because of the pains of death, but upon several other accounts it is an awful thing forever to take leave of all that is in this world, to leave friends and relations, to have a period put to all business and designs in the land of the living, and to their present state of existence. It is an awful thing to go into eternity, to go into a hitherto-unseen world. One had need not only to have a strong hope of their good estate, but even to be absolutely certain and to have the peculiar presence of God, and a more than ordinary manifestation of his love in order to take away all the dread of these things.

God must be with them in a more than ordinary manner, if they are quite above the fear of all ill when they walk through the valley of the shadow of death. God often favors his people with a more-than-common assistance and light in that time of need and so to support their spirits that they are not overcome by the torrents of death. Sometimes he gives them such light as carries them clear beyond all fear, makes them to triumph gloriously over all the pain and darkness of that hour. But when it is so, 'tis because God gives peculiar light. However, there is always a vast difference between the death of the righteous and of the wicked. Generally the godly have peace and comfort in their death and a joyful hope that when they die they go to their best beloved and their dearest friend and shall enter into the heavenly society, and they shall be blessed forever in the enjoyment of God the Father and Jesus Christ and shall thenceforward be filled brimful with the Holy Ghost. Proverbs 14:32 says, "The wicked is driven away in his wickedness: but the righteous hath hope in his death." There is a great deal of difference between him who is a dying and is sensitive, he is going directly to the furnace of God's wrath to be there forever, and him who hopes through the grace of God and love of Christ to enter into eternal blessedness.

And though it be possible that a godly man may be in great darkness when he is about to die, yet there is a great difference between the death of such an one, and one who dies in a natural condition. For death to the one puts an end to all his darkness and lets his everlasting light shine where there is no more fear or torment, no more pain or sorrow, and tears are wiped from their eyes. Revelation 21:4 says, "And God shall wipe all tears from their eyes; and there shall be no more death, neither sorrow, nor crying, neither shall there be any more pain: for the former things are passed away." Whatever sorrows the godly meet with in this world, or whatever darkness or fears they may have upon a deathbed, yet "blessed are the dead which die in the Lord from henceforth: Yea . . . they rest from their labours; and their works do follow them" (Rev. 14:13).

4. Another thing implied in considering our latter end is considering and meditating upon the last judgment that we are to be the subjects of. This will be the latter end of the world and the conclusion of this state of things. This world is not made to last forever, and there is a time when it will have a period put to it, and God will call to an account the inhabitants of it, how they have lived upon it. God has told us of this judgment, and since we ourselves are to be the subjects of it, therefore this judgment greatly concerns us. He has given us in his Word a description of it for this end—that we may consider it and be stirred up to provide for it. Ecclesiastes 11:9 says, "But know thou, that for all these things God will bring thee into judgment."

God has told us by whom this world is to be judged, even by Jesus Christ the God-man, and in what glory and majesty he shall descend in the clouds of heaven with all the holy angels with him. He has told us how suddenly and unexpectedly it shall be. He has told how the dead should be raised at the sound of the trump of God, and how the godly shall be caught to meet the Lord in the air and be separated from the wicked, the one placed on the right hand, the other on the left, and how every faint thing shall than be brought to light, and the books shall be opened, and all shall be judged out of those things that are found written in the books. We have an account of what sentence shall be pronounced upon both the one and the other, and how the world shall at that day be set on fire and shall be dissolved in devouring flames, and the heavens shall depart and be rolled together as a scroll.

Surely these things are great enough to be considered by us. It is worth the while to take pains to provide against that day, especially considering that this case is the only time that it will avail us anything to consider of it. It is foolish to neglect the consideration of it because it is a great way off, for it is the same thing to us as if it were as near as our death. For then it will be determined how it will go with us at that day of judgment, and when that day comes, it will as much concern us.

It will be as much to our misery if we are not prepared and as much to our benefit if we are ready for it as if it were to be tomorrow.

5. Another thing that is implied in our considering our latter end is considering our last state, our eternal condition. There are two states that are the last states of mankind. The one is a state of perfect holiness and perfect happiness, the closest union and most intimate communion with God and Christ Jesus and the most dear fellowship with saints and holy minds forever, being perfectly blessed in both soul and body. And there is another state that is the last state of the greater part of mankind that is quite the reverse of this. It is a state of perfect separation from God and eternal removal from all his goodness, and a state of enduring of his displeasure and the fierceness of his wrath. This will be in a place where there is nothing to be seen but dismal tokens of God's anger in a company of devils and wicked, miserable spirits, being miserable both in soul and body forevermore.

Certainly if it be so in everyone's wisdom to consider it and be wholly influenced by the consideration of it. The thing is so great that it can't but have influence if it be duly considered.

We should often consider what it would be like to be rejected of God, cast away from him as the object of his loathing and have the almighty God, eternally and without ceasing, executing his vengeance on us. We should often consider the dreadful descriptions that are given of hell in the Word of God, and what an amazing consideration it is to think of suffering to such an extremity, not for a month or a year or an age but forever and ever. And on the other hand, what a blessed thing it will be to live in a perfect fullness of happiness and pleasure with certain security that we never lose it, that no creature shall ever deprive us of it.

Now it is great imprudence and folly to neglect the consideration of these things. We shall briefly sum up the reasons of it under the four following heads:

1. He who doesn't consider his latter end is exceedingly imprudent because he is careless about obtaining his greatest interest and avoiding his own latter undoing. Prudence may be defined as that habit of mind whereby a man is guided and influenced to make choice of the best methods for his own true advantage. He who doesn't consider and provide against death and eternity, however careful he may be of his worldly advantage, is negligent of his greatest happiness and foolishly orphanages himself into absolute and everlasting destruction. He minds only his present gratification. He follows his present ease and pleasure, and regarding what will become of him at last he is trying to obtain the pleasures or profits of the world, and by that means he at length loses them and loses himself too. He loses all his worldly goods and cuts himself from ever obtaining any other part of good, and is past help, immersed into all sorts of evil, and this is for want of considering because he carelessly went on and would not consider where he was going.

2. He is careless when he has a very fair opportunity of securing his great interest. Men are at liberty to choose. God has set life and death before them, and it is left for their choice. A Savior is offered to them upon condition that they will fix themselves to him and give themselves to him.

3. Their imprudence appears in that they are careless though the opportunity be uncertain. It would be no strange thing if the opportunity should be at an end within a month or a week or even a day. For we know not what a day may bring forth, if there be an opportunity of a very good bargain, and if it is uncertain how long it will last. Man will be in hope they won't let joy slip, but yet so imprudent are many that they take no care to improve the uncertain opportunity to save themselves from the eternal wrath of God.

4. They neglect to prepare for their latter end for a matter of nothing. They be not careless about preparation for death because they are

pursuing some other good as great as that and which they stand as much in need of but for those trifles—those vanishing, unsatisfactory enjoyments that can stand in no comparison with it. Some for the sake of food to nourish, and raiment to clothe the body, will neglect both body and soul so as to suffer both, to sink down into everlasting burning. Others sell heaven and run into hell for the sake of strong drink, others for the sake of the gratification of lasciviousness, quit all spiritual delights in the enjoyment of everlasting love of Christ and consign their bodies to eternal torments. Others for the sake of extravagant mirth and jollity will run the venture of weeping and wailing and gnashing of teeth to endless ages. Such madness is in the hearts of those who don't consider their latter end.

APPLICATION

Everyone is exhorted to consider and prepare for their latter end. It is such folly and great imprudence to neglect this as we have shown. You be entreated not to be guilty of such great imprudence. I would especially entreat those who live careless and vicious lives, who neglect duties of religion such as secret prayer and reading the Scriptures and are persons not of a sober but vain conversation. Do be wise and consider your latter end. Consider what will be the issue of your present life. Are you so stupid as to look only at the present moment and have no consideration of a hereafter? Don't you care what becomes of you when you die? Is that the reason that you no more consider your latter end? If you do but consider, your reason will tell you that trouble and misery hereafter will be as hard for you or no.

'Tis not at all more eligible to suffer tomorrow than today. You will hate pain and sorrow and torment as much when you come to die and after you are dead as you do now. You will not be at all more insensible of pain in that world that looks to you like a dream. Then in this world it will not look like a dream when your time comes, but you will be as one awakened out of a dream, for a person's sense and perception will be abundantly quicker and more lively hereafter than at present.

Be entreated to be so prudent and careful of your own comfort and interest as to consider and prepare for your own death and not to put it off. You can't but be sensible that you shall be glad of it, if you do it and that you will bewail it if you don't do it. You expect to repent it. Why therefore will you do it? You won't repent if you be not convinced that it is foolish and imprudent. If you expect to be convinced of that, how grave is your folly in doing that which you expect you to be convinced is exceeding foolish! You know very well that if you were upon your deathbed and were sensible that you were going into eternity, you would not approve of many things that you now allow yourself in. Yea, you intend to bewail it and condemn yourself for them, and yet such is your folly that you practice them from day to day.

Be exhorted to consider of eternity, of your own eternity. Consider this, that God has given you a being not among beasts that perish, but among those who have immortal souls, and that seeing you have already a being, you must have a being henceforward forever, and that your being won't be in a state of indifference in a middle state and a changeable state always, but that after a while, it will be fixed and will be one or the other of the extreme states. There is an eternity that belongs to every man. Take the whole of duration of every man as eternity. You began that duration already, and why should you take care for the first forty or fifty years of it and not take care of the rest? If your whole duration was to be but a thousand years, you would be imprudent if for the sake of care and pleasure for the first forty or fifty years, you should expose yourself to misery through all the rest. But much more so when for the sake of pleasing yourselves for the first few years, you will be tormented all the rest of eternity.

Is it because the other part of your duration is to be in another world, and you don't think it so much worth the while to concern yourself about it for that? But how unreasonable is that, for misery in another world will be as bad as if it were in this world, and happiness will be as good to you.

I have chosen to speak upon a subject of this nature because of the deaths that have lately happened, and the threatening sickness of others, hoping that God's providence with his world might work some effect upon you. Persons are apt enough in time of spreading sickness and mortality to be afraid of their lives. Commonly at such times, many persons are stirred up to see a greater appearance of religion than at other times. Though they are generally as sailors in a storm, as soon as the storm is over, they are quickly returned to their old course. But God may make such dispensations issue in the thorough reformation and conversion of some and oftentimes does. But those who will neither be awakened by God's Word nor providence are set to a great degree of hardness and have great reason to fear, lest they should be some of those who will be suddenly destroyed, and that without remedy.

3

~⊷⊜ ⊜⊷~

It Is a Matter of Great Comfort and Rejoicing to Anyone in Whatever Circumstances He Is In, When He Can Say That He Knows His Redeemer

For I know that my redeemer liveth.
JOB 19:25

This is an example of a sermon that Edwards originally preached in Northampton and then preached again during his years as a missionary to the Housatonic Indians at Stockbridge. It was first preached in 1740 and then preached again in 1755.

This is a message designed primarily to bring great comfort to the saints. Edwards makes clear that whoever we are, whatever we do or do not possess, whatever the state of health we are in, and whatever our circumstances (and he describes many such examples in detail), if we belong to God and know him as our living Redeemer, then we have many reasons to rejoice. The soul with whom it is thus, says Edwards, dwells on high.

In an extended application, Edwards wastes no opportunity to exhort those in a Christless condition to compare their current state with that of a person so privileged.

The sermon manuscript is a typical, though lengthy, duodecimal booklet, consisting of forty-nine leaves with no evidence of damage. In the body of the sermon, there is some evidence of deletions, additions, and corrections in Edwards's own hand, but nothing on the scale of a major rework of the sermon as a whole. The application is lengthy, consisting of twenty-seven pages.

In saying these words, "For I know that my redeemer liveth," Job seems to have an eye to the reproaches that his three friends cast upon him and so much insist upon—that he was a hypocrite and a wicked man. He says in the twenty-third verse, "Oh that my words were now written." That is, "Those words that I am now going to say which are said in the verse of the text and two next verses, I know that."

He wishes that these words were written and so graven that they might never wear out to the end, that it might be remembered that he said them even 'til the event proves them to be true. That men at the latter day, when Christ should come and stand upon the earth, might remember how positive he was interested in him and that he would then appear as his Redeemer, notwithstanding all the uncharitable and reproachful suggestions of his three friends to the contrary. Then it might be seen who was in the right—they who said he was a hypocrite or that he who was so positive to the contrary.

Job's worth is accordingly fulfilled. God so ordered that these words should afterward be written in a book by the direction of his own Holy Spirit. This is where they have remained for more than three thousand years and are more durable than if they were engraven with an ink pen and lead in a rock. They will remain 'til his words are fulfilled, 'til Job's Redeemer stands at the latter day on the earth. Then he whose body has long ago been destroyed with worms shall see God in his flesh and shall see him for himself.

There are two things that I would now take notice of concerning these words of Job.

1. What is the privilege that he professes himself—that he knows that his Redeemer lives and be the subject of.

2. How much he has when this privilege is professed. How precious the matter of his profession is to him that he should so deserve to have his words by which he makes his profession so written or engraven, that they may remain forever in indelible characters. He speaks of his privilege with an air of triumph as that which he comforts himself in. He glories in the midst of his great affliction under which his skin was already destroyed with sore boils all over him from the crown of his head to the sole of his feet, and wherein he was so deserted by his former friends and so disposed and reproached by them as a wicked man and a notorious hypocrite.

DOCTRINE

It is a matter of great comfort and rejoicing to any person, whatever circumstances he is in, when he can say that he knows that his Redeemer lives.

I would take notice of the several things contained in this profession and show how it is a matter of great comfort and rejoicing to anyone when they can say thus.

First, I would show what is implied when anyone can say that he knows that his Redeemer lives.

1. It implies that he knows that Christ is the appointed Redeemer and Savior of men. It implies a knowledge of Christ's divine mission that he was no imposter but indeed a person sent from God to reveal

his mind and will. It implies a knowing that he is the Messiah as he professed himself to be and that he is the person whom God has pitched upon and sent into the world and that he might be the Savior of men from their sins and from eternal destruction. It implies what Peter professed in John 6:69, "We believe and are sure that thou art that Christ, the Son of the living God."

It implies that he knows the truth of the gospel and that it can be said of him what Christ said of his disciples to the Father in John 17:7–8, "Now they have known that all things whatsoever thou hast given me are of thee. For I have given unto them the words which thou gavest me; and they have received them, and have known surely that I came out from thee, and they have believed that thou didst send me."

It implies a knowing that the Scriptures are the Word of God and that the Word is true and that the way of salvation revealed in the Scriptures is the very way of life and that there is no other name given under heaven whereby we must be saved but the name of Christ.

2. Another thing contained in the knowledge that is professed in the text is knowing that Christ lives. This signifies four things:

Knowing that he is in possession of life in himself. It implied in Job's time that he was the living God, that he was not as those idols that the heathen worshiped, things without life. And now in the days of the gospel it implies that we know that Christ is risen from the dead and so is alive as the God-man. And so that it is true what Christ cries of himself in Revelation 1:18, "I am he that liveth, and was dead." If Christ were not risen he could not be our Savior. The apostle Paul says in 1 Corinthians 15:17, "If Christ be not raised, your faith is vain; ye are yet in your sins," and they who are fallen asleep in Christ are perished.

Knowing his sufficiency as the author and fountain of life. The sufficiency of false gods is often represented in Scripture in that they were things without life, dumb idols, lifeless sticks and stones, and so not able to help those who trusted in them. But the sufficiency of the true God and his ability to save those who trust in him is often represented in that he is the living God, and the sufficiency of Christ to save us and give us life is represented by the same thing. He is a sufficient Savior because he is a living Savior: "Wherefore he is able also to save them to the uttermost that come unto God by him, seeing he ever liveth to make intercession for them" (Heb. 7:25).

Christ tells his disciples in John 14:19 that because he lives they shall live also. He is sufficient for them as a fountain of life to them. And in this, Job comforts himself that though he should die and worms should destroy his body, yet his Redeemer lives and is sufficient to restore him to life that he might still see his Savior in his flesh at the latter day.

3. *Knowing his faithfulness and unchangeableness as a Savior.* There are many who have formerly appeared to be friends to others who live still, but yet that friendship does not live as men. They live, but as friends they are dead. Job professes his faith in that Christ not only lives himself but lives as his friend and Redeemer. His promise lives, his word is established as a pure record in heaven, and his faithfulness to his promise lives. His mercy lives. He is a Redeemer of the same grace and mercy that ever he was. His love to him who believes on him lives, for whom he loves he loves to the end. He hath loved them with an everlasting love.

He loves as the fountain of their good, a living spring whose stream never dries up. This Job comforts himself in. He in himself alone was a mutable being subject to great changes. He had passed under great changes already. He was suddenly brought down from a state of health and wealth and great earthly glory, to a state of the greatest meanness and poverty and distress and wounds. His skin was destroyed with sore boils, and he should still be the subject of a greater change. His body that was now diseased should die. Those worms that were on his body had already devoured his skin: "My flesh is clothed with worms and clods of dust; my skin is broken, and become loathsome" (Job 7:5). And his body should yet become the subject of a greater change, in that the time would soon come when the worm that had destroyed his skin should destroy his body. But though he was subject to such changes, yet that was his confidence—that his Redeemer was unchangeable.

Knowing that he is an everlasting Savior. That he will live forever and that his power and his mercy and his wrath will be forevermore. This Job comforts himself in. He wishes that his words were so written or engraven that they might remain forever as his Redeemer shall live forever. Though he should die and be devoured with worms, yet therein he rejoices that his Redeemer should never die but should live forevermore, agreeable to Revelation 1:18, "I am he that liveth, and was dead; and, behold, I am alive for evermore."

The third thing contained in the privilege spoken of in the doctrine is knowing that Christ is our Redeemer. Thus Job professed not only that he knew that Christ was a Redeemer and that he lived, but also that he was *his* Redeemer. That when he should see him standing on the latter day on the earth, "I know that my redeemer liveth." It implies not only that we know that Christ is a divine and glorious person but that he with all his glory is ours. Not only a knowing that he lives but that he lives for *us*. That he is risen from the dead and ascended into heaven in our name and as our forerunner. That he has loved us and lived for us, agreeable to the profession which the apostle Paul made in Galatians 2:20, "Who loved me, and gave himself for me."

'Tis a knowing not only that he has promised such and such unspeakable blessing to them who believe, but knowing that we do believe and so that the promises are made to us and that the glory shall be bestowed upon us.

I come in the second place to show how it is matter of comfort and rejoicing in all circumstances when any person can say thus.

1. 'Tis reasonable ground of comfort and rejoicing in all circumstances, whether persons are rich or poor, if they can say as truly Job did in the text, they have reason to rejoice. If they are destitute of those conveniences and comforts of life that others have and meet with great difficulties and are driven to great straits, are often hungry and have not food to satisfy their hunger and know not which way to turn to provide themselves clothing for themselves and their families, yet if they can say that they know their Redeemer lives, they have enough. They are richer than earthly kings commonly are. They have food to eat that others know not of that is of a most refreshing and satisfying nature. They feed lavishly and dine highly, for they dine upon the bread which came down from heaven; they dine upon angels' food.

If they are looked upon as mean and are despised in the world, are less regarded than their neighbors, their words are not so much heard, they have not much respect shown them—yet if they can say, "I know that my Redeemer lives," they have reason to set their hearts at rest about the esteem of men. God has given better honors than that which is of men. They are highly advanced in honors; they are God's children and heirs to a glorious crown.

If they labor under infirmity of body and a broken constitution and are some of those who never eat with pleasure and don't know what it is to enjoy health and the common benefits of life that others do, yet if they can say, "I know that my Redeemer lives," they have enough to strengthen them with strength in their souls. They have that in their spirits that may well sustain their infirmity and make them strong in weakness.

If they have painful and destroying diseases and have words from days and nights appointed to them, yet if they can say, "I know that my Redeemer lives," they have that which may well quiet them and comfort and make them exceeding glad in all their tribulations. Though they have outward pain, yet they may have inward pleasure and peace that passes all understanding.

If they are exercised with bereavements and God has taken away very dear friends, pleasant companions, or children, or God has taken from them loving and prudent parents who were great comforts and blessings to them, yet if they can say, "I know that my Redeemer lives," they may have comfort in their mourning. They have no reason to mourn as others. Their hearts have no cause to sink under their bereavements. The consideration that their Redeemer lives may be sufficient to give them the oil of joy for mourning and the garments of praise instead of the spirit of heaviness.

If they think of their sins, if the dreadful corruption of their hearts is discovered to them and the sins of their practice in all their multitude and in their blackest aggravations stand before them staring them in the face, yet if they can say, "I know that my Redeemer lives," they need not be distressed with their sins. Let them be never so many and great. The view of them may well humble them but not discourage them in the least. Instead of sinking with the thoughts of their sins, they may well thereby have their hearts so much the more employed in praise and glorying in God's mercy and the love of Christ and cry triumphantly, "I have an advocate with the Father, even Jesus the Christ, and in the Lord Jehovah have I righteousness" (see Isa. 12:2; 1 John 2:1).

If the town or land where they live is threatened with public calamities and judgments, either with sickness and the grievousness of war, they may glory in this and say, "God is our refuge and strength, a present help" (Ps. 46:1). "We have a strong city; salvation will God appoint" (Isa. 26:1).

If they are exercised with the temptations and attacks of the devil, yet the consideration may well fill them with courage and carry them above the fears of their painful, cruel adversary and laugh at all his rage and give them strength to trample underfoot the young lion and dragon.

If they are the subjects of cruel profanation and are delivered up to the hands of tormentors, yet if they can say, "I know that my Redeemer lives," they may notwithstanding rejoice and be exceeding glad and have courage to pray in the dungeon and triumph in flames.

If they are on a deathbed and there is no prospect of any other, but then soon leaving all things here below and parting with all their dear friends and leaving their bodies to be eaten with worms, yet they may with joy use Job's language in the text and context, "I know that my Redeemer lives." If they should see the world coming to an end, yet if they could say, "I know that my Redeemer lives," they might even then say, "I will not see, though the earth be removed and the mountains fall" (see Ps. 46:2).

2. If anyone can say, "I know that my Redeemer lives," it won't only be just ground of comfort, but it will actually and infallibly give comfort and rejoicing in all circumstances. All who can say, "I know that my Redeemer lives," at some particular season can't say so at all times. Faith is not always in that degree of exercise in them, but when it is, it infallibly has the effect to give comfort and rejoicing to the soul. Nothing in their circumstances can keep them from their joy. Romans 15:13 says, "Now the God of hope fill you with all joy and peace in believing," and when faith is in exercise to such a degree, the soul is steadfast and immovable in all storms and tempests.

The soul with whom it is thus, dwells on high, and his place of defense is the mountains of rocks. His bread and his waters are sure and fail not. He is like a tree that spreads its roots by a river that always supplies it with sap and therefore even flourishes in the greatest drought. Jeremiah 17:7–8 says, "Blessed is the man that trusteth in the LORD, and whose hope the LORD is. For he shall be as a tree planted by the waters, and that spreadeth out her roots by the river, and shall not see when heat cometh, but her leaf shall be green; and shall not be careful in the year of drought, neither shall cease from yielding fruit."

We read of joy unspeakable and full of glory from that sight that faith gives. First Peter 1:8 says, "Whom having not seen, ye love; in whom, though now ye see him not, yet believing, ye rejoice with joy unspeakable and full of glory." So we read of rejoicing in hope of the glory of God through the influence of faith and glorying in tribulation in Romans chapter 5.

When there is reached this full assurance of understanding, it will infallibly be accompanied with the spirit of adoption. This is the spirit of love that delivers from and casts out every fear and is the seat and earnest of the Spirit in our hearts and his witness that we are the children of God.

The following reasons may be given of the doctrine.

1. He who can say, "I know that my Redeemer lives," knows him to be better than all, for as has been observed already, 'tis implied that he knows that he is the Christ, the Son of the living God. He sees in him that glory and excellency that is above the glory of all other things and sufficient to satisfy his soul.

This beauty is so great, so divine, that the light of it when it is so clearly seen is above all things sweet. It fills the soul with a light so divine and powerful that it is impossible but the soul should be withal filled with peace and pleasantness. A lacking deliverance and sorrow is not consistent with such light. What can be better to the soul than to see the face of the only begotten Son of God who is full of grace and truth, and while the soul has that sight, it will have comfort. In vain is the rage of Satan or any of his instruments to the contrary.

And besides there being this truth implied, the soul at the same time that reflects the divine glory of this face, and knows him to be better than all, also knows that he is his Redeemer and can say, "My beloved is mine, and I am his" (Song 2:16). It must needs give it comfort. Whatever else it is deprived of—if the believer is destitute of riches, years, and of food and raiment, or if he be deprived of earthly friends—yet if he sees and knows that he has Christ and that he is and will always be his and never can be deprived of him, this must cause him to possess himself in quietness and confidence.

2. He who can say, "I know that my Redeemer lives," knows that his Redeemer is over all and able to do all things for him. If he be persecuted, he knows that his Redeemer is above his persecutors. If he be targeted by the devil and he sees that the powers of hell are against him, he knows that his Redeemer is above all the devils in hell and that he is able to deliver him from their hands.

He knows that his foundation is sure and his refuge stronger and that his Redeemer is round about him as the mountains are round about Jerusalem, and that his name is a strong tower and his salvation that is appointed for his walls and bulwarks is as mountains of brass.

If he has affliction in the world and is in the middle of storms, he knows that his Redeemer is above the storms of the world and can restrain them and quiet them when he pleases. 'Tis but for him to say, "Peace, be still" (Mark 5:39), and all will be. If he be tossed like a vessel on the tempestuous sea, he knows that his Redeemer is in the ship and therefore knows he cannot sink.

If death approaches with its most grave and ghostly countenance, yet he knows that his Redeemer is above death and therefore is not terrified with it, but can look upon it with a calm, pleasant countenance and not fear death.

3. He who can say, "I know that my Redeemer lives," knows that God loves him and pities him under all suffering. He knows that he has loved him first before he loved him, that he still loves him and will love him to eternity. He knows that he is the object of the free and unchangeable love of his Redeemer, and he knows that as a father pities his children, so his Redeemer pities him under affliction and that

he renews his soul in adversity and that a woman may sooner forget her sucking child than Christ forgets his children. That he has graven him, as it were, upon the palms of his hands and that in all his affliction he is afflicted. And this must needs be a most supporting and comforting consideration under all affliction.

4. He who can say, "I know that my Redeemer lives," knows that his Redeemer will fulfill his promises to him. He finds in his Word very great and precious promises, and they are precious to him. He is persuaded of them and loves them. He knows that he will never lose him or forsake him. He knows that Christ will not forsake his people and never will cast off his inheritance. He knows that he will defend him and will not suffer him to be utterly cast down. He knows that he will order that which he sees to be best for him and that he will never take away his loving-kindness from him, nor suffer his faithful one to fail. He knows that none can ever pluck him out of Christ's hands.

He knows that Christ will at last make him a conqueror over all his enemies and will subdue them under his feet and that the time will soon come that he will wipe all tears from his eyes. There shall be no more death, neither sorrow, nor crying, and he is persuaded that "neither death, nor life, nor angels, nor principalities, nor powers, nor things present, nor things to come, nor height, nor depth, nor any other creature, shall be able to separate us from the love of God which is in Christ Jesus our Lord" (Rom. 8:38).

APPLICATION

1. This may well lead those who are in a Christless condition to reflect on their unsuitable state that is so exceeding distant from that privilege spoken of in the doctrine. So blind are you and dark is your mind with respect to spiritual things that you don't yet know whether Christ be a Redeemer or no of God's appointing or whether there be any Redeemer at all. You have all your days been told of a Redeemer

and been instructed in the doctrine of his salvation. But you never know and don't now know whether there be a word of truth in all that you have heard about him. 'Tis a question that you never yet have fully resolved whether Christ be the Son of God. You have always halted between two opinions with respect to it, and so you do to this very day.

You have all your days been in the school of Christ, but you are one of them who have been ever learning and never yet come to the knowledge of the truth. And though Christ be the most glorious object that ever was exhibited or manifested in this world and be the light and glory of heaven and the brightness of God's glory, yet you have always been blind and never would see any form or comeliness in him or beauty wherefore you should desire him.

You are ignorant of him as the Light and Fountain of Life. You don't know that he lives. You be not determined in your mind whether he rose from the dead or not. And you not only don't know that he is your Redeemer, but you do not care that he is not. You have no interest in him. You are without Christ and without any Redeemer. You are a poor, undone, perishing sinner and have none who you have any interest in to appear before God for you.

You stand in as much need of a Redeemer as others. You are a poor captive in the hands of the devil. You are a poor prisoner in the hands of justice and have no interest in any Savior. Those who can say, "I know that my Redeemer lives," have that which may abundantly comfort them whatever circumstances they are in. But what comfort can a poor creature in your condition take under any circumstances? What comfort can you have in the thoughts of dying without a Redeemer? The thought of it may well be amazing to you. What can you have to give you any reasonable comfort when you consider how many sins you have been guilty of and have no mediator to make satisfaction for you? Your sins may well appear more terrible than so many devils to you.

What reasonable comfort can you take under any affliction when you have to consider that those afflictions are from the hand of an angry God and that you have no Redeemer to stand between God and you? And if you have any comfort in your miserable state in outward prosperity, your rejoicing is madness to you. You have no reasonable comfort in anything in the state that you are now in.

2. This doctrine may lead such persons to consider their folly who trust in such redeemers as shall perish. They who trust in Christ and know that they do so may say that they know that their Redeemer livesm whatever changes they pass under, and though they should die and worms devour their bodies. Yea, though heaven and earth should come to an end, yet still their Redeemer lives. But what will they do who trust in man whose breath is in his nostrils, that make flesh their arm, what will they do who trust in their own righteousness? What will become of this and the hope that is built upon it when death comes? The hail shall sweep away such dying refuges, and the waters shall overflow such hiding places. Death that will cut them off will at one blow cut off all their confidence and dash their false hopes in pieces: "For what is the hope of the hypocrite . . . when God taketh away his soul?" (Job 27:8).

3. I would hence exhort those who hope that they have an interest in Christ to seek that assurance of faith and hope that Job expresses in the text, that they may be able to say with him, "I know that my Redeemer lives." And here I shall particularly reflect on the last thing that it was observed was implied in such a profession—knowing that he is your Redeemer or being assured of an interest in him. Consider the following:

If you have an interest in Christ and yet don't know it, in many respects you will fail of the benefit of it while in this world. He who has an interest in Christ and doesn't know it can't have the benefit of it. He is under great restraint in his rejoicing in Christ. He dare not rejoice in him as his Savior. When he does rejoice in him and gives himself obediently for a while to salve himself in Christ's love, yet such a thought as this is ready to come across him, "It may be I am only a hypocrite. I have been taking comfort in the love and promises of a Savior, but it may be I am deceived and have comforted myself in that which doesn't belong to me and instead of rejoicing were full of sorrow and trembling from the consideration of my miserable condition."

As long as the saints are at a loss whether Christ is their Redeemer or no, it tends to make them afraid to take comfort when they read these things in the Scriptures that hold forth the wonderful mercy and love of Christ to believers. They will be afraid to take the best of them lest they should take to themselves that which doesn't belong to them. And if they do sometimes allow themselves to take these things to them, it is with restraint and fear lest they do what they have no warrant for. They dare not so much as give God thanks for giving them an interest in Christ, though that be so much the greatest mercy that ever they received, for fear they thereby give God thanks for a mercy they never received.

Christ came into the world to die that he might deliver those who through fear of death are all their lifetime subject to bondage. But the saints who don't know that they have an interest in Christ will be subject to bondage through fear of death. Still they will shrink at the thoughts of dying, for they know that death will finish and determine all things that relate to their salvation. That then they must appear before an all-seeing, heart-searching Judge who will pass a sentence upon them that can't be altered. And that if they should be found mistaken, then it will be too late to rectify the mistake; and if they are mistaken, they shall be undone forever. And therefore not being certain whether they are in a good estate or no, the thoughts of dying must needs be terrible. 'Tis a great thing to leap off from this stage into eternity, to launch forth into that boundless ocean. He who is going to fetch that leap will be afraid unless he be fully assured that he has good security as to the event.

It is enough to terrify the soul to leap forth into an uncertain eternity. And thus doubtless many truly godly persons have lived under a great deal of fear and sorrow and also have had much sorrow and exercising fear on a deathbed and so bereaved of much of the sensible benefit of their interest in Christ while they lived, and never could fully take the confidence of it 'til after they were dead because they died not knowing that Christ was their Redeemer. They hoped he was but were not assured of it. This may well stir us up earnestly to seek that we may obtain a certainty of an interest in Christ.

Let it be considered how much more seeking assurance would be for your comfort than any of those temporal good things that men are wont to spend their time and strength in the pursuit of. You don't begrudge to labor hard all the year round for the obtaining of temporal good things, for those things you exercise your skill and contrivance for and those things you willingly labor under the burning heat of the sun in the forenoon for. For those things, you will expose yourselves to the freezing cold of the winter and will go forth in rain and snow. For those things many of you also make long journeys and are long absent from home and suffer a great many difficulties abroad and are not sparing of your strength, nor are you ever weary but continue still to pursue the same things. But if you could obtain that which Job makes profession of to know that your Redeemer lives, how much more comfort might you have in it than in all those temporal things.

It would be better to you than the most flourishing estate. It would be a greater comfort to you than to have the most plentiful grass, the greatest bargains, and the greatest stores of good things in your houses. It would afford you a great deal more benefit than to think that you had plentifully laid in for the winter and the greatest abundance stored up in your barns and cellars and had also wherewith will to set off your children or to set them up comfortably in the world and to leave them large portions when you died.

If you could say, "I know that my Redeemer lives," then you would have this to think of—that you know you were well provided for against the day of death and the day of judgment. You would know that you had, for time and eternity, and could say with the psalmist, "The LORD is my shepherd; I shall not want" (Ps. 23:1). I have a table prepared for me, and my cup runneth over, and though I walk through the valley of the shadow of death, I will fear none evil. Such thoughts as these would cast a light upon all your enjoyments and all your circumstances, and you could not help rejoicing evermore.

What could be more joyful to a man than to know that he is free from the eternal dreadful destruction that the greater part of the world is exposed to? To know that he is out of the reach of the sting of death and the power of hell. To know that there is a glorious, almighty God and this God is his God. To know that Christ is the Judge of heaven and hell and yet to know that he is his Redeemer. To know that there is a day of judgment and also to know that then he shall stand at the right hand of Christ. To know that there is a heaven of eternal glory and to know that this is a kingdom prepared for him. To know that God has loved him before the foundation of the world, that his name was on Christ's heart then, and that he died out of love to him and will love him to eternity.

Such consideration will surely give strong consolation and will tend to make everything pleasant to him. Such an assurance will be a great help to you to come with boldness at all times to the throne of grace, for then you will know that when you go to God, you go to a Father, and you won't be afraid to call him Father. And when you speak to Christ, you won't be afraid to use such a style as this,

"My Lord," "my Redeemer," nay, "dear Savior," and this will make prayer and other duties of religion pleasant to you. This will generally tend to make the Lord's Supper a delightful ordinance to you, for you will know that person and whose body and blood is there represented as your Savior and that that death and those sufferings that are there commemorated were for your sake and that when you take Christ's body and blood and eat and drink, you take what is your own. You eat that bread that came down from heaven for you. You drink that blood that was shed for you.

This assurance will greatly open the way for a more fruitful and sweet converse between you and your soul. It will make the promises of the gospel abundantly the more sweet to you when you know that those promises are made to you and the Bible is all over full of those precious promises. It will be a sweet book to you. And then your life will be filled up with the sweetest and best and most desirable and reasonable comforts, and your life will close with peace and comfort and nothing doth make you afraid.

Seeing that you don't begrudge to take much pains with so much affinity and constancy for the enjoyment of this world, why will you not take as much pains for that which, if you obtained it, would yield you so much more comfort than any or all of them.

Let it be considered that such an assurance would not only be most comfortable but also very profitable to your soul. It would be a great strengthening to you against temptations. It would give you courage to go through difficult duties and to bear sufferings for Christ's sake. For what can tend to give the child courage more than for the father to stand by speaking comfortably to him, manifesting his love and acceptance?

If you know that Christ is your Redeemer and know that he has loved you from eternity and that he has laid down his life for you, it will greatly fill your heart in love to him. It will tend to quicken and warm your heart and greatly to enliven your graces and engage your heart in Christ's service. The apostle Paul, speaking of his labors and sufferings for Christ's sake, says in 2 Corinthians 5:14, "The love of Christ constraineth us." The consideration of Christ's having loved him and died for him had a powerful comforting influence upon him to engage him in the service of Christ. It will cause you to do your duty with the greatest cheerfulness and will draw you on in the way of holiness that you may not only walk but run in the way of God's commandments.

It will be a great help to our heavenly life if you know that Christ who is in heaven at the right hand of God is your Redeemer and your Savior. It will have a tendency to keep your heart there and to take it off things that are here below.

This is a privilege that many of God's servants have attained to. Job professes it, and David often professes it in the Psalms. He often speaks positively that the Lord is his Shepherd (Ps. 23:1) and "the portion of mine inheritance and of my cup" (Ps. 16:5). The apostle Paul often speaks in the most positive terms, "I know whom I have believed" (2 Tim. 1:12). And he says positively in Galatians 2:20 that Christ died for his sins and that for him to live was Christ and to die would be gain (Phil. 1:21). And near the close of his life, he speaks confidently, "I have fought a good fight" (2 Tim. 4:7). And not only the eminent saints that we read of in the Scriptures, but there have been many in all ages of the church who have attained to this privilege.

'Tis not a privilege attainable only by a few but that which in the use of proper means might ordinarily be attained by the saints. That is evident because 'tis a privilege that is set forth in Scripture for all to seek. All are commanded to seek it. Second Peter 1:10 says, "Give diligence to make your calling and election sure." And not only so but those who have it not are much blamed that they have it. Second

Corinthians 13:5 says, "Know ye not your own selves, how that Jesus Christ is in you, except ye be reprobates?"

This would not be unless the saints might in the use of due and proper means with proper care and diligence ordinarily attain. It is manifest by those Scriptures that assurance is a prize that God has set up for all Christians to run for. Striving after it is part of the work that all Christians have to do. If they be not attained, they are much to blame.

Now how much May these considerations will quicken to think how excellent the privilege and to think that is attainable and that you may reasonably hope to attain it in the due use of proper means in order to it. And so you come to say as well as holy Job, "I know that my Redeemer lives."

But I proceed now briefly to consider what are the proper means to be used in order to attain to this privilege. And before I come to particulars, I would observe in the church. To use self-examination alone without any other means is not the way for persons to attain to this privilege. There be fair rules of trial given in the Word of God and the way in which God has made of the qualifications of those who have an interest in Christ be very full and clear. Self-examination ought by no means to be left undone. Yet, says Christ, one can use no other means to obtain otherwise, but only to examine themselves, however good rules may be given for them to examine themselves by and however strict and frequent they only be an examination of themselves.

But in order for a person to enjoy this glorious privilege, four things are required:

1. That troublers be cast out and kept out. Some persons secretly allow themselves in some practice or way that is disagreeable to a Christian spirit and Christian rules and offensive to the pure Spirit of God. Some lust that has some secret evil covered over with false pleas and carnal reasonings. It will be in the heart as Achan was in the camp

of Israel. It will be a continual troubler that will cause God to hide his face and will darken evidences of grace, and the light of God's countenance and assurance of his favor is not to be expressed. All the self-examinations in the world won't satisfy the soul of all its good efforts 'til the Achan is destroyed, and when that is slain, another must not be admitted.

There must be the careful and strict watch kept up against all ways of sin either in our labors towards God or man, either at home or abroad, alone and with company, in God's house or elsewhere. And there must be a close walk with God in a way of closeness. They who walk closely with God will be in the way to have much communion with him and to know their interest in him. The psalmist says in Psalm 119:6, "Then shall I not be ashamed, when I have respect unto all thy commandments." This implies that then he should behold, being assured of his own sincerity.

2. Another thing requisite is that grace be not in low degrees. If persons have only very small degrees and exercises of grace, the consequences will be that it will be differently seen. This is the very reason that many saints live so much in doubt. Their souls are sickly, and grace is in a very feeble state in them. They have very much exercises of it, and hence they can't be satisfied fully whether they have any or no.

But if persons are strong in grace and have commonly the benefits of grace, it is easily seen and known. Grace is a very distinguishable thing from everything else. The reason why sometimes it is so difficult to distinguish it is that there is so little of it to be seen. But when its exercises are vigorous and lively, they plainly show themselves. And consider the stronger grace is, the more clear the eye to discern and distinguish between that which is true and that which is counterfeit. And the more gracious the soul is, the more does Christ delight to commune with it and manifest himself to it, and the more will he bestow his grace and blessings on it. So that thought of grace and the lively exercises of it every way find to promote assurance.

Therefore those who would obtain assurance should not rest on past attainments but should press forward with all their might, striving earnestly after higher degrees and actings of grace. They should make this their great and main business. Their lives, their strength, and their all should be devoted to it.

Thus they should seek greater acquaintance with Christ, that they may see more of his divine glory. We must first see how glorious a Redeemer he is and how happy we should therefore be if he were our Redeemer before we see and know that he is our Redeemer. We should strive after a strong faith and the lively actings of it, for a true hope is the daughter of faith. Faith is the root of which hope is the branch, and according to the strength of the root, so is the branch. There never is a true assurance of hope without an assurance of faith. If we would know that Christ is our Redeemer, we must first know that he is the Redeemer whom God has appointed and that he lives and is a sufficient, faithful Redeemer, able and willing to save to the uttermost. And we must strive that we may grow in love to Christ. The spirit of love is the spirit of a child that cries, "Abba, Father" (Rom. 8:15). 'Tis the spirit of adoption and when it is in strong exercise, it casteth out fear and gives assurance. "There is no fear in love" (1 John 4:18).

There is nothing that does more naturally tend to encourage and assure the heart than to feel the strong and lively actings of a holy, childlike love to God. It naturally and ineffably causes us to look on God as our Father when we feel such lively actings of the spirit of a child toward him.

Such a lively exercise of the spirit of adoption or spirit of love is the very thing that in Scripture is called the seal of the Spirit: "And grieve not the holy Spirit of God, whereby ye are sealed unto the day of redemption" (Eph. 4:30). "In whom ye also trusted, after that ye heard the word of truth, the gospel of your salvation: in whom also after that ye believed, ye were sealed with that holy Spirit of promise" (Eph. 1:13). And the earnest of the Spirit: "Who hath also sealed us, and given the earnest of the Spirit in our hearts" (2 Cor. 1:22). And the witness of the Spirit with our spirit: "that we are the children of God" (Rom. 8:16).

This Spirit that casts out fear is that which enables the saints to glory and triumph in tribulation (Rom. 5). 'Tis a strong faith and strong love that causes the souls to rejoice with joy unspeakable and full of glory. "Whom having not seen, ye love; in whom, though now ye see him not, yet believing, ye rejoice with joy unspeakable and full of glory" (1 Pet. 1:8). And it is not to be expected that persons should obtain assurance in any other way than by obtaining the strong, lively actings of love to Christ in the soul so as to swallow up all carnal affections and desires.

Again, another grace that you must earnestly seek that exercise of is humility and poverty of spirit. There is no grace whatsoever that has so many promises of comfort and the tokens of God's presence and favor more to in the Scriptures as such a spirit as this. Isaiah 66:1–2 says, "Thus saith the LORD, The heaven is my throne, and the earth is my footstool: where is the house that ye build unto me? and where is the place of my rest? For all those things hath mine hand made, and all those things have been, saith the LORD: but to this man will I look, even to him that is poor and of a contrite spirit, and trembleth at my word." Isaiah 57:15 says, "For thus saith the high and lofty One that inhabiteth eternity, whose name is Holy; I dwell in the high and holy place, with him also that is of a contrite and humble spirit, to revive the spirit of the humble, and to revive the heart of the contrite ones." Psalm 34:17–18 says, "The righteous cry, and the LORD heareth, and delivereth them out of all their troubles. The LORD is nigh unto them that are of a broken heart; and saveth such as be of a contrite spirit."

If you indulge a spirit of pride, a spirit of high count of your own godliness or of any other qualifications or an ambitious, revengeful spirit, a spirit of high resentment in your behavior among men, you will not be likely ever to obtain a strong assurance. But if you would obtain this, you must earnestly seek that you may be meek and lowly of heart and be more and more as a lamb or dove or a little child.

You must seek the increase and exercise of these graces in a diligent, constant, and laborious attendance on all the appointed means of grace and performance of all duties of piety and charity. You will never be likely to come to any great strength of grace unless you will progress in it in something of a constant, steady manner, and in order to this your watchfulness and diligence and labor and prayer must be constant.

3. Another thing ordinarily requisite in order to assurance is an abounding in holy fruits. The goodness of the fruit confirms the goodness of the vine both to ourselves and others. Isaiah 38:3 says, "Remember now, O LORD, I beseech thee, how I have walked before thee in truth and with a perfect heart, and have done that which is good in thy sight." Second Timothy 4:7 says, "I have fought a good fight, I have finished my course, I have kept the faith." The testimony of our own consciences with respect to doing good works and living a holy life is spoken of by the apostle Paul as that which tends to give us assurance. First John 3:18 says, "My little children, let us not love in word, neither in tongue; but in deed and in truth."

And hereby we know that we are of the truth, and shall assure our hearts before God. And the apostle Paul mentions diligence in a holy life as that which tends to give full assurance of hope. Hebrews 6:9 says, "But, beloved, we are persuaded better things of you, and things that accompany salvation, though we thus speak." Holy works, and especially works of charity and self-denial, are those that are means to reward with special tokens of his presence and manifestations of his love and favor.

4. The next thing that is requisite to assurance is frequent and strict self-examination. Some persons soon know what a condition they are in, and the reason is they never thoroughly organize. They don't take thorough pains to reacquaint themselves with the role God has given to us to try ourselves by. They have a hope that it is well with them, and they are too lazy and contented with an uncertain hope. They have not obtained any certainty, and they are too willing to go without it and be not thoroughly engaged to inquire what their state is. Rules of trial were given that we might use them and try ourselves by them.

Christians should often be examining themselves. They ought to deal truthfully, looking to God to help, by the influence of his Spirit. He would help them oppose the wickedness and deceitfulness of their hearts. He would search them and try them and lead them in the way everlasting.

4

That It Is the Temper of the Truly Godly to Delight to Exalt God and to Lay Themselves Low

Not unto us, O LORD, not unto us, but unto thy name give glory.
PSALM 115:1

This is the first of three examples of sermons from the Psalms, a favorite source of messages for Edwards. Though there is much here on the twin themes of abasing ourselves and exalting God, this sermon seems to be principally a reflection on the first part of the text.

Beginning with the foundation that the godly will delight in such merely because they delight in seeing God exalted, Edwards spends the rest of the sermon outlining the many ways in which the godly will delight to exalt their Lord.

The sermon manuscript is a clean, oversize booklet, consisting of seventeen leaves with no evidence of damage or changes.

This psalm is a psalm of praise unto God for the deliverance of the children of Israel out of Egypt, or some signal victory of theirs over their enemies, or some other great deliverance. The psalmist praises God in that manner which is always most acceptable to God. Even by acknowledging their insufficiency and inefficiency, thus to work deliverance for themselves. That it is not by their own strength or wisdom but only by the power and mercy of God. It is not our own sword or bow by which we are thus delivered but by God's strength and because he hast sought for us.

We may easily perceive the frame the psalmist is in. Thus being full of a thankful sense of the mercy, of the salvation, and of a humble sense of his own insufficiency, he breaks out at once, "Not unto us, not unto us," repeated over again, but "Unto thy name give glory." These humble acknowledgments of the godly are those sacrifices that are truly acceptable to God that do really come up before him as a sweet-smelling savor. They are better sacrifices in the sight of God than thousands of rams and ten thousands of rivers of oil.

You may take notice that the psalmist is, as it were, glorying in triumphing over his enemies, but after what manner doth he triumph over them? Not by boasting of his own strength and telling his enemies of their weaknesses, but as it is written, "He that glorieth, let him glory in the Lord" (1 Cor. 1:31). He glories in the greatness of Israel's God and in the meanness of pagan gods. Verses 2 and 3 of Psalm 115 say, "Wherefore should the heathen say, Where is now their God? But our God is in the heavens: he hath done whatsoever he hath pleased." This is our God; he dwells in heaven. He hath delivered us. But as for their gods, see verses 4 and 5, "Their idols are silver and gold, the work of men's hands. They have mouths, but they speak not: eyes have they, but they see not." This is the psalmist's way of boasting and triumphing.

There are three things to be taken notice of in the passage in order to our receiving the improvement that is offered to us therein:

1. How the psalmist lays himself and his people low: "Not unto us." He disclaims all the power and all the glory and all the wisdom of bringing about the salvation referred to, though God had done it by

them, and made them a means of their own deliverance. He rejects and casts off all the praise and honor of it as that in the boast which belongs to him. He will not entertain a thought that tends to the exalting of himself and his people in his own esteem.

2. How the psalmist exalts God: "But unto thy name give glory." It belongs unto God and that wholly and solely. 'Tis God who has done whatsoever he wouldest that we cannot do what we will but depend on him for his help.

3. The delight that the psalmist seems to take in thus abasing himself and exalting God. This appears in the repetition of the phrase, "Not unto us, not unto us." He seems to be full in the matter. He has not the least inclination to assume the glory to himself, but to abhor the thoughts of it and delight in attributing all to God.

DOCTRINE

It is the temper of the truly godly to delight to exalt God and to lay themselves low. It is natural to a godly man as a godly man to delight in this. 'Tis not only a mere transient glance of affection after some great deliverance from a greatly feared danger, after a dangerous fit of sickness, or some dangerous accident, or the like, but it is the continued nature and disposition of the godly man. Not but that it may be otherwise with him at such times, but the thing is not because he has not such a disposition and temper so to do but because this disposition is not in exercise. The godly man then doesn't act when the godly man does. Otherwise, it is not the godly man who acts but the body of sin. If every man thus acted contrary to true grace, at some time was a wicked man, we should have none but wicked men in the world, because every action of corruption, small or great, is contrary to true grace. But this is what we say, that it is the spirit and temper of the godly man to delight thus to act. Here we shall show that they delight to exalt God and that they delight to abase themselves.

1. It is the temper and disposition of a truly godly man to delight in exalting God.

They delight in seeing him exalted. They are to see God reigning on the throne of his glory, exalted up on high. They love to have him do whatever is his will and pleasure in the armies of heaven and among the inhabitants of the earth. They care that he should do just what he pleases. They rejoice in it that God is the governor of the world. It is a happy and joyful consideration to them that God reigneth. This was spoken of what is a joyful piece of news to the godly. Isaiah 52:7 says, "How beautiful upon the mountains are the feet of him that bringeth good tidings, that publisheth peace; that bringeth good tidings of good, that publisheth salvation; that saith unto Zion, Thy God reigneth."

The godly man not only loves that God should reign over others, but that he should reign over him too, and that with an uncontrollable power. He is heartily willing that God should be a sovereign King over him. He had rather be ruled by God and have God for his King, than be in all respects at his own disposal. "Ye are not your own . . . ye are bought with a price" (1 Cor. 6:19–20). And the believer had rather have it so than otherwise. He had rather be God's than his own. He had rather that God should have an entire right to him, body and soul, than have a right to himself. He loves to have God for a lawgiver and would rather that God should give him laws than not. He loves to have God dispose of him in his providence. He can delight in thinking that he is in the hands of God. That is the language of his soul, which proceeds from the soul with delight and pleasure. "Lord, I am in thy hands, deal with me as seemeth to thee good."

He delights to exalt God in his own heart. He will not presume to sit on the throne of his own heart but chooses rather that God should sit there and he himself at the footstool. The sinner sits in the throne of his own heart. He takes God's place, will be governed by none but himself. But the truly godly man invites God to sit in the highest place in his soul and delights to see him placed there and instead of being against. He wonders that God will even condescend so much as to take up his abode in his heart, although it be in the throne of it. He rejoices to see God possessing the best apartment in his heart, the best room of his soul, and greatly admires that the great Jehovah will even so humble himself as to dwell there.

Before he was converted, while he was yet a rebel against God, he would not admit God into his heart. He proudly possessed the throne himself and held the scepter of his own soul. But since God has graciously enlightened him, how doth he immediately quit his seat, give place to God, and deliver up the scepter to him and with pleasure cast himself down to the footstool. He finds vastly more pleasure now in the dust before God than he did before in the throne.

He will no more suffer his carnal reason or his own private interests, his own pleasures, or his affection to friends, or any other affection to reign in his heart, for he considers that God's is the kingdom, the power, and the glory. He will make all these lie at the footstool. Formerly he used to delight in suffering his lusts to reign, but now he delights to see them God's captives and to place them under his feet. 'Tis his temper to delight to have higher thoughts of God than of anything else. He is not careful lest he should think too highly of God but grieves that he can think no more highly of him. He delights to bring his understanding, his will and petitions and give them to God, give him entire possession of them, and offer them as sacrifices to him. He himself brings these Christ's enemies that would not, that he should reign over them and slay them before him (Luke 17:29).

He loves to attribute to God the glory of what he is, what he has, and what he does. The believer delights in giving the praise of all that he has, all that he is, and all that he enjoys, to God. He acknowledges that it comes from him and that it is all the fruit of his sovereignty and is not owing to himself. That it is not owing to his own strength to get it or to his own merit to deserve it but alone to the mercy of God in being willing to give it and to his power in procuring it. Thus he cares to give God the glory of all his temporal things, even his common enjoyments. He is not as some are, living continually on the bounty of God and not considering who they are owing to, nor sincerely once praising him for them.

But especially it is the joy of his heart to give God all the glory of his spiritual enjoyment. He loves to give him the whole praise of his redemption and salvation, admires of God's goodness in choosing him from all eternity. Admires that he should be of his distinguishing goodness, chosen out from among so many, to be made the vessel of honor and subject of glory. He wonders at God's goodness in sending his Son to redeem him. He likewise admires at his grace in calling of him to Christ by his Holy Spirit. He delights to acknowledge that his conversion is not at all owing in any respect to himself but to the grace of God alone.

So he loves to give God the glory of all his works whereby glory redounds to God. He is not for attributing anything to his own power or goodness. When he overcomes a temptation, he exalts God that his grace was sufficient for him. When he doth a good work by feeding the poor or otherwise, he takes none of the glory of it to himself, as if he had done some great thing that made him worthy of God's love, and therefore he will not sound a trumpet before him to give notice of it, as if he gloried in it, but will do as secretly as possibly he can, for he knows that he doth only his duty.

He desires not that any should know of it but God and to him he will say, "Not unto me, O Lord, not unto me, but unto thy name, who hast enabled me to do any good work, be the glory." He makes him uneasy when his heart is apt to be lifted up therewith as if it were owing to him. He is not inclined to boast of what he doth before men, but his heart is never more lifted up with joy than when he can with his whole heart give all the glory to God. He considers that it was not so proper, he himself who did as Christ dwelling in him, as the apostle says in Galatians 2:20.

'Tis the temper of a godly man to delight to live so that God may be honored by his life. Men exalt God in their lives when they live chiefly for him and make him the chief end of their lives. When they live in obedience to his commands and delight so to obey his commands because they are his commandments, and because obedience to them is submission to him. They exalt God in their lives by manifesting a fear of his displeasure. They thereby declare to the world how fearful God's displeasure is. They exalt him in their lives by living a life of faith in him, of hope in his mercy, trust in his goodness, when they trust in him in difficulties and they delight in him in affliction.

'Tis a godly man's spirit and temper to delight to exalt God amongst man. They are glad when God is highly esteemed in the world. They rejoice when they hear God spoken highly of, and they will do all that they can to beget such a high esteem of God in the minds of men. They will leave no stone unturned, that if possible they may be the means of bringing it about, that God shall be rightly thought of by others as well as themselves. And how glad when his endeavors succeed! How doth his heart rejoice when he can give a lift towards the rearing up of the kingdom of God amongst men.

He will exalt God amongst men by endeavoring all that possibly he can in his place and station, that sin and wickedness may decay, and holiness and religion may flourish and prosper. By endeavoring by his life, strength, and wisdom to reclaim persons from wicked curses, that men may be brought over to Jesus Christ and to live a holy life. He with delight will exalt God amongst them by showing his regard unto the worship and ordinances of God, by his regard to his public worship, his holy sabbath, and his ministers.

He delights to exalt God by speaking of him to his praise and honor, by talking of his wondrous works and making known his judgments amongst the saints. He will also bring glory to God's name amongst men by procuring it by his earnest prayers to God for the advancement of his kingdom, the flourishing of religion, and the manifestation of glory. Thus it is the temper of the godly to delight to exalt God.

2. It is the temper of the godly to delight to abase themselves and lay themselves low before God. The joys of humility to them are their best and most pleasant joys. How pleasantly, how sweetly doth the godly man feel. What sweets doth he experience when he finds himself in the most humble frames, when he is more especially enabled to lay himself in the dust before God. When he is annihilating himself in God's presence and lying at his footstool. He loves to empty his soul of himself that God may fill it, that God may be all and he nothing. He can never lay himself low enough to satisfy himself.

He loves to abase himself before God by humiliation for his sin. He loves to humble himself before God for it. It is not because he is forced to do it. He doesn't humble himself in this respect or as an enemy that is conquered who is compelled to submit himself by force of arms whither he will or no, perhaps with the greatest regret. No, but he delights to yield to God and to lie low before him. 'Tis not his grief that he must humble himself but that he can do it no more. He rejoices that he can find so much humiliation in his own heart, but he grieves that he can find no more.

He delights to have his heart broken all to pieces at the remembrance of his sins. It is his joy when he can feel this sort of sorrow. Here is a paradox and a mystery that men should rejoice in sorrow. But thus it is with respect to this sort of sorrow, even godly sorrow for sin. What believers experience most of, they experience great delight. Repentance is a Canaan for delights because the godly man loves to repent and be humbled. They love to have their head like waters and their eyes a fountain of tears, that they may mourn for their transgression. They delight in having their hearts melted down before God.

3. It is the temper of the godly to delight to abase themselves before God by acknowledging their own meanness. They are far from delighting to extol and exalt themselves. They are not like the hypocrite who delights in making himself appear as well as possibly he can in God's presence—dressing himself up in his fine clothes and putting on his own righteousness. He doesn't care to come before God except he can bring something of his own to show.

But the believer delights in coming like a beggar in his own rags, for he knows he has nothing else to offer to God. His concern is not how he should make himself appear as well as possibly he can before God, but how he may if possible present all his own unworthiness and sinfulness. He is rather concerned because he can't make his confessions and acknowledgments adequate and proportionate to his unworthiness. He is willing to confess that he has nothing and that he is nothing—yea, worse than nothing. He delights to own and acknowledge before God that he has nothing of his own.

He loves to be ashamed and blush in God's presence and never appear so vile in his own eyes, but that he is willing to acknowledge it all before God. He delights in acknowledging that he is thoroughly vile and sinful and unworthy of the least regards of God. He quits all claim to mercy through his own deserts and chooses to have mercy as free and undeserved.

Thus we have briefly shown what kind of temper the truly godly has. This is their true disposition thus to delight to exalt God and abase themselves. They have that within them that naturally inclines them to do thus. Here we would not be misunderstood as if we intended that none were godly but what at all times found this temper and spirit in exercise. For the godly have their times of weakness and infirmity wherein the remainders of the contrary principle prevails over this temper, but still it is the temper of their mind. This is their inward disposition. However, they may at some times act contrary to it. Christianity inclines them, so nothing else so far as that has possession of their hearts.

APPLICATION

Of examination. You have heard what temper the truly godly are of. That it is their spirit and disposition to delight to exalt God and to abase themselves before him. Wherefore, let all examine themselves by this, whither they are truly godly or not. Let all examine and see what temper they themselves are of lest they should deserve that rebuke which Christ gives in Luke 9:55, "Ye know not what manner of spirit ye are of." This is a disposition that belongs alone to the godly, never to sinners, alone to the hearty, sound, and sincere and never to hypocrites. To the true believers in Christ and never to the self-righteous, yea and is the very thing that distinguishes a sincerely godly person from a self-righteous man, and the best distinguishing mark, for most certainly he is not a wicked man, a self-righteous man. He is not a hypocrite who loves and delights in abasing himself and exalting God.

How contrary is the disposition of a wicked man to it in whose heart pride, obstinancy, presumption and selfishness reigns instead of this humble, Christian, sweet and Godlike disposition. How set are they from delighting to exalt God and to lay themselves low, whose only care is how they shall please their private appetites, how they shall exalt themselves, caring nothing what becomes of God's honor and glory. Instead of delighting to exalt God in their own hearts and in placing him up on the throne, and delighting to lie at the footstool, he haughtily sits on the throne himself. He will be governed alone by himself, will not submit to God's commandments, nor hearken to his dictates but will rather set up his own carnal reason, his pleasure, his worldly profit, and his sloth and negligence and act according to the dictates of these. He will make the commands of God turn aside because it is in the way of his worldly business, or for the sake of his pleasure, or for the gratification of slothfulness.

How far are these from delighting to exalt God in their hearts and their lives, and to make all their private concerns stoop to him. How far are the wicked from delighting to abase themselves. How far are they from caring that God should have all the praise and honor and they have none. Truly they are strangers to this kind of pleasure. If they do what they think is a good work, a commendable and laudable action, how far are they from being willing that God should have all the praise. They are for having some of it themselves, or else they think 'tis lost if they feed the poor or relieve the distressed. They are not content to keep to the rule of the gospel nor to let their right hand know what their left hand doeth. They are not contented that God alone should know of it. It doesn't content them to so think that God who seest in secret will reward them openly. But they are for publishing of it, that they may have the applause of it; otherwise they think they have done it in vain.

How far are wicked and self-righteous and hypocritical men from delighting to acknowledge that they have no righteousness, no strength of their own. How far are they from delighting to have their heart broken all to pieces for their sin and to feel themselves humbled to the dust before God. Truly these pleasures and delights are what they know nothing of.

Wherefore let us examine ourselves concerning this matter, whether we love to abase ourselves that God may be exalted. We have heard the explication of this disposition. One would think there should be no great difficulty to find out whether we have it or no. Let us put the question, Do we really love and choose to renounce all our own worthiness and the worthiness of all that we do, and to acknowledge freely and fully and heartily, that it is good for nothing that God's grace may be exalted? Wicked men had as like say it in their prayers as not. They are free to say with their lips in prayer that all their own righteousness is as filthy rags and that they are poor, miserable creatures unworthy of the least of God's mercies. But the question is whether we really love the heart's acknowledgment. Are they freely willing not to have any mercy merely on the account of their worthiness? Do they love to be saved altogether freely?

Do we choose that God should be all and that we ourselves should be nothing? Do we love that God should possess the throne and sway the scepter in our hearts? Do we long to be more humbled and abased before God? Is a humiliation and contrition our delight? If so, we may doubtless with humility rejoice in it, that God has chosen us from all eternity and has called us out of darkness into marvelous light. Then we will give God all the praise thereof, or all they will delight to do, are such as the doctrine speaks of.

Use of instruction. I would draw one inference from this doctrine. It is so that the temper and spirit of a godly man is to love to exalt God and abase himself. Hence we may learn that a godly temper is undoubtedly wrought by the Spirit of God. How much is it against man's natural disposition to love to abase himself? It is quite contrary to it. It is therefore quite beyond the powers of nature to bring man to this temper and fix it in him. This must undoubtedly be the supernatural work of the Spirit of God, for what else can ever bring a man to love to lay himself low that God may be exalted? Surely none else but he who made the soul of man can then alter and change and put a new nature into it.

So contrary to that disposition which is natural to all men universally, yea, there is hardly any disposition stronger in man by nature than that which is contrary to this, even a disposition to exalt themselves. But the godly are of such a temper as not only to abase themselves but to love and delight so to do, and to take great pleasure in it. Therefore here are the undoubted marks of the finger of God, and plain evidences of the effects of his Holy Spirit powerfully working in man's heart.

Use may be of exhortation. First to all such as depend on their own righteousness, to exhort them to let go their hold. You see how distant you are from the spirit of such as are in a state of salvation. They don't delight and pride themselves in their own goodness and the goodness of their works but delight in the contrary. They are not endeavoring to dress themselves in the apparel of their own goodness but come in beggar's rags before God, for they come to beg a garment of him, even the righteousness of Christ. They had rather be saved freely upon the account of no goodness and pity than for the works that they do. They delight in such a way of salvation. They love to have their hearts broken for their sin. They love to lie low and in the dust and take no pleasure in less exalting thoughts, wherefore by this such may see how far they are from a godly disposition. Let them be exhorted therefore not to hope for salvation in the state they are in for the present but seek another disposition of mind and get into another state.

To all in general. It is so that it is the temper of the godly to love to exalt God and abase themselves, to be thus exhorted to seek and pray for such a disposition. Here we shall briefly tell you what it is that makes the godly love thus to abase themselves that God may be exalted. From what principle it is that this spirit arises, which may be a direction and guide to us in our pursuit of such a disposition.

1. It arises from love of God. We love to have exalted and lifted up that which we love. The godly have a dear love to God, and therefore it is that they can with delight give him that highest place in their soul, the delight to obey him. Choose rather to do it than not. Therefore it

is with delight they can say, "Unto thy name give glory." Therefore they love to exalt him by their praises. Therefore they love to acknowledge that all they have and all they are is from his goodness and have no ambition to have the glory of it to themselves.

We love to acknowledge the kindness of them whom we love. Therefore it is that the believer loves to acknowledge that all the good he enjoys is a free gift and undeserved, yea, would be surprised to find that it were not so. We love to acknowledge the free gifts of those who are dear to us. It is more pleasant to receive a gift from such than a debt. It puts greater joy into a lover when something is given him freely by the person loved, than when a debt is paid. Therefore believers had rather accept salvation as a free gift from God than as a debt, than as what is due from God because he loves God. Wherefore seek love to God that you may have the same temper.

2. This disposition is from repentance. The believer remembers how he sinned against God in times past. How he was proud, haughty, and obstinate; how he used to sit in the throne in God's place and serve his own lusts instead of God; how he used rebelliously to dishonor and affront God. He now sees his own vileness for it, and he can never lay himself low enough for it. He can never satisfy himself by abasing himself before God for it and confessing of it. He loves now to humble himself for he sees that he ought to be exceedingly humbled. He longs to humble himself more and more and to exalt God whom he has dishonored in time past and therefore will seek all opportunities to exalt him.

Wherefore seek repentance for sin. Endeavor to forsake baseness of disobeying God and obeying lust. Endeavor to see the baseness. If you truly do this, you will find such a frame of soul that will also ever after cause you to love to humble yourself and lay yourself low and to exalt God.

This temper to love to exalt God and debase themselves arises from gratitude. The believer considers what God has done for him, reflects on his wonderful mercy, the greatness and the multitude. A principle of gratitude makes him delight to exalt God for it. He considers how God has humbled himself that has condescended to have mercy on him and help him. Therefore gratitude makes him delight to do that which is no condescension but his broader duty even to humble himself for sins and lay himself in the dust for it.

He considers how Jesus Christ, who is God, humbled himself and lost heaven and lived in ignominy upon earth, and became obedient unto death, even the death of the cross for him. Therefore, gratitude moves him to humble himself and to love to lay himself low before God, since his Son made himself so low for him as to be in the form of a servant and a malefactor. Therefore, seek to be affected with those wonderful instances of the greatness of God, and let not your heart be as a stone. Be not more ungrateful than the beasts, and you will find that abhorrence of yourself and those high thoughts of God as will make you to delight to exalt and honor him and to lay yourself low.

3. Exhortation is to all who have this temper. Be exhorted to increase more and more in this temper and disposition. 'Tis an excellent and heavenly temper; 'tis that which makes you shine much brighter than other sort of men who are sinners and hypocrites. Be not lifted up at any thoughts of your own goodness or worthiness. Give all the praise for "who maketh thee to differ from one another? and what hast thou that thou didst not receive?" (1 Cor. 4:7). When you do good works, be not elated in your own minds, but let God have the praise. Seek not the applause and commendation of men. Let God have the praise, and you shall praise of him hereafter. Delight in having your heart broken for sin. Delight in humbling yourself at the seat of mercy, and let it be your delight to exalt God in your heart and by your acknowledgments.

How just and reasonable it is that we should so do. It is the way to have the consolations of God's Spirit.

1. This disposition is attractive unto God when he sees a person of such an excellent disposition. It draws the eyes of God upon you, and not only so but draws him down from heaven into his heart and soul. God will delight to make his abode in such a soul and fill it with comfort. He has said in Psalm 138:6, "Though the Lord be high, yet hath he respect unto the lowly." Isaiah 57:15 says, "With him also that is of a contrite and humble spirit, to revive the spirit of the humble, and to revive the heart of the contrite ones."

2. This is the way to have the guidance of his Holy Spirit in all your ways. God has said that he will guide the meek in his way. Psalm 25:9 says, 'The meek will he guide in judgment: and the meek will he teach his way."

3. God will love to help to exalt and honor such. Luke 14:11 says, "He that humbleth himself shall be exalted." It seems that this disposition more peculiarly affects the Almighty's bounties. It is the only way to have God as a Father to us in this world. To keep us in all our ways, to provide for us, to keep us from evils and dangers, and to be our comforter in afflictions and the answerer of our prayers. God takes most pleasure in the prayers of the humble (Ps. 10:17).

4. And this is the way to be advanced to glory hereafter. Yea, the lower you lay yourself by humility in this world, the higher will you be exalted in glory in the other. This is so well-pleasing to God that it not only draws the eyes of God—yea, holds his eyes fixed as it were with admiration and holds the King in the galleries. Yea, this grace of humility, this link of the chain of the graces of the spouse, not only ravishes his heart and brings light and all spiritual blessing down upon the believer in this world but soon causes the gates of heaven and the arms of God to open and attracts the rivers of pleasure. It causes the tree of life to bend to yield her fruit and all the blessing of Jerusalem

above to flood in upon him, speaks not as a private person only but either as respecting Christ or his mystical body.

So in this psalm in particular the psalmist seems to speak not only in his own name of God's saints and people in general wherein the true church giveth to God and glories and triumphs in him before the heathen. God's people boast and glory but not in themselves in their own strength, courage, wisdom, or riches. They boast not that Israel was a wiser nation than the nations of the neighboring or that they had better courage, more riches, or a greater multitude in more fruitful land but that they had a more glorious, powerful, wise, and merciful God than they.

They observe nothing in themselves though they were so much advanced above all other peoples on the face of the earth, especially in David's and Solomon's time. But they will glory in their God before those who had no other than senseless rocks and stones for their gods, as from the second verse of Psalm 115, "Wherefore should the heathen say, Where is now their God?"

They remember God's dominion. They don't think that he sets his eye upon them because they are better or more in number than other people but because he loved them. They assume not the glory to themselves but give it all to God. It matters not whether there be any particular victory obtained over the heathen and in this manner praises and triumphs over them or God's blessing to that nation in general in distinguishing them from all other people and in divine privileges advancing them above them and the mighty works wherewith they were brought out of Egypt. Spoken of in the foregoing psalm or whether great, swelling words of their adversaries threatening to destroy them might give occasion that through faith and trust, to glory in God their help in affliction, being assured of their safety as it might occasion to this request that God would defeat them and destroy their enemies and save them and so glorify his own name and not them.

5

⊷⇒◎ ◎⇐⊶

That We Ought to Make Religion Our Present and Immediate Business

I made haste, and delayed not to keep thy commandments.
PSALM 119:60

T his is an undated sermon that Edwards preached to show what true religion really means. He wanted to make abundantly clear that it involves both a person's inclinations and actions, habits and exercises, both internal and external.

He then describes the various reasons this way of living is to be our present and immediate business. To delay such behavior is, according to Edwards, the greatest abuse of God's mercy and patience. He makes a special plea to young people to be converted to Christ while they are still young and so avoid God's leaving them in their sin in an unconverted state.

The sermon manuscript is an oversize booklet, consisting of twenty leaves. There is no evidence of damage, but some changes to the text have been made by Edwards. The application consists of nine leaves.

When we find holy and righteous men in the Scriptures solemnly making profession before God of anything in themselves, pleading it as an instance and argument of their integrity or as praising God for granting them such a disposition, or enabling them to do such actions, it is the same thing to us as if we were directly instructed in our own duty. And such professions are to have the force of commands with us. Therefore, when the psalmist says, "I thought on my ways, and turned my feet unto thy testimonies. I made haste, and delayed not to keep thy commandments" (Ps. 119:59–60), it is the same thing as to everyone of us as if he had said, "Think on thy ways and turn thy feet into God's testimonies, make haste and delay not to keep God's commandments." Here we may observe:

1. The substance of this profession of the psalmist is his obedience and observation of God's law, living according to that revelation which God had made of himself. This is perhaps more plainly implied in the foregoing verse, by that expression, "and turned my feet unto thy testimonies," meaning by God's testimonies that testification or revelation which God had made of himself and his will.

By keeping God's commandments is to be understood the whole of religion, both in its inclinations and actions, its habits and exercises, both internal and external. Religion is more frequently in the New Testament represented by the names of its internal exercises, faith and charity and the like. In the Old Testament this is called keeping the commandments of God, being more agreeable to the imperfect state of the church under the law of Moses.

2. We may observe the circumstance of time and manner of the psalmist's thus doing. He did it speedily and immediately; he made haste and delayed not. He thought on his ways, as he says in the foregoing verse. He considered his life and actions and wherein he found his ways were wrong, he immediately rectified them. The first thing he

did was to repent and reform. He saw the evil of the way he was in and prayed not to allow himself a little further gratification of his flesh or sinful desires. He stayed not 'til this or that business was done but, without any hesitation or delay, betook himself to his duty. The Word, therefore, teaches us some important truths.

DOCTRINE

We ought to make religion our present and immediate business. The proposition is so evident of itself that a proof would be needless if it be our duty to obey God's commands. 'Tis our duty to do it without delay, for while we delay to obey them we disobey them. God's commands in the meantime are neglected where he gives no indulgence. We shall endeavor to illustrate the truth of the doctrine by the following considerations.

1. It appears that we ought to make religion our present and immediate business because 'tis the business for which we came into the world. God raised us out of the dust of the earth for this enjoyment. For this his hand formed those curious frames of our bodies and breathed into the habitation as he prepared our understanding and immortal souls. 'Tis for this that we are set above the beasts of the earth by a power of reason and reflection and are made rulers over them and possessors of this land or world. We might have served to inferior purposes as well if we had been made sheep. If it were not for this, there would have been no need of introducing the animal in the image of God into the world at the end of the six days' works. 'Tis for this end that the sun daily arises upon us, that the rain descends, and that the earth brings forth for us, and for which all the brute creatures which are in the earth, the sea, or the firmament of heaven are subservient to us.

Surely then we ought not for any time to neglect or to delay this business, seeing that whilst we so do, we live to no purpose. The candle of life burns in vain. We eat and drink, and our heart beats, and our blood runs in our veins for nothing. The wheel wears out at the cistern, and we gradually draw near to the grave. In the meantime we do nothing as that which we were made for.

As long as we neglect this business, however we may otherwise employ ourselves, we spend our time unprofitably. All other business is subjected and subordinated by God because all the inferior ends of our being are subordinated to the chief and are good only as they have regard to that highest end. Whatever business men exercise themselves in, yet if they don't bring forth the fruits of righteousness, they are looked upon by God as barren trees and cumberers of the ground (Luke 13:7).

2. Religion is a business infinitely of the greatest importance. 'Tis what the common sense of all men dictates—that things of the greatest importance should be first taken care of. The utmost that any other employment or exercise respects in this life, it affects us only while we stay here, whether that be a longer or a shorter time. If we obtain any good by the pursuit of it or if we sustain loss or damage through its neglect, it can last us no longer and perhaps not near so long as we live here. Yea, it is very uncertain whether we shall obtain that worldly good at all that we propose by it or whether or no the event won't be quite contrary to our desires and expectations.

But the least that the business of religion has respect to is an eternity. Eternal misery ensues from the neglect of it and everlasting happiness from its pursuit and practice. If we through delay should happen to lose our opportunity, as it very often happens, then there is no help or remedy but that we must be everlastingly miserable. No repentance or tears or after labors will avail us anything, either to the obtaining of that eternal good that we had an opportunity of obtaining.

Now 'tis as certain as anything can be that the least misery that is everlasting is more dreadful than the greatest that has an end. It would be our prudence to pursue the least happiness that we shall never be deprived of rather than to neglect it for the greatest that we are certain of in a short time of losing. The misery that we avoid and the happiness that is attained by godliness is not only infinitely exceeding that which is earthly in its continuance but in its degree and height. The losses and afflictions of time are to be despised in comparison to damnation because they are but for a few moments. So they are as nothing when compared with those flames as to greatness of torment.

If it can be supposed that we shall for the present be least happy for neglecting the world for the sake of religion, yet in a few years we shall be never the worse for it. But we are sure of losing the better forever, and surely 'tis a pain of prudence to undergo a little short inconvenience for the sake of a great and lasting good.

But then we are not sure of being the worse for religion in any respect. Yea, we have great reason to expect to be happier even in this world. If we don't enjoy more of the world, we are sure of having more peace and contentment and the blessing of God in what we do enjoy, which is better then abundance. However, had not we better run the venture of foregoing some outward delights, than of missing of heaven, or of suffering a little for the present than of enduring God's wrath always? If we miss our opportunity, this punishment is sure to us; and if we hear God's voice today while it's called today and diligently want the worship of God, happiness forever is as sure as the word and oath of God.

3. It appears that we ought not for any time to delay or put off our religion because all our time is God's. All our time is his because we ourselves are his. He has made us and given us all our powers of action. All the while we delay the work of religion, we unjustly rob God. And all the while we live, he preserves our life and he requires that the life which he upholds should all of it be devoted to him. He gives us our power of thinking, and we cannot think a thought without

him. He preserves our powers of acting, and 'tis in him we live and move, and surely our thoughts and actions ought therefore immediately to be given to him. We have not one moment of time but what God gives to us.

If we procrastinate religion to another season, we in the meantime steal from God. This year is his as well as the next. If we live 'til that time, it will be because God feeds us and clothes us. 'Tis God's wool and his flax, his corn, his wine, and his oil that sustains us while we live in sin against him. Hosea 2:8–9 says, "For she did not know that I gave her corn, and wine, and oil, and multiplied her silver and gold, which they prepared for Baal. Therefore will I return, and take away my corn in the time thereof, and my wine in the season thereof, and will recover my wool and my flax."

4. By delaying religion 'til another season great contempt is cast on God's authority. It becomes us when we receive commands from those who are our rulers and very much our superiors, not only to obey exactly but forthwith and without delay, that we may show the cheerfulness and readiness of our obedience. But how provoking is it when the almighty God himself commands for us that are not worthy to be his servants! Will we be slow in obeying, especially when he expressly requires present and immediate obedience? When God says "now," we should not say, "Not now, but when I have a more convenient opportunity, when I have more leisure from my own business, and when I find a greater disposition to it than I do now." When God says "today," to delay for weeks, months, and years—and the excuse is that there are other things to mind, or he feels very much indisposed to such things as God's commands—man doesn't love the work that God sets him about.

Is not this enough greatly to increase God's displeasure and to rouse his justice and bring down his wrath upon such? This is especially true, considering that God's commands are so much inculcated and accompanied with promises and threatenings, as well as gracious invitations and entreaties. What prince will bear this of a subject? What master would bear it in a servant? What prudent parent would bear it in a child?

5. In putting off religion, we manifest a great slight of God's glory and excellency. Hereby is God set last and in the lowest place as if he were least of anything to be regarded. His business must be done last as if it were no great matter whether it were ever done at all and other things were much more to be regarded then he. This is the language of their practice: God has his demands, 'tis true, but this world and our appetites have their demands, and God must wait 'til they are served first. Even sin and Satan must have their share before God.

So the sinner puts later on God's right. Every filthy lust and desire must be served before him, and every creature is exalted above the Creator, and the high and mighty God must come in the rear of all such contempt as this. Those who delay to keep God's commandments do most certainly cast upon God. They delay to hearken to God for the sake of their ease, their sensual and sinful pleasures. Placing God lowest in their affections and last as ten times. Giving sin and the world their youth, their strength, and the bloom of their life. God must be turned off with old age, with decrepit years, a decayed mind and body and must even take up with that or have none at all. Or perhaps only a little time upon their deathbeds, when the frame is breaking to pieces and they are taking their leave of the world, then they would devote themselves to God and live to him. Malachi 1:8 says, "And if ye offer the blind for sacrifice, is it not evil? and if ye offer the lame and sick, is it not evil? offer it now unto thy governor; will he be pleased with thee, or accept thy person? saith the LORD of hosts."

6. Delaying to keep God's commandments is the greatest abuse of God's mercy and patience. What an abuse is it because we read that God is gracious and merciful and long-suffering and slow to anger. To

take occasion from thence to dare to go on in sin against him, to disobey, dishonor, and affront him because he is merciful, because he is a gracious being who is willing upon repentance to forgive our faults—this is to render unto God evil for good and to be the more his enemy because he is inclined to pity and help us.

If we did not hope that God is so merciful a being that he would hear us and pity us—though we do allow ourselves to sin against him and provoke him for some time longer—we dare not go on in sin with such freedom. We should fear his wrath and anger and should be more careful, but this is that which encourages men. They think that prayers and tears will do as well afterwards as now, and so they give themselves a liberty, but how ungrateful this is. This in Scripture is called despising God's goodness: "Or despisest thou the riches of his goodness and forbearance and longsuffering; not knowing that the goodness of God leadeth thee to repentance?" (Rom. 2:4).

Though other reasons might be mentioned, yet those that have been mentioned are sufficient to make the doctrine evident to us. We ought to make religion our business immediately and without delay

1. We ought not to put off religion through our own indisposedness to the duties of it. Men's own sloth and indolence and their indisposedness to those duties that are required of them is a very common reason why religion is put off and delayed. They cannot but be in some measure convinced of the sins and folly of it, but yet they find such a resistance and opposition of their nature against it that they still delay and a little longer procrastinate. The infinite majesty, holiness, and authority of God and the strict bands of our duty to him be of greater weight with us than our own dispositions are.

How great our indisposedness to duty may be, yet surely 'tis more against our inclination if we are reasonable creatures to suffer hellfire. If we suddenly should be brought to look into the grave, as we know we may be, then we should feel more of it, except we are very much hardened indeed, and should find a prevailing inclination for the time to come to deny ourselves.

We ought to consider why it is that the business of religion is so contrary to our inclinations. Is it because of the labor of it, and do we not labor in other things of infinitely less concern? Do we express so much as to get our daily bread without labor? And can we afford to labor for God and for our own immortal souls? Or is it because our natures are so sinful and corrupted that everything that is our duty that pertains to holiness and to God is so contrary to us that we can't bear it? If it be so, certainly we ought not to nourish and pamper such a disposition but with indignation to suppress and contradict it. And further, how will it help this indisposedness to religion to put it at a distance? Shall we be less opposite to it hereafter than now? No, 'tis so far from that that our contrariety to it grows the longer 'tis neglected. If we now betake ourselves to our duty, we shall experience some painful mortification at the first. But it's worst at first. After a while duties would become easier to us. If we are truly converted, they would become our pleasure and delight.

2. Religion ought not to be delayed for any other case or business. We can't say that we have not the time to mind the affairs of our souls because no business is of such importance that it ought to crowd out godliness. We ought not to be so taken up with business that is earthly as to neglect or be diverted from that for which we were created. If we never have sought God, it concerns us now immediately to seek him. But terms and merchandise ought not to hinder our accepting Christ's invitation. This appears from what we have already said of the importance of religion.

3. We ought not to delay for the sake of any sinful pleasures. The sensual man hears such suggestions as these within himself: "If I resolve immediately to set about religion, I must at once be deprived of all such and such pleasures and delights. I must never more gratify

such a dear inclination. Must never more expect to enjoy such a darling lust. I must always be forced to restrain myself from all the pleasures of the world, must keep my mouth with bit and bridle. Must make a covenant with my eyes. Must lock up my senses and shut out pleasure and merriment. And why should I do this so soon; why in such haste? Is it not better to enjoy those pleasures a little longer? Shall I not have time enough to prepare for death some years hence?"

What need of devoting so great a part of life to such a melancholy and joyless employment as that of religion? But if we regard our duty more than our pleasure, or if we regard our eternal pleasure more than our earthly, or indeed if we curtail our happiness even in this life and our pleasure on this side the greater, we should not heed those temptations. There being nothing that tends so much both to regulate and heighten our satisfaction here as godliness. The pleasures of sin bring such as bitterness in the latter end. Thus we ought so to make religion our present and immediate business, that no indisposedness or aversion to it, no worldly care or business, no lusts or pleasures ought to delay it.

APPLICATION

The improvement we shall make of the doctrine is chiefly to exhort all to make religion their present and immediate business. Let all hearken to the voice of God which is to them this day without delay to forsake sin, to throw up at once all sinful pleasures. Let Satan no longer have our service and the exercise of those powers that God gave us for a more excellent employment and nobler purposes. Let us not daily run the venture of our damnation and let the consideration of our duty and those arguments that have been set before us have some influence upon us. Let us consider that God's eye is continually upon us and how provoking must it needs be to him to see us notwithstanding all his instructs to continue in disobedience. Let gratitude to our daily benefactor cause us to exercise care that we don't sin against him from whom we have all our supplies of all the good we enjoy.

Consider how miserable we sometimes should be if God should delay his mercy and should not make haste to help us. If we are exercised with strong pain and cry to God for help, how impatient are we of delays. We want speedy relief and ease, and how miserable should we be if God were as slow in helping us as we be in obeying him. While God defers help our bodies suffer, and while we defer obedience, God's honor suffers. Which is of greater importance? When we labor under any calamity, we would have God make haste in showing mercy to us, but we make no haste to obey his commands.

How miserable we would be if God should withhold the common gifts of his providence during the time that we put off our duty to him. If he denied us our meat, drink, and sleep and all our defenses from the security of the weather were denied us, the light of the sun and the produce of the earth 'til we should turn our feet into his testimonies, doubtless 'twould quicken us. Although we are so slow of doing anything for God as long as we find that he supports us and gives us life and ease without it. But how just would it be with God if he should do thus? Is God obliged to bestow those blessings upon us to make that time comfortable to us that we spend in sinning against him? Is God bound to feed and nourish us to make us strong to serve Satan? Is he bound to give us corn and wine and oil to offer up to Baal?

These things conquer the unreasonableness, but be convincing to everyone delaying to make religion his business. But if you are not swayed by plain and evident duty and make no difficulty of doing things that you know in their own nature are most base and vile, let your own interests influence you. All men indifferently would avoid pain and misery and have happiness. Therefore, consider in the next place:

1. One would think 'twould be enough to say to you that 'tis a work that must be done first or last and when it's done we are safe and we need not be any longer in fear. When we lie down, we may think with ourselves that if we should die before we wake again, we are ready for it, and we need not fear that we shall lift up our eyes in hell being awakened in torments. If we are taken with any dangerous illness, we need not be amazed with the dreadful hurry of thoughts and fears. Whatever will be the issue, we may be sure of the grace and help of God. If sickness sends us to the grave, we have this to comfort us— that it won't send us to hell.

When we go about the ordinary affairs of life in which men are frequently exposed to pardon and fatal accidents, we may think with comfort if we should suddenly be snatched out of the world by a fall or any unhappy occurrence, we can't be snatched out of the merciful hands of our Redeemer. We need not fear being hurried into endless torment before we have time to turn a thought or to say, "Lord, have mercy on my soul," as it often is with men who are suddenly killed by accident. If we are called in God's providence particularly to expose ourselves to danger, we may encourage ourselves that providence calls us to this undertaking. If it proves fatal to us, we shall be found in the way of our duty and whatever becomes of our soul's state.

How blessed is such a soul's condition and how miserable are those who are out of it who are uncertain every day. How near they are to the term of their lives and are certain that if it should happen any way that their lives should be taken away while they are in the present state, they are in hell in spite of all the world and must be there forever.

2. What reason have we to fear that if we refuse to hear God's voice when he calls upon us that he will refuse to hear us when we cry unto him? Our time of finding is not always. There is a time wherein God may be found and wherein he is near. Isaiah 55:6 says, "Seek ye

the LORD while he may be found, call ye upon him while he is near." This implies that there is a time wherein God will not be found. Ezekiel 8:18 says, "Therefore will I also deal in fury: mine eye shall not spare, neither will I have pity: and though they cry in mine ears with a loud voice, yet will I not hear them."

We can't have too high and exalting thoughts of God's mercy. But yet we may have wrong thoughts of it—thoughts that are inconsistent with the honor of his majesty, authority, and justice. This is a wrong thought of it, as far as we have reason to conclude that God generally hears those cries of sinners upon their deathbed who have 'til then neglected religion.

3. Let us consider how many instances there arose of dying persons lamenting their delaying to keep God's commandments. If everyone of us have not seen many such instances, yet by what we have seen and heard, we may know that they are very frequent. Persons who are dying and as it were, in the middle between both worlds, are most likely to have a true and impartial sense of things of this nature. The words of dying persons ought to take hold on us because we ourselves must at a time appointed be dying persons. Except we hearken to them who have gone before us, we shall all be forced to set our feet to their testimony and to take up the same lamentation.

4. Let us consider what it is that we delay religion for, or wherein religion will be easier or in what respects will it be better setting about it hereafter than now. Have we an aversion to the duties of religion now? If we delay longer, we shall have a greater aversion.

And because religion is laborious and painful, that we defer it will never be less laborious. We can't be religious now without taking pains, and we shall not find that we have less to do hereafter, but more. For by continuing in sin, we make work for ourselves. Is it because we have a mind to enjoy more of the pleasure of sin? We shall not have a lost mind then. Sinful appetites don't decrease but increase by being gratified. Nor will lust that is gratified in youth wear out of itself in old age. The longer your mind is set on earthly things, the more earthly minded you are likely to grow, and the more will your thoughts be entangled in earthly things. Religion will not hinder you but help you in all your lawful business. Thereby you may hope for God's blessing not without a promise. Matthew 6:33 says, "But seek ye first the kingdom of God, and his righteousness; and all these things shall be added unto you."

But last this exhortation may be directed particularly to those who are in youth. Be exhorted to make haste and not delay to keep God's commands and now to make religion our business. 'Tis not only because those who are young are ready to think that there is time enough before them that they neglect religion, though that is the thought of the heart of most in youth. But they seem to think that religion is not properly the business of youth. They think that mankind doesn't generally so much expect that young persons should be religious. However, it may not be credible to be old and wicked yet that 'tis no shame to be void of serious religion and chiefly to mind the things of this world when young, while the spirits are vigorous and the tide of the blood is high, and nature is in its bloom.

They think the world expects no other than that now they should a little indulge themselves and their appetites and that they be not much to blame, nor very provoking to God or man, although they don't darken the spring of their life with the gloom of religion and the mortifying duties of holiness. They see that it's contrary to common custom and unfashionable to be thoughtful and serious and godly in youth and think the contrary credible. How much less, say they, would they be regarded by the gay world, and where must they go with all their seriousness and religion for companions? And if they could find any, what should they do with such dull, mopish company?

Whether any care to speak out thus or no, yet 'tis to be feared that 'tis really the thought of many young people if they think anything about it. 'Tis indeed deplorable that it should be thus amongst Christians who profess to believe that godliness is the business of their lives and that they are born for no other end but to be holy, but it is not thus.

These things are much for want of a true notion of holiness and from mistaking of it to be an unlovely, dark, and obscure thing that dulls and depresses the mind. For want of a sense of its contrary, excellent, and joyful nature whereby it would add to the bloom of their youth and greatly heighten and increase their joy, instead of depriving them of the verdure and cheerfulness of that age. And let it be considered that whatever is the custom and thought of the world—whatever they may think of an indulgence that is given to youth to transgress— yet God gives no such liberty. He expects that youth itself be improved as a special talent committed to them above others. God gives no more liberty for not directing the prime of our days to them than he did to the children of Israel to withhold the firstfruits which was what he more especially required.

But their own interests and safety plead no less for young persons speedy seeking God's face than their duty. Consider that if you defer religion 'til youth is past, you are certain if you die in youth of being miserable forever. And if you live 'til you are old, you are not certain of ever being converted. And how dreadful will it be to live 'til old and die at last in sin! To have a long life of sin to answer for and to suffer for is much more dreadful than to die in youth, yea, though you die in sin in youth. And if you live in sin in youth, 'tis much less probable that you will be converted afterwards because the heart grows harder and harder the older you are. There is the greater likelihood of God leaving the sinner and giving him up to sin.

And if you are converted afterward, you are sure of repenting of this very thing—that you did not do your work when young. You are sure of making work for repentance 'til that time comes and making your work of reformation and conversion much more difficult, and of having the bitterness all your days, of thinking that you devoted your early and best days to sin. And you will probably have less peace and joy, less of the comfort of the Holy Spirit. And your dying hour may be darkened with your remembrance of your sinful youth. You will have less time to do service to God in the world and will probably not make such progress in holiness. If you escape hell, yet you will have a less reward in heaven. Surely if there were only this, that was the advantage of being early religious—that we shall be forever advanced higher in glory. 'Twould be worth our while for an addition to that happiness which is eternal, interminable, and infinite. And if all these things are so—as most certainly they can't be objected against—how much is it our wisdom to remember our Creator in the days of our youth.

We may close this discourse with a few directions on how immediately to set about the work of our souls.

1. Consider the nature and tendency of your present sinful course of life. True reformation is always begun in mature and serious considerations. The psalmist tells us in the verse foregoing our text that he thought on his ways and then he turned his feet into God's testimonies and delayed not to keep his commandments. 'Tis thoughtlessness and inconsideration that uphold a course of sin. There is such madness and folly in an allowed neglect of religion. That did men but consider themselves, they could never rest in it. If you want to do what you should consider of, consider of those things that you have heard at this time. If duly pondered in your thoughts, they can do no other than convince you that 'tis your duty and prudence to choose God's commandments immediately. Take off your thoughts sometimes from the world and compel them to dwell on serious subjects. There is a

natural power which men have over their own thoughts to restrain them from some things, at least in some measure, and to exercise them about others. Let this power be exerted by you.

2. Immediately fly and avoid all those things that have been particular hindrances and temptations to prevent your being religious—whether these be ill conversation or any particular practice that, however innocent in itself, you find the temptations of it too mighty for you. Flee from those things which will be a great hindrance to you or whatever else upon consideration you may conclude will be as pullbacks or stumbling blocks in your way.

3. All known sin must be immediately forsaken. The keeping of one darling lust, of one sinful pleasure, though comparatively small, if it be a known evil is enough to render all ineffectual. The man who still lives in sin and is not reformed has not turned feet into God's testimonies. He who allows himself in the breach of one command is as if he broke all. James 2:10 says, "For whosoever shall keep the whole law, and yet offend in one point, he is guilty of all."

4. Diligently use those means that God has appointed for our instruction and conversion. The Word of God was given to us to be read and doubtless is what is above all things adapted to obtain those great ends. The preaching of the Word was appointed not merely to strike the ears but to be attended to in order to practice, and God's ministers were designed for guides to us in matters that concern our souls.

5. Let God be sought frequently and carefully by prayer. The business of religion, a business that immediately respects God and religion, is vain without some communication between God and our own souls. God has appointed prayer for the maintaining of this intercourse. Let us seek to God for his grace, his pardon, and his acceptance, if ever we hope for it. A course of sin makes the least course into prayer. And a diligent and constant attendance on prayer will keep us from avowed sinning.

6

⊷⊷⊷⊷ ⊷⊷⊷⊷⊷

That God Is Everywhere Present

Whither shall I go from thy spirit? or whither shall
I flee from thy presence?
PSALM 139:7–10

This sermon, also undated, is the last example of Edwards's sermons from the Psalms. Edwards himself introduces it as a meditation upon God's omnipresence and omniscience. He describes
something of God's being, his nature and working. Even though it is
done in typical Edwards fashion for such subjects, yet when it comes
to the application, the first reason he gives is that the subject matter
might awaken sinners.

Edwards explains that God's omnipresence means more than God
is near. He is even in those who provoke him to anger. Edwards further shows the dreadful danger that sinners are in when he states that
God possesses those parts of the body which they use as instruments
of sin.

The sermon manuscript is a typical duodecimal booklet, consisting of twenty-two leaves with no evidence of damage and only limited
examples of changes. The application consists of ten pages.

This psalm is a meditation upon God's omnipresence and omniscience. The psalmist seems to be carried out with an admiring sense of it. He therefore dwells upon it and upon the effects and manifestations of it throughout the psalm. And in these verses he considers it with relation to himself as God's creature and one subject to his providence and judgment. He considers with himself how impossible it is for him, as for any creature, to get from God so as to be hid from him, or be out of his way.

In this light:

1. He considers God's omnipresence more generally in these interrogations: "Whither shall I go from thy spirit? or whither shall I flee from thy presence?" That is, "I can nowhere hide myself from thee."

2. He also considers it as it were by parts and terms, according to the threefold difference of distance. That is difference in height and depth and parallel distance. He divides the world or the whole infinite space into three: that which is above which he calls heaven, that which is below which he calls hell, and that which is distant on every side which is the uttermost parts of the seas. He could never ascend so high into heaven or should go never so great a distance above that he could get out of God's reach. Things that are very high are far out of our reach but not out of God's. Or if he descend so low into the earth, even down to hell, he would not be hid from him or out of his way. Or if he should take the wings of the morning and fly to the uttermost parts of the sea—if he should fly with the light of the rising sun that immediately spreads from one horizon to another and is spread abroad at an immense distance in a manner so if he could fly as swift as the morning light and go as far as not only the ends of the earth but to the uttermost parts of the sea which is beyond that, yet he should yet be in God's hand.

DOCTRINE

God is everywhere present. Here we shall first explain how God is everywhere present and then bring some arguments that prove that he is so.

1. God is present everywhere in his being and essence. There is no place where God in his being is not. There is no other being but what is confined with respect to the place of its existence. Some creatures are of most extent a mighty space beyond our imagination. This globe of the earth, if we attempt to conceive of it, appears a thing of a mighty bulk. Some other of the heavenly hosts are immensely greater in bulk. The sun is a body in comparison of which the earth is but a little speck, but this is as nothing in comparison of the whole universe or only of the visible part of the universe, which far exceeds our comprehension. It is almost beyond the power of numbers to express according to the certain discoveries of learned men. It must needs be of an amazing extent, and how much farther it extends than has been yet discovered. How far beyond the remotest parts of it that can be seen by the naked eye or assisted by artificial helps we can't tell. But this we know, that it can't be infinite.

An infinite thing can't be made up of finite things. However large it is, it doesn't come at all the nearer to infinite for that. A pebble or a grain of sand is as near infinite as the world is, but God is infinite. Although a body be finite, yet we unavoidably conceive mere space which is a positive thing but only room as having no bounds but there is no part of space where God is not. God fills the world. In Jeremiah 23:24 God says, "Do not I fill heaven and earth?" He does not only fill heaven and earth, but he is where the world is not. The heaven of heavens are spoken of as the utmost bounds of the world, but yet they cannot contain God: "Behold, the heaven and heaven of heavens cannot contain thee" (1 Kings 8:27). God is where the world is and where the world is not. Everywhere where the world is not, God's essence is as much beyond the utmost boundaries of the creation as it is beyond the bounds of a little ball.

As some created things by the vastness of their bulk are in many parts of space at the same time according to their different parts, so many by their swiftness and activity can be wholly in many places successively in a very little time. Thus the angels whom God has made as a flame of fire and as a flash of lightning for swiftness, they can be in the highest heavens and upon the earth in a very limited time. But God is in all places at one and the same moment of time.

God not only is where other things are not but also where they are in the same places where other things are amongst them. It would imply a contradiction to suppose that two could be in the very same place at the same time. If any body possesses any part of space, 'tis impossible that any other body should come there 'til that be removed. 'Til that body removes from its place, it will keep all others out of it. God is not excluded by other things but is there where other things are, not only round about them but in them. We are in God. Acts 17:28 says, "In him we live, and move, and have our being." And God is in us and in every part of us. He is in us and he is through us. "One God and Father of all, who is above all, and through all, and in you all" (Eph. 4:6).

We must take heed that we haven't so gross a notion of God's immensity and omnipotence. We must not conceive of it as if part of God were in one place and part in another as great bodies are. God is not made up of parts, for he is a simple, pure essence. If we say that God is in this house, it must not be understood that *part* of God is in this house but God is here. 'Tis not part of God who is in us, but God is in us.

2. God is present everywhere where any other being is by his operation and influence. God is in the continual exercise of his infinite power and wisdom everywhere throughout the whole creation. Every

moment 'tis a continual act of infinite power to uphold things in being. When we look upon anything that we can behold, we see the personal operation of infinite power. The same power that made things to be, that first moment that ever they were, is now exercised to make them to be this moment and is continually exercised to make them to be to be every moment that they are. God's preservation of the world is nothing but a continued act of creation.

We read that God created all things by the word of his power, so we read that he upholds all things "by the word of his power" (Heb. 1:3). And by that he made all things so "by him all things consist" (Col. 1:17). And as it is the continual operation of God to uphold things in being, so it is the divine operation that keeps them in action. Whenever a body moves or a spirit thinks or wills, it is the infinite power and wisdom that assists it. God has established the laws of nature, and he maintains them by his continual influence.

When we see the sun shine, we see God's present operation and that which is the effect of his former operation but that is from his immediate influence every moment. So when we see the heavenly bodies move, or when we see the sea ebb and flow and the rivers run and the trees grow and animals move and act and we ourselves live and breathe, we behold God's present work. Whenever there are any natural actions or motions in things with life or without life, then God is present by his operation. And with respect to ourselves, it is because God is in us that our blood runs, our pulse beats and our lungs breathe and our food digests and our organs of sense perform their operations.

When we look at the sun, moon, and stars above, or look upon the earth and the things below, if we look so much as upon the stones under us, we see infinite power now in exercise thereof at that place. So if we look upon ourselves and see our hands or feet and the members, these have an existence because God is there and by an act of infinite power upholds them. So that God not only is everywhere but he is everywhere working where any created thing acts or is. And if we look on things aright, we may as properly see God act as we can see man when we see him walk or work.

But although God is present everywhere and with respect to his essence present everywhere alike, yet there are different kinds of the divine presence. He is present after a different manner in different places and with different creatures.

1. He is gloriously present in heaven. We are always informed that "God is in heaven" (Eccl. 5:2), that he dwells there. God is in heaven, and therefore we often read of God's coming down from heaven. It is said that Christ came down from heaven when he was incarnate, as if God's place to dwell is there, nowhere else but in heaven because God is present there after a manner that he is nowhere else nor anything like it by a peculiar manifestation and communication of himself. His glory dwells there. There they see him and converse with him more familiarly than Moses did. Heaven is called the city of the great King, the house or temple of the living God, the throne of God. The Holy of Holies where God dwelled amongst the children of Israel was but a shadow of it.

2. He is gloriously present in his church and with his people on earth. He is present with them by the gracious influences and operations of his Spirit. This is the same kind of presence as his heavenly host in every imperfect degree. There are different ministers of God's gracious presence with his people there. His presence by communication and presence of manifestation, God may communicate himself to those who at the same time he doesn't manifest himself to. There is the sanctifying presence of God, and his comforting presence are different things, though they generally go together. The saint always has the Spirit of God dwelling in his heart to sanctify him. He never leaves us in this respect, but he may withdraw from us as to his comforting presence and hide his face from us.

3. God is present by his common goodness and bounty with mankind in general. Though man is in a fallen state and condition, yet it is evident that he has not forsaken the earth by that abundant bounty and goodness which he disperses abroad in the world. His gracious communications he disperses of his goodness to all nations of men and by his goodness is yet present in this lower world that is so exceedingly corrupted.

So that the different kinds and degrees of God's presence may be thus summed up, this is his essential presence which is everywhere alike, both where created things are and where they are not. And there is his influential presence or presence by his operation which is his presence by his common goodness, and thus he is present in this world of mankind. There is his sanctifying presence by the indwelling of his Spirit in his church and with all his people at all times. There is his comforting presence with his people at the same time, and there is his glorious presence in heaven. Even in hell God is present essentially and by his power and operation, but it is in a dreadful, tremendous manner that he is present there. Christ said thus, that God was in himself as Alpha and Omega, that he is in the world as author and governor.

That he is as the angels as their pleasure and beauty. That he is in the church as the Father of a family. That he is in the soul as a bridegroom in his chamber. In the just as a helper and protector. In reprobates as terror and torment.

We proceed now to give the reasons why it must needs be that God is everywhere present. We shall not here insist upon testimonies of Scripture. Several have been already mentioned, but upon reasons taken from the divine nature other attributes of God to evidence that he must be omnipresent.

1. God is a necessary being, and his being everywhere present will follow from thence. When we say that God is a necessary being, we

mean that he is not a being whose existence flows not from another greater beside himself but that he is because it is in itself considered an impossibility or a contradiction that God should not be. It is not only a necessary consequence from the creation and the like, that God should be, but it is in itself necessary that he should have an existence. It is not only necessary that God should go on to be, seeing he once is, but there is a necessity prior to any consequence. It was necessary from all eternity that God should be, and he also necessarily is just what he is and no otherwise.

Now if it be so, it will follow that God is everywhere, for if it be absolutely necessary that God should be in any place it is necessary that he should be in all places. If we suppose that God is so far extended that his presence only fills such a determinate place, then I ask what necessity was prior to all determining causes that he should be so far extended and no further.

If you say it chanced to be so that God should be so great and no greater, but that overthrows the supposition of God's being a necessary being, for chance and necessity are very inconsistent things. If you suppose God is finite and there are bounds to his existence, then it must be because of one of these things: Either because some cause made him so great and no greater nor less, or that he only chanced to be so great, or that it is in its own nature impossible that God should be greater or less than such a finite greatness. The two former are against the supposition of God's being a necessary being; the latter is a gross nonsense.

2. God is an unchangeable being, and it follows from this that he is everywhere. For if he were in some places and not in others, he would be changeable. For instance, if he were only in some finite place, he would be capable of motion, of moving from place to place which is change, for everything that is finite is capable in its own nature of motion.

3. God is omnipotent and therefore must be in every place. If God is omnipotent, he is able to do everything in all places. But if he be not in all places, he cannot do this, for nothing can act where it is not. If God be not everywhere, then where he is not, he can do nothing 'til he is there. If God be almighty, then he is able to create another world beyond this and a thousand more, but he can't do it except he be there where we suppose these worlds must be. If God be not infinite, then he can't create and uphold and govern worlds any further than his existence is extended. So his power would be reduced to the same bounds as his existence. Other reasons might be given, but these are sufficient to show that God must be present everywhere.

APPLICATION

1. Use of awakening to sinners. It is an awakening and even an amazing consideration to think that they live and move in that God who is angry with them every moment. He is not an enemy at a distance from them, nor is he only near to them, but he is in them and they in him. He is in them and through them wherever they go, and yet they provoke him to anger. They daily disobey him and do acts of contemptuous, willful rebellion against him, affront him every day. He doesn't only stand by them and look on when they do it, but they are in him. He possesses every part of their body which they use as instruments of sin against him.

If they can hide themselves from men and get into corners and secret places, yet they are in God. If they would fly from his presence, let them fly where they will; they are still in his presence. If they could enter into heaven, he is there. If they creep under the earth quite down to hell, he is there. If they travel to distant countries, to other continents, they can't fly from him; they are still in him. If the mountains should fall on them and the rocks cover them, they would not be hid from his wrath. Other enemies may be fled from. If men are provoked, there are ways of securing ourselves from them. If a king is provoked, those who are the objects of his displeasure will oftentimes fly into other countries, and then they are out of the way. But it signifies nothing to endeavor to fly or to hide from God (Amos 9:1–4).

So that there is no such thing as flying from God. God is not only present with sinners wherever they are as to his essence, but as to his creation God has also created them, and he creates them every moment. 'Tis the immediate, infinite power of God who continually upholds those hearts in which they design wickedness and those tongues by which they speak wickedness and hands by which they work wickedness. 'Tis his immediate power that enables them to think or to speak or breathe, and yet all they do is to sin against God and provoke him to anger.

One would think that when you look upon your hands and consider that God by his mighty power keeps them in being, you should not dare to put them to any wickedness and that you should tremble at the very thought of it.

2. In this doctrine is matter of great comfort to the saints—that he who is their friend and Father is always present with them and in them, that they live and move and have their being in him who loves them with a great and everlasting love. Our earthly friends can't be always with us. We are often called to part with them, but God is a friend always at hand, always with and in those who are his.

Let those who have given themselves to God and have chosen God to be their God consider this: that they are in him who is favorable unto them and delights in them and always consults their good and feeds their welfare. They are in him, and none can separate them from him. Wherever they are, they are still with God.

This is great matter of consolation to them whatever danger and difficulties they are brought into—that they are with God, that he is right at hand, so that they need not be terrified with any amazement.

They are in him who orders all things and who loves them so that he will surely take care of them and order things well for them. If they pray to him in their difficulty and beg his help, he is present to hear their prayers. They need not go far to seek him or cry aloud to make him hear. He is in them and hears the silent petitions of their hearts and is with them.

If they are in solitude and are very much left alone, if they have lost all their earthly friends and are left desolate, if they are banished from their native country and obliged to fly into the wilderness, it may be a matter of great consolation to them that however they are deprived of the company of earthly friends, God is with them. They can't be bereaved of that friend who is more than all. None can banish them from the presence and society of God. A Christian never needs to be lonesome as long as he is in the company of such a one.

If a Christian is journeying or has occasion to remove from place to place, he may consider that all the way that he goes, God goes along with him. Wheresoever he is, there is God. Or if he be carried into captivity—it is a doleful thing to be carried from all friends and acquaintances into an enemy's country, and it may be amongst a barbarous people—yet there is this comforting consideration for them: God is in all countries, that all lands are his who 'tis their friend and not their enemy.

If a Christian dwell in a mean cottage or be cast into a prison or a dungeon, yet God dwells with those who are of a humble and a contrite spirit, however mean and base the place is where they dwell. God's presence is in prisons and in dungeons as well as anywhere else. And if they are involved in any difficult business or undertaking, nothing can give greater comfort and courage than to consider that God is at their right hand to help and assist them. Or if a Christian is dying and going out of the world, going to leave all things here below, he has this to support him—that he is not going to be separated from God.

His soul leaves this lower world, yet it will go where God is. For God is in the other world as well as this world. Yea, he is going to heaven where is God's glorious presence, his peculiar dwelling place, his own house or temple where they shall see him and dwell with him forever.

It is a matter of great consolation to them that Christ their Redeemer is everywhere. That he who has loved them and died for them and washed them in his own blood is with them in all places. He who has undertaken for them and has given himself to be their helper and Savior, whenever they are weary and heavy laden with sins and their consciences are afflicted. They may consider that they have Christ to fly to at all times, who is ready to undertake for them. When they are in spiritual darkness, there is he who is the Light of the world nigh unto them. Whenever they pray to God, Christ is ready to perfume their prayers with the incense of his merits and intercession. Romans 10:6–8 says, "Who shall ascend into heaven? (that is, to bring Christ down from above:) Or, Who shall descend into the deep? (that is, to bring up Christ again from the dead.) But what saith it? The Word is nigh thee, even in thy mouth, and in thy heart."

Saints have little reason to be afraid of dangers, if they have faith as the disciples had who were in the storm when Christ was in the ship. But that you may have the comfortable sense of the presence of God and of Jesus Christ, it is needful that you follow these two directions:

1. Be exceeding careful not to drive away the comfortable presence of God by sinning against him. God as to his essential presence can't be driven away, nor wholly his sanctifying presence, but you may grieve God by your sins so as to make him withdraw from you as to his comfortable presence. Though God be always present with you, yet if you grieve him by carelessness and negligence or by a worldliness or by sinful passion or giving way to any sinful, unchristian disposition, you may make him hide his face from you and lose the comfortable

sense of his presence with you. You may be left in darkness and sorrows and see no light and be surrounded with many terrors and fears and be in a great measure without the support of God's Spirit. God will never leave his people 'til they leave him. They shall enjoy the light of life except they do the works of darkness. God delights to manifest himself to those who keep themselves pure and undefiled, but he doesn't love to come near to spiritual filthiness. Iniquity is an abomination unto him.

2. If you would keep alive a comfortable sense of the presence of God, you must often converse with God in prayer. If God be with us, yet if we don't converse with him and have nothing to do with him, we be not likely to have much comfort of his presence. If there but be little conversation between a saint and God, he will forget that God is present with him; he will lose the sense of it. If he doesn't converse with God by prayer, God will not converse with him. So there will grow a strangeness, but be expected that God will not be at hand at all times to teach and instruct and to comfort as otherwise he would be.

The third use is of exhortation in several branches:

1. If it be so that God is everywhere present, then stand in continual fear and awe of God. If you were in the presence of an earthly prince, you would stand in awe. You would be afraid of behaving yourself so as to be displeasing to him. You would as soon eat fire as to disobey and affront him. And will you not see to do that which is displeasing to him—who is the great King of heaven and earth—in his presence before his eyes?

You are afraid of ordinary men; you dare not be seen by them in these and those wicked practices. You dare not practice them when they stand by and look on. Yea, you are afraid of a little child and many men stand a great deal more in awe of children than they do of the great God. They dare not do those things before a child who can just speak plain what they boldly commit before God's eyes. How unreasonable and stupid and how perverting is this! What dreadful presumption it is. God will make such to know that it is more dreadful a thing to disobey him in his presence than to disobey any earthly prince in their presence, however light a matter they make of it now.

Consider therefore of this matter when you are about to commit sin. Consider with yourself that God is here. You now live and move in God. The darkness and the light are both alike to him. Although now he lets you alone, yet he won't forget it, but he will have a reckoning with you for all your miscarriages. Ecclesiastes 11:9 says, "Know thou, that for all these things God will bring thee into judgment."

2. Let us avoid all manner of guile and hypocrisy. Let us see to it that we make no pretence to anything in religion but what is real. Don't let us make any pretences in prayer or in any other duty that is not true, for God is everywhere. He knows how the case is with us. He is always by us and in us and searches the secret closets of our hearts; he knows what is there and what is not. However we may blind men's eyes, we can't delude God with any of our pretences. Let them never be so sure and plausible. He knows our thoughts afar off. His eyes are as a flame of fire. 'Tis not clouds or darkness or roofs or walls or caverns of the earth that will hinder God's seeing of us.

If persons are hypocrites and hide themselves under deceitful garments, they may appear no other than to have their garments at last to be pulled off and to be forced to walk naked so men should see their shame and that they may see their filthiness and pollution.

3. If it be so that God is present everywhere, let us be exhorted to walk with God, to stay close to him and not depart from him after the example of Enoch (Gen. 5:24). Let us endeavor to know God, to get acquainted with that being whom we have our being in. Let us seek after a spiritual union with God. Reconciliation to him and his friendship and forever that we may walk well with him as a friend with a friend. Let us continually seek his gracious presence that he may not

only be essentially present with us but present by the holy and sweet indwelling of his Spirit. In all our business and affairs let us go to God and consult him and make known our case to him and commit our way to him that he may direct our steps.

Let us always behave ourselves as in the sight of God, shunning all evil, seeking and pursuing God, and conforming ourselves to his image. After we have walked with God, God might take us as he did Enoch to dwell with him forever in his glorious presence.

7

God Stands Ready to Forgive Every Sinner upon His Heartily Confessing and Forsaking His Sin

He that covereth his sins shall not prosper: but whoso confesseth and
forsaketh them shall have mercy.

PROVERBS 28:13

This is a sermon that Edwards preached to the Stockbridge Indians in March 1752. It consists of a very clear presentation of how real confession of sin results in a real forsaking of that sin, which results in our receiving forgiveness. He takes great care to explain the nature of real confession, that it is not just words. As sincere and humble confession of sin is made, there will be an accompanying sense of the hatefulness of that sin, especially as it pertains to God's holy nature, together with a sense of God's wrath against sin and of his great mercy. True confession is confirmed true by a genuine forsaking of sin and a choosing instead of a life of holiness and obedience.

The sermon manuscript is a typical duodecimal booklet, consisting of thirty-two leaves with no evidence of damage, but it does contain many corrections and additions from Edwards.

Though the gospel was never fully promulgated 'til Christ came, yet it was revealed sufficiently for the salvation of the people of God under that legal dispensation that went before. There are many gospel promises to be found in the Law of Moses and throughout the other parts of the Old Testament. The terms of the gospel—faith and repentance—were not then kept hid. We have often promises of pardon upon repentance, as we have here in the text upon confessing and forsaking of sin, which are the two genuine expressions of repentance and the proper acts of a penitent soul.

DOCTRINE

God stands ready to forgive every sinner upon his hearty confessing and forsaking his sin. I would show what it is heartily to confess sin. It cannot be supposed that by confessing sin in the text is only meant a saying in words, "I acknowledge I have done this or that, and I acknowledge I have done sinfully in it." Words are but wind and are easily spoken. If men might have pardon upon only saying such words, this would not only make the gate of heaven very wide and be an encouragement to an unrestrained wickedness, but it would be to make that which very commonly is only a lie to be the condition of pardon.

We never find such great things as pardon and salvation connected with the saying of any words or with anything that is merely external. Men may confess in words a thousand times, yea, and make other appearances and shows of repentance; they may often keep days of fasting with pretence of humbling themselves for their sins; they may fast twice a week and yet be never the nearer to pardon. Therefore in order to the confessing in the sense of the text, there must be really a pretence and show of what there is in confession.

1. They must be sensible of the sins that they confess. In confession of sin that is a pretence of this, they say they have sinned. When they confess particular sins, they say they have sinned in doing thus and thus. In so saying, they must speak their hearts. They must say as they think and not lie to God. There must be a conviction of sin when they confess that they are sinful by nature. There must be a conviction that it is really so and a sense of it. They must not only say that their nature is corrupt, but they must see that it is so and see wherein it is so.

There must be a conviction of their actual sins. They must not only say that they have done wickedly in this and that act or practice or manner of life, but there must be a sense of it. There must be a reflection on their past sinful courses and acts and a sight of their contrariety to the law of God. It must not only be said to God, "We have done wickedly; we have lived wicked lives," but they must see wherein they must have their sins set in order before their eyes in order to hearty confession.

2. In order to have hearty and sincere confession, there must be a sense of the evil of the sins that are confessed. In confession there is a show as though they acknowledged that what they have done was evil, unreasonable, and hateful. And there must be really such an acknowledgment the heart must be sensible that they are hateful.

For men to confess their sin, as though they owned them to be very odious, vile, and detestable things, and at the same time think them to be eligible and desirable, is but a mocking of God. A person cannot truly acknowledge that which he is not sensible of for what is acknowledging, but a person's expressing his sensibleness of a thing. For a person to acknowledge or confess the hatefulness of his sins is to express his sense of the hatefulness of it. If he has no such sense, then he cannot truly confess it.

They therefore who do in sincerity confess their sins will see the hatefulness of that corruption which is in their hearts, and they will see the loathsomeness of their lusts and of their sinful ways, and that they are worthy to be avoided and renounced and shunned. Note Job's confession, "Behold! I am vile" (Job 40:4).

3. In confessing to God there is an appearance if they do it sincerely which implies their sense of the evil of sin as against God. If they were only sensible of the evil of such and such acts, considered in themselves absolutely without any relation to God, why will it not content them to bewail and lament their sins by themselves? Why do they go to God to bring their lamentations before him?

The language or show of their so doing must be that they are sensible of the evil of what they have done, as it is against God. They have wronged God and affronted and dishonored him. And that is the reason it does not contemn them to lament their sins by themselves, but they confess it to him because he is nearly concerned. God they have injured, and therefore to him would they confess.

If there be a sincere confessing of sin to God, there must be a sense of the evil of sin as committed against God. The hatefulness and vileness of it is contrary to his nature, and therefore they must see a sense of the excellency and glory of his nature that it is contrary to.

There is also a sense of the unreasonableness of sin as contrary to God's will and as contrary to God's glory. Leviticus 26:40,42 says, "If they shall confess their iniquity, and the iniquity of their fathers, with their trespass which they trespassed against me, and that also they have walked contrary unto me. . . . Then will I remember my covenant with Jacob, and also my covenant with Isaac, and also my covenant with Abraham will I remember; and I will remember the land." Thus David when he confessed expressed his sense of sin as against God: "And David said unto Nathan, I have sinned against the Lord" (2 Sam. 12:13). So in Psalm 51:4, "Against thee, thee only, have I sinned, and done this evil in thy sight." So Nehemiah said, "Both I and my father's house have sinned. We have dealt very corruptly against thee" (Neh. 1:6–7).

4. In confessing sin to God, there is an appearance of a sense of God's displeasure for sin, and therefore if confession be sincere, there is really such a sense. We confess to God because we are sensible he has been displeased and provoked, and therefore we come to humble ourselves before him to seek reconciliation. He who truly confesses to God is therefore sensible of God's holy and pure nature whereby he abhors sin and is much displeased with it. They are sensible of his greatness and majesty which they have affronted and are therefore sensible that God is angry with them. Thus the church confesses, "Behold, thou art wroth; for we have sinned" (Isa. 64:5).

5. A sincere confessing of sin implies a sense that God's displeasure is just. There is an appearance and show made of this in confessing of sin to God. If God has no just cause to be displeased, then there is no need of confessing. If this be not confessed that they have given just cause of his anger, nothing is confessed.

Therefore, those who do sincerely confess their sins are sensible that God might justly be angry with them and punish them and follow them with his wrath and curse. They are sensible that they have deserved the displeasure which he manifests and as great a punishment as he threatens and are sensible of their own utter unworthiness by reason of sin of any mercy of favors and that they have nothing of their own to plead for themselves why God should not proceed against them in wrath. Thus, Job confesses in Job 40:3, "Behold, I am vile; what shall I answer thee? I will lay mine hand upon my mouth." He was sensible he had no excuse to make for himself. Nothing to plead in his own behalf. Thus also, the church confesses, "The LORD is righteous; for I have rebelled against his commandment" (Lam. 1:18).

6. He who heartily confesses his sin does it with humility and abasement of soul for his sins. There is a show of persons humbling themselves in their confessing of their sins. They make as though they had a humble sense of their own unworthiness. And as though

they were willing to lie low before God and to take shame unto themselves. And therefore he that heartily confesses his sin doth so indeed.

He is little and vile in his own eyes and has a sincere disposition to lie in the dust at the foot of God. There is a gracious humbleness and brokenness of heart, a disposition to set God high and to lie at the footstool. So it was with the repenting and confessing prodigal in Luke 15:18–19: "Father, I have sinned against heaven, and before thee, and am no more worthy to be called thy son." So it was with Job in Job 42:6, "I abhor myself, and repent in dust and ashes." So it was with the penitent publican in Luke 18:13. Thus Ezra confessed in Ezra 9:6 and said, "O my God, I am ashamed and blush to lift up my face to thee, my God: for our iniquities are increased over our head, and our trespass is grown up unto the heavens."

7. In hearty confessing of sin, there is an apprehension of the mercy of God to pardon sin. This is our encouragement to confess our sins—that God is merciful and there is hope for us in his mercy that we may be pardoned. We confess seeking mercy and reconciliation as the publican did in Luke 18:13, "And the publican, standing afar off, would not lift up so much as his eyes unto heaven, but smote upon his breast, saying, God be merciful to me a sinner." Though he was so sensible of his own wretchedness and unworthiness and was so filled with shame in a sense of his sin, yet he despaired not of mercy.

Therefore, they who act sincerely in confessing have an apprehension of the mercy of God in Christ whereby he hath a sufficiency for our pardon. Thus Daniel in his confession of sin professes a sense of the mercy of God to pardon. He said, "O Lord, to us belongeth confusion of face, to our kings, to our princes, and to our fathers, because we have sinned against thee. To the Lord our God belong mercies and forgivenesses, though we have rebelled against him" (Dan. 9:8–9).

Let us consider what is the forsaking of sin.

1. The heart must forsake it. There is naturally a union between the heart and sin and that union must be dissolved. There is naturally a dear friendship that the heart hath for sin. This friendship must be broken. The soul is wedded to sin, but there must be a divorce. The heart must forsake sin in three things.

The heart must forsake sin in its choice. Men naturally choose sin as what they delight in, as what is naturally and agreeable to them. It is their element, their nature inclines to it, and they can't bear to part with it. The natural man chooses sin as his food; he has a thirsting desire after it. He feeds upon it every day and seeks it as naturally as the body of man craves food. Natural men choose the temporal advantages, ease, honors, profits, and pleasures of sin. Some or all of these are for his portion.

But if ever they truly forsake sin, they forsake it and renounce it in their choice and choose what is contrary to it. They choose God and choose a life of holiness and obedience. They renounce sin with all its advantages and pleasures and choose a life of holiness with all the disadvantages and temporal difficulties that attend it.

God sets before men life and death to choose in that he sets before them sin and holiness which are virtually life and death (Deut. 30:15).

The heart must forsake sin in its affections. Wicked men's affections are debased to embrace this foul monster. Their affections cleave to it. The objects of their lusts are the objects of their strongest and most violent affections of their loves, their desires, their complacencies, and their hopes. They go out after those objects above all other objects.

But when men do truly forsake sin, those affections forsake those objects which they loved before. That which before they thirsted after is become now loathsome to them. They delight not in it. That which they had their complacence in is now their burden. What they rejoiced in before, they now mourn for and go mourning under the remains of it. Their affections are turned another way. They now love God and delight in holiness and hunger. They thirst after righteousness and rejoice in holy exercises and have their chief joy and complacence in holy objects.

The heart must forsake sin in purposes and resolutions. There is a sincere purpose of heart in them who do truly forsake sin, of forever abandoning former ways of wickedness. Of utterly disallowing lusts that have been formerly indulged, no more returning to former sinful ways whatever circumstances they should be under and whatever difficulties their adherence to the ways of virtue and holiness may be attended with.

2. The other part of forsaking of sin is forsaking it in life and practice. He who truly forsakes sin actually departs from it in deed as well as in disposition. This is the proper evidence of his forsaking it in heart—that he forsakes it in act. Men may think themselves willing to forsake their sins and abandon their lusts. That when it comes to the trial will not do, they will not take their leave of their sins. If they do it in some measure, yet they won't do it wholly. They can't bear to have any more acquaintance or conversation with those old friends and wholly to treat them as enemies and to give them no entertainment, neither secretly nor openly. If they part with them for a while, yet they are not willing to part with them forever.

A person may think himself willing to part with an old friend. Yet when it comes to a trial, he may find it otherwise when he comes to the parting point, may find such affections rising towards him that shall overcome him and draw him to his embraces again. Or if he doth for the present seem to go away and to part with him, yet when he has been absent awhile, he may find himself not weaned. He has such an inbred love for him that shall work so strongly as to make him repent and return to him again and renew his old friendship.

Or if he does seem to continue in a degree to abstain from his company so that he won't do it openly or so frequently, yet his friendship may not be broke, but he may still maintain a kindness for his old friend and may indulge that friend by some secret intercourse. He may meet his friend in the dark sometimes and in a secret place, and there he may gratify his old remaining affection to his friend, though he seems to others to have forsaken him wholly. Or if he is restrained by fear or some such thing from ever coming to so full and free a conversation with him, yet he may indulge a friendship to his old friend in other ways, by still maintaining some more distant conversation with him. Friends may give each other testimonies of each other's love, though they be not allowed to come together.

If a man makes profession of renouncing friendship with one whom he formerly loved, 'tis his practice that must show it. If he does indeed forsake him and treats him ever after as an enemy, then there will be reason to believe him—that he really has forsaken him in his heart.

So 'tis forsaking sin in the deed that is the proper evidence of forsaking it in heart. If men utterly renounce it evermore, fight against it, and will in no case harbour it or give any entertainment to it under any pretence whatever and will not allowedly have to do with it in the light or in darkness, in thought, word, or act in one way or another, as long as they live. And will never be persuaded to return to it by all affrightments or allurements, that man doubtless has forsaken sin in his heart and his practice shows it.

They who do truly forsake sin never statedly allow of any known sin, nor can they make a trade of any sort of wickedness whatsoever. No known wickedness can be said to be any godly man's course or practice. 'Tis against the plain Word of God: "They also do no iniquity: they walk in his ways" (Ps. 119:3). First John 3:6 says, "Whosoever abideth in him sinneth not."

God stands ready to pardon any sinner whatsoever if he will but thus confess and forsake his sin. If they are but sensible that they are sinners by nature and practice and are sensible of the evil of what they have done against him, and are sensible how they provoked him, and that they might justly for their sins be held under his wrath and curse, and are humbled in an abasing sense of their sins, and come to him for pardon in an apprehension of his mercy in Christ to pardon them, and do forsake their sins in heart and in life, God insists upon this, and he insists upon no more. But let men's sins have been what they will, if they come only up to these terms, God will surely pardon them. He will wholly blot out their sins and remember them no more. They shall be buried forever as it were in the depths of the sea, that they shall no more appear against them.

These things hath God often declared. Pardon is often promised to each of those distinctly. It is promised to a hearty confessing of sin. Job 33:27–28 says, "If any say, I have sinned, and perverted that which was right, and it profited me not; he will deliver his soul from going into the pit, and his life shall see the light." First John 1:9 says, "If we confess our sins, he is faithful and just to forgive us our sins, and to cleanse us from all unrighteousness."

Thus, as soon as ever David said to Nathan after he had been guilty of adultery and murder, "I have sinned." Nathan replies to David, "The LORD also hath put away thy sin; thou shalt not die" (2 Sam. 12:13). This is agreeable to what David declares in Psalm 32:5, "I acknowledged my sin unto thee, and mine iniquity have I not hid. I said, I will confess my transgressions unto the LORD; and thou forgavest the iniquity of my sin."

So pardon is often promised for forsaking of sin. Isaiah 55:7 says, "Let the wicked forsake his way, and the unrighteous man his thoughts: and let him return unto the LORD, and he will have mercy upon him; and to our God, for he will abundantly pardon." Jeremiah

36:3 says, "It may be that the house of Judah will hear all the evil which I purpose to do unto them; that they may return every man from his evil way; that I may forgive their iniquity and their sin." Ezekiel 18:21–22 says, "If the wicked will turn from all his sins that he hath committed, and keep all my statutes, and do that which is lawful and right, he shall surely live, he shall not die. All his transgressions that he hath committed, they shall not be mentioned unto him."

God insists upon this, that men should confess and forsake their sins in order to pardon. If he should forgive men who be not sensible to the evil of sin and neither do forsake, God would thereby greatly dishonor the holiness of his nature. By thus pardoning and embracing an impenitent sinner, he would embrace wickedness itself which he cannot do, for evil shall not dwell with him. And then again, he would give those his grace who won't receive it, which would be very unsuitable, because impenitent sinners refuse to receive the pardoning grace of God in Christ. They won't entertain it and accept it and therefore 'tis no way fit they should have it.

If God should bestow his pardoning grace upon an impenitent sinner, he would thereby dishonor his grace. He would expose it to contempt by giving of it to them who will no way thankfully receive it. That will not give him the glory of it but despise the pardoning grace of God. Therefore, God insists upon this—that men should heartily confess and forsake their sins, and he insists upon no more. He is ready to accept this without any satisfaction at all made by the sinner. 'Tis only to acknowledge their sin and to forsake it. And thus there are no other reasons to be given but that God is infinitely gracious. That God will forgive all sinners only upon their repentance is not to be attributed to anything but infinite grace. What marvelous grace is it that so great a God should forgive sinners.

'Tis not to be attributed to any need that God stands in of us, or to any influence anything has upon him, out of himself or besides his mere and sovereign grace. This is agreeable to God's design of glorifying his grace manifested in the gospel, hereby the freedom of pardoning grace appears that we may be free from all the dreadful effects of sin only upon forsaking it.

The terms of the gospel are faith and repentance. Pardon in the New Testament as well as in the Old Testament is promised upon repentance. Thus repentance we find denominated from this effect of it, repentance for the remission of sins. Mark 1:4 says, "John did . . . preach the baptism of repentance for the remission of sins," so repentance and remission of sins are joined together again. Luke 24:47 says, "And that repentance and remission of sins should be preached in his name." Acts 2:38 says, "Repent, and be baptized . . . for the remission of sins." Confessing and forsaking are but the expressions of repentance.

Objection: Is not this to make two conditions of justification? The gospel seems to make the condition of justification but one, and that is faith in Jesus Christ.

Answer: Faith and repentance are implied in each other. True repentance implies faith in the nature of it. There can't be repentance without faith. As we have shown, that one thing implied in a sincere confessing of sin to God is a sense of the mercy of God in Christ to forgive sin. So true repentance as the catechism teaches us is from an apprehension of the mercy of God in Christ. So faith includes repentance in its nature, for in faith there is a receiving of Christ as Savior from sin. But the act of receiving of Christ as Savior from sin implies a forsaking of sin or renouncing. Persons can't seek and accept a Savior from sin if their hearts don't renounce sin.

We destroy sin by the act of faith because true faith is a penitent faith and therefore the apostle Paul says in Galatians 2:17–18, "But if, while we seek to be justified by Christ, we ourselves also are found sinners, is therefore Christ the minister of sin? God forbid. For if

I build again the things which I destroyed, I make myself a transgressor." Seeking to be justified by Christ in faith implies a destruction or renouncing of sin.

Faith and repentance are one and the same conversion but only considered two ways or in different respects. Repentance is conversion considered with respect to the turn from that which is sin. Faith is conversion considered with respect to the turn to that which is Christ. Conversion is a turning from sin to God by Christ, a turning from sin is repentance, a turning to God by Christ is faith. It is not two turnings or conversions but one conversion. But only when we speak of repentance we have respect to what a man in that conversion is converted to. In conversion the soul acts with respect to two contrary objects. There is its act towards sin in renouncing—that is repentance. That is its act towards God in coming to him through Christ—that is faith. But 'tis one conversion.

So that though the gospel sometimes seems to speak of repentance as though that were the proper condition of pardon, at other times of faith as the condition, we need not understand that there are two conditions or that the Scriptures disagree with itself. Proverbs 28:13 says, "But whoso confesseth and forsaketh them shall have mercy."

APPLICATION

Of confessing. Learn how fair and gracious God's terms are when he requires nothing of sinners whatever sins they have been guilty of against him but only that they would confess and forsake their sins. What could God require less? And how unreasonable would any be to expect to be forgiven when they refuse to confess or refuse to forsake their sins, to expect that God should forgive them when they obstinately continue in their sins?

There is a great deal of finding fault with God's terms in the world. But the doctrine shows us how unreasonable it is. What would those persons have who find fault with those terms? This shows how inexcusable sinners are who will not heartily confess and forsake their sins, and how conspicuous will the justice of God be in executing full punishment upon such sinners. This will be manifest, that all their lifetime God offered to pardon and release them from punishment only upon their confessing and forsaking their sins and this they refused. How will the mouths of such persons be stopped before the judgment seat, and how will saints and angels praise the justice of God appearing in their destruction?

Objection: But I can't heartily confess and forsake my sins if I would. Repentance is the gift of God, and none can turn from their sins but whom God enables. And this is the reason that they find fault with these terms that they are such that they can't perform if they will. To this objection I answer:

Answer: If you truly will, 'tis not true that you cannot confess and forsake your sins. If you truly are willing to confess and forsake, you can. There never was any man yet who was willing who found himself unable. He who gives a willingness always gives ability at the same time. When God works to will, then he works to do. And therefore there is no man here who has this to plead in excuse for himself or by way of objection against God's terms, that he is willing and desirous to confess and forsake his sins but he can't. I am bold to determine there is not one such person here.

To be willing is what is wanting. If you were but willing, there would be no want of power. How can there be anything else wanting in order to confessing and forsaking sin but only a willingness? The not doing of it must be from nothing else but refusing to do it.

If you cannot heartily confess and forsake your sins, it is not true that you are willing. I make no doubt of it but that there are some here present who cannot truly confess and forsake their sins. But then there is not one of them who is willing. Those who cannot don't desire if they choose not to do it. For to will to forsake sin is forsaking in heart, and if the heart forsakes it, the difficulty is overcome. If men have forsaken sin in heart, a forsaking it in practice will follow naturally.

If you are of such a disposition that you cannot confess and forsake your sins, this shows how desperately wicked you are. This shows how wicked you be, if you are so wicked that you can't be sensible of the evil of your wickedness and are so set upon wickedness that you can't forsake it. And surely 'tis a very odd way of excusing wickedness to plead that you are so wicked that you can't forsake your wickedness.

If a man can't help hating his father or mother, that shows how great his hatred is. Nobody would look upon that as a good excuse for so doing. But he would be looked upon so much the more vile and the object of everyone's indignation if there were any who hated you without cause and his spite and malice were so deeply rooted that he could do no other than hate you and could not help showing of it every now and then upon occasion by reproaching you and abusing. He hated you so desperately that he could not avoid it. You would not think the fixedness of his unjust hatred of you an excuse for the abuses you suffered from him. But on the contrary, you would have the greater indignation towards him.

Or if some men had very greatly abused you some way, you would expect that they should be sensible of their fault and acknowledge. But if the man were of such a proud spirit and so senseless of his fault that he could not heartily confess his fault to you, you would not think that to be an excuse for him. On the contrary you would look upon it as an aggravation and would be the more angry with that he should be of such a base spirit that he could not have a sense of his fault when he had so much reason to be sensible of it.

But yet you will plead such things as these as an excuse for not heartily confessing your sins to God and not forsaking of them, as though you were not to blame and as though God has no cause to find fault because you are of such a perverse, obstinate disposition that you can't repent. As though you were the party that had cause to find fault with God for his expecting any such thing and not God with you for refusing it. So unreasonable a creature is man.

Of self-examination. Let us all examine ourselves to see whether we ever have truly confessed and forsaken our sins or whether we have ever truly repented of our sins. If we have truly repented, our sins are remitted to us, and we are in a state of peace and reconciliation with God. If we have not repented, sin still lieth at the door.

There is a true and a false repentance. There is a repentance unto salvation, and there is a kind of repentance that many do depend upon that will not stand them in stead. Wicked men by the force of natural principles may go a great way and in many things may imitate the truly penitent, as in Saul and Ahab and Judas whose repentance will not avail them. Here I would take notice how far a hypocrite may go and then mention some other things wherein the difference appears.

1. A hypocrite may be convinced of the folly of particular sinful ways and practices that he has been guilty of. He may have other notions about things that he has had and may see that 'tis his best way not to live any longer as he has done and so be another mind about it than he used to be. He may see so much of the ill effects and consequences of such and such wicked practices that he may be sensible that 'tis best to avoid them. Saul at length was convinced, "I have played the fool, and have erred exceedingly" (1 Sam. 26:21).

Yea, a hypocrite may for a time have a sense of the folly of wicked practices in general by reason of the wrath and vengeance of God that he is exposed to. The dog may be sick of what he hath eaten for the present and may vomit it up.

2. One who is not a true penitent may have grief at the thoughts of the wickedness he has committed and wish that he had not done it. Judas was sorry that he had betrayed his Master and wished that he had not done it, as is evident by his actions. His grief of mind was very great to the degree of horror. But yet it was so far from being true repentance that it was only a foretaste of the grief and darkness of a state of damnation. 'Tis said of the children of Israel after they had murmured at the report of the spies and Moses had told them of the evil that God would bring upon them, that the people "mourned greatly" (Num. 14:39). 'Tis not the degree of grief that makes repentance true and saving. The damned in hell will mourn and wail at the thoughts of their sins to an exceeding degree, and wicked men may have something of the same kind of grief here and yet not be true penitents.

3. A person may confess his sins to God and men with much affection and yet not be a true penitent. A hypocrite may confess. Thus Pharaoh confessed his sin in Exodus 9:27–28: "And Pharaoh sent, and called for Moses and Aaron, and said unto them, I have sinned this time: the LORD is righteous, and I and my people are wicked. Intreat the LORD (for it is enough)."

Judas confessed his sin, according to Matthew 27:4, "I have sinned in that I have betrayed the innocent blood."

Saul also confessed his sin in sparing Agag and the best of the sheep and oxen alive when he went to destroy Amalek: "And Saul said unto Samuel, I have sinned: for I have transgressed the commandment of the LORD, and thy words" (1 Sam. 15:24). A hypocrite may confess with tears. Saul confessed his sin with affection and many tears. "And Saul lifted up his voice, and wept. And he said to David, Thou art more righteous than I: for thou hast rewarded me good, whereas I have rewarded thee evil" (1 Sam. 24:16–17).

So the children of Israel confessed their sins before God once and again and with tears, but yet God did not forgive them: "Then ye answered and said unto me, We have sinned against the LORD" (Deut. 1:41). And then again after that as we read in verse 45, "And ye returned and wept before the LORD; but the LORD would not hearken to your voice, nor give ear unto you." So that to shed tears about our sins, though they be shed very plentifully and before God in confession to him, is no sign of sincere repentance.

4. There may be external humiliation in people's behavior and yet not true repentance. Persons may have a melancholy countenance and may hang down their heads and may keep days of fasting and may appear humble in their apparel besides confession and tears and yet not be a true penitent. So it was with Ahab: "'And it came to pass, when Ahab heard those words, that he rent his clothes, and put sackcloth upon his flesh, and fasted, and lay in sackcloth, and went softly" (1 Kings 21:27). So that upon it God says to Elijah, "Seest thou how Ahab humbleth himself before me?" (1 Kings 21:29).

5. Besides all this they may take up resolutions of amendment and yet not be true penitents. So did the children of Israel in the wilderness. Often Moses had told them how God would deal with them for their murmuring at the relation of the spies as in Deuteronomy 1:41: "Then ye answered and said unto me, We have sinned against the LORD, we will go up and fight, according to all that the LORD our God commanded us." So Saul took up a resolution to reform in 1 Samuel 26:21: "Then said Saul, I have sinned: return, my son David: for I will no more do thee harm."

6. They may actually finally forsake some sins and yet not be true penitents. It seems that Ahab, who had been so dreadfully addicted to idolatry, forsook that sin before his death and returned to it no more

after that humiliation of his that we read of and yet was no true penitent.

7. And lastly, a person may reform of all known external sins for a while. The sow may be washed clean for the present all over from her mire. The sinner may not dare to allow himself in any known sin in any of his external behavior or neglect any known external duty. The most powerful lusts may be restrained and kept under, and they may refrain from their dearest iniquity for a while. Judas's iniquity was his covetousness, which was the cause that he was so grieved at the spending of the box of precious ointment in the anointing of Christ. This reason is given of it that he was a thief and had the bag and kept those things that were put therein (John 12:6). It appears again by his selling his Master for thirty pieces of silver. And yet he had for a while seemingly left all his worldly possessions to follow Christ. He was one of those whom Peter speaks of when he says to Christ in Mark 10:28, "Lo! we have left all, and have followed thee."

But I would next take notice of some things wherein the difference between true and false repentance appears.

1. Sorrow for sin in false repentance is from self-love. In true repentance it is from love to God. Men who are not truly penitent may be sensible of the folly of their wicked ways because they may see they hurt themselves by it, have brought upon themselves temporal calamities, and have brought guilt upon themselves and exposed themselves to misery in another world, and may be sorry for it upon that account. 'Tis because he is concerned for his own interest.

But the true penitent is sensible that God is an excellent and glorious being, most worthy to be honored and obeyed, and that 'tis most becoming of the creature to have the greatest respect to his holy command and to be obedient to him in all things, and therefore is sensible of the unreasonable nature of sin as 'tis an expression of a disregardful spirit towards God and is against his command and is that which dishonors God.

It is contrary to God, and therefore, what he can't have any favorable thoughts of. It is what God hates and therefore what he hates. It is what is displeasing to God and therefore can't be pleasing to him. The true penitent has a taste and relish of the excellency of the holiness of God. It is taken with that beauty of the divine nature, and therefore whatever is contrary to holiness is hateful to him.

Upon such like accounts as these, the true penitent mourns for the sin that he has been guilty of and not only because he has wronged his own interest either temporal or eternal.

2. The sorrow of false repentance is ordinarily from the threatenings of the law. The true penitent's sorrow is from the discovery of God's glory and grace in the gospel. The children of Israel's repentance in the wilderness, after they had murmured at the report of the spies when they returned and wept before the Lord, was wrought by terrors by God's threatenings that they should never enter into God's rest and that their carcasses should fall in the wilderness. Their hearing of these things made them to mourn greatly.

So it was in Saul in his seeming repentance after he had spared Agag and the best of the sheep, and of the oxen, and of the fatlings, and the lambs, and all that was good. When Samuel told him how he had displeased God and how God had rejected him, then he cried, "I have sinned against the LORD."

So it was with Ahab when Elijah told him that God would bring evil upon him and cut off all his posterity and make his house like the house of Jeroboam, the son of Nebat, and that he who died of Ahab in the city the dogs should eat, and he who died in the fields the fowls of the air should eat. Then we are told, "When Ahab heard those words, that he rent his clothes, and put sackcloth upon his flesh, and fasted, and lay in sackcloth, and went softly" (1 Kings 21:27).

So it was with Judas. His repentance was only legal from the terrible apprehension of the wrath of God against him which cast him into despair.

But there is something else that causes the true penitent's mourning for sin of quite another nature. That is the discovery of the glorious excellency and grace of God and love of Christ in the gospel. The discovery of these things doth melt down the heart in repentance and a gracious mourning for sin.

The discovery of God's mercy in Christ overcomes the heart that before was obstinate in sin and makes it quit its hold and wholly to renounce it. Joel 2:13 says, "Rend your heart, and not your garments, and turn unto the LORD your God: for he is gracious and merciful, slow to anger, and of great kindness, and repenteth him of the evil."

3. A false penitent's forsaking sin is forced, but a true penitent's is free. The false penitent is driven from sin, but he loves sin as well. He still entertains an inward friendship for it, but he dare not enjoy it. He is driven from it by fear and by the sight of the rod. But the true penitent forsakes it by choice. His heart is alienated from it. He desires not to have anything more to do with it.

The false penitent is driven. The true penitent is drawn. He forsakes. He is drawn away from it by the discovery of the beauty and comeliness of God and of his holiness. It hurts and grieves the soul of a false penitent to part with his sin. He is sorry that there are such dreadful consequences attending sin that he can't enjoy it any longer. He is sorry God so strictly forbids it. The true penitent doesn't desire to have anything more to do with sin. He desires not that the law of God should allow it. He forsakes with freedom and delight.

The false penitent forsakes sin only for the sake of the ill consequences that sin bears for him. But the true penitent forsakes for the sake of the evil that there is in sin itself and for the deformity and odiousness of the nature of sin and because it is taken with the beauty of the contrary holiness.

4. A false penitent may have transient affections about his sins. But the true penitent hath his very nature alienated from sin. The nature of the hypocrite is the same for all his affections. His tears argue no change of nature. The swine that is washed has the same swinish nature. But the true penitent is become a new creature. He is sanctified in soul, body, and spirit. So changed from that which before was his element, it is now distasteful and odious to him. There is a habitual hatred and opposition in his heart towards sin.

5. The alienation from sin in true repentance is universal and persevering. The heart is alienated from all sin. Whatever has the nature of sin and is forbidden of God for that reason is renounced. A hypocrite may have a kind of hatred of some particular evil. A natural man may hate pride, or he may hate lying or stealing. He may hate a begrudging spirit, and he may have a kind of hatred of some practices that he has formerly lived in. But this hatred is not of sin as sin, or as against God. 'Tis from some other considerations, and this appears because he doesn't hate all sin that he knows to be sin.

There are other sins that he delights in. There are some who are very offensive to God who are dear to him. From whence it appears that 'tis not for the sinfulness of anything that they hate it, for if it was that they would hate everything that was sinful, so far as it was known to be so.

But the true penitent is alienated from every way of sin. If anything be known to be sinful and displeasing to God in all his past life, that is enough to alienate him from it. The true penitent is alienated from outward evils and from spiritual evils, and he is finally alienated from sin. He has taken an everlasting love of it. The hypocrite, though he seems to part with sin for the present, yet there is no final parting. Though he may be restrained a considerable time, yet the union and friendship is not broken and therefore will be very liable to return to sin again.

Here before I dismiss this use, I would advertise you that in what I have said, I would not be understood that none who is a true penitent is ever influenced by the same principles in sorrowing for sin as the hypocrite is. There is very often a mixture of natural principles with gracious ones. A true penitent may mourn for sin from self-love but then that is not all. There is another mourning besides this. He also mourns from a principle of love to God.

A true penitent may be influenced to forsake sin from the terrors of the law. But if he is, this is not true repentance. 'Tis the influence that the discovery of the glory and grace of God in the gospel has upon him to make him mourn for sin and forsake it that renders it genuine and truly gracious.

A true penitent may in his affections be influenced partly by the same natural principles that the hypocrite is, but then there is something worldly. A true penitent may be driven from his sins with fear. But he is not a true penitent because of that but because he is drawn with love.

A true penitent at some times may have the workings of very little else besides natural principles. He may have the same kind of workings as a hypocrite has and grace may be very much asleep. At other times he has gracious principles chiefly at work and natural principles be surmounted. But however these last things that have been mentioned must be in a man in order to his being a true penitent, he must sorrow for sin from love to God from a sense of God's excellency and grace. He must forsake sin freely and of choice. His nature must be alienated from sin, and he must be alienated from it universally and finally. Whatever other things may be in him, these must be in him.

Grace may have an indirect influence upon natural principles to set them to work. A man may be the more under the influence of the threatenings of hell and the promises of heaven for grace because grace makes him believe the truth of them more than otherwise he would do.

There are many who seem to be somewhat concerned how they shall obtain the pardon of their sins because they are afraid of the wrath of God and eternal damnation. You are told how in the text and doctrine. The terms are the fairest and most gracious imaginable. Do but truly confess and forsake your sins, and you shall find mercy. Let your sins have been what they will, you who have been long seeking, you who are grown old in sin and fear, God wants to move you to do it now without any delay. Consider these things:

1. To defer repentance when God calls upon you is very provoking to God. God requires it now. Will you harbor that enemy of God in your bosom when God commands you to deliver it up?

2. All deferring of repentance increases the hardness of the heart. Easier pulling up a plant when young than after it has stood long and is rooted deep in the ground.

3. Still persisting in sins will increase the moment of your sins, your own guilt and the anger of God.

4. Life is most uncertain.

5. Repentance is the gift which it is most likely God will give in the time he appoints and not in that which we appoint, so there is no occasion for us to put it off. But we ought to repent today while it is called today. If we neglect it when God calls for it and while we may repent, there is danger that God will not enable us thereafter. 'Tis a sign that you have no sincere purpose of repenting at all. Do but deceive yourself. 'Tis a sign of a man who never seriously intends to pay his debt when he puts them off from day to day.

6. If we were certain of a future repentance, it would be unworthy to deal with God. We be not willing God should deal so with us. We take it ill to be dealt with so one by another.

7. We should account it rudeness in men to act so in temporal affairs. House on fire. If one had accidentally took poison. Bit with a rattlesnake.

8

⊷⊜ ⊜⊶

The Day of a Godly Man's Death Is Better Than the Day of His Birth

A good name is better than precious ointment;
and the day of death than the day of one's birth.

ECCLESIASTES 7:1

Edwards preached this sermon in June 1734. It is one of those biblical statements that flies in the face of what Edwards calls "commonly entertained notions"—namely that times of birth are usually regarded as happy times, whereas the coming of death is not usually regarded in quite the same way by natural men.

Edwards takes this simple statement and explains in detail why the coming of death for the godly is far better than his birthday: Eternal life takes over from natural, mortal puts on immortal, and as Edwards states, "he receives the life of angels."

Not wanting to be misunderstood, Edwards acknowledges that spiritual life obviously began at conversion. So to make it abundantly clear what he is arguing, he adds that this being so, on the day of his death, the godly person receives the life of glory.

Edwards applies this doctrine to those who are in grief through the loss of loved ones, that their grief might be moderated. He reminds his hearers that though the death of the godly might bring us sorrow, yet we must remember that it brings them real joy and is all to their gain. He also applies this truth to those who need to get into such a right state, that the day of their death may be so to them.

The sermon manuscript is a typical duodecimal booklet, consisting of twenty leaves with no evidence of damage. In the body of the sermon there is little evidence of deletions, but Edwards has made several insertions and additions by his own hand.

There is in this text (Eccl. 7:1) a twofold comparison made—between a good name and precious ointment and between the day of death of a godly man and the day of his birth. And it may be worthy to be inquired why those two comparisons are thus put together. Why doth the wise man observe that a good name is better than precious ointment and that the day of death for a godly man is better than the day of his birth? What connection is there between them, or what relation have they one to another? Doubtless there was some relation that the wise man had in his eyes, and it seems to be thus.

It may be observed here that the day of a man's death is preferred to the day of his birth, in like manner as a good name is preferred to precious ointment. The reason of it is that on the day of anyone's birth they were wont to ointment the newborn child with ointment but on the day of a good man's death he left a good name behind him. It is evident that it was the custom among the Jews on the birth of a child to use ointment, to anoint the child, for 'tis this custom that is alluded to in the sixteenth chapter of Ezekiel, verse 9. God tells Jerusalem how he passed by her in the day she was born and was cast out into the open field in her blood and none took care of her to wash or supply or swaddle her. But he took care and washed her with water and anointed her with oil.

It was the custom of the Jews to anoint their newborn children after they were washed and anointed with ointment and sometimes with very precious ointment or ointment that was perfumed with fragrant spices. But this precious ointment that children were anointed with when first born was not attended with so sweet a savor as that good name that a good man left behind him when he died. That same wherein observes that when a good man dies, he leaves a blessed name and memorial behind him as in Proverbs 10:7, "The memory of the just is blessed: but the name of the wicked shall rot." When a wicked man dies, he goes out like a stinking wick. He leaves an ill name behind him. But when a godly man dies, he leaves a sweet odor. Behind a good name there is sweeter and better than the most fragrant perfumed ointments than the children of princes are anointed with when first born.

Thus we see the reason why these things are here put together by the wise man—precious ointment and the day of one's birth and a good name and the day of death. We also see why the day of death is said to be better than the day of one's birth, since a good name is better than precious ointment.

But here another question needs to be resolved—why the wise man says the day of death is better than the day of one's birth. Sometimes the day of a man's death is the most awful day that ever he saw. 'Tis the day of his condemnation. 'Tis the day of his entering into eternal misery, and 'tis more commonly so than otherwise. How then can the day of a man's death be said to be better than the day of his birth? I answer that we must still observe the connection between the latter and the foregoing part of the verse. It is only intended that the day of his death is better than the day of his birth who, when he dies, leaves a good name that is better than precious ointment. He whose memory is blessed and not he whose name rots and stinks. To him who loves a good name better than precious ointment and desires it, his death is better than the day of his birth.

DOCTRINE

The day of a godly man's death is better than the day of his birth. This is as contrary as possible to the notions commonly entertained by men who look on the day of a man's birth as a happy day but the day of death as the most sorrowful and doleful day that man ever met with. There is nothing that man has so great a dread of and such terrible apprehension of as death. 'Tis generally looked upon as the end of all good to a man in entrance in a doleful state of oblivion and darkness and eternal separation from all enjoyment. They consider death only from its appearance. Death puts an end to a man's being in this world and all worldly enjoyments and is attended commonly with great pains and agonies and many melancholy circumstances. It makes an awful alteration in the body; it makes the countenance ghostly. It deprives of all sense and notion; it makes the flesh loathsome, is shut up in the dark and silent grave. It returns to putrification and turns to the earth.

Men beholding these things have an awful impression thereby in their minds and awful thoughts of death fixed in them. And it is a strange paradox to the world to tell them that the day of a man's death is better than the day of his birth. But this is with the godly and that on a twofold account: (1) On the account of the glorious change that is made in their circumstances by death, and (2) on the account of the comfort and joy that sometimes attends the approach of their death.

The day of a godly man's death is better than the day of his birth on account of the glorious change. Though there be a very awful change in the outward appearance and in the circumstances of the body, yet there is a very glorious change in the circumstances of the person, so as to render it a more happy day than the day of that birth.

1. A pious person on the day of his death receives a better and more blessed life than on the day of his birth. The birth of a person we look upon as the beginning of his life, for the life be in a measure received before, yet 'tis then that life is first exercised and enjoyed in the world. And the day of a person's birth is looked upon as a joyful day because then another human creature is come into being and begins his life. Life is looked upon as the greatest good and is most praised by men. What is esteemed more precious than life? But when a godly man dies, he receives a better life than when he is born. We call it death. It signifies the end of life or the abolishing and destruction of it, and it is so in appearance. But it is in reality the beginning of a more glorious life. Therefore, God, who sees things as they are, doesn't call a godly man's decease by the name of death, but the Scripture calls it sleep. Thus it is said of Stephen who was stoned to death in Acts 7:60, "When he had said thus, he fell asleep." So 1 Corinthians 15:18 says, "They also which are fallen asleep in Christ." So in many other places.

And Christ, not accounting the decease of a godly man worthy of the name of death, says that he who believes in him shall not die. John 6:49–50 says, "Your fathers did eat manna in the wilderness, and are dead. This is the bread which cometh down from heaven, that a man may eat thereof, and not die." And John 6:51 says, "If any man eat of this bread, he shall live for ever." A godly man's death is indeed more like a resurrection or a rising from the dead than like death. The present life is but a state of death in comparison of that glorious life that a godly man enters into when he dies. He enters into the more glorious and blessed state. He does, as it were, awake out of sleep and therefore this change is implied in Psalm 17:15, "I shall be satisfied, when I awake."

The present life is a state wherein the godly are exceeding changed with the flesh and with sin. They are in a great measure hammered and deadened and rendered insensible and inactive in comparison of what they are in another world. In the day of a man's birth, he receives the bodily and natural life; but when a godly man dies, he receives the life of angels. He is made a partaker of the glorious life of Jesus Christ. When a man is born, he receives a short, fading, and uncertain life, but when a godly man dies, he receives eternal life. When a man is born, he then becomes mortal; but when he dies, he receives an immortal life. The life that a person receives on the day of his birth is not worthy to be called by the name of life in comparison of that which the godly receive at the day of their death. The godly who are dead now live. They live now indeed and never lived before with that which is worthy to be called with the name of life.

They have a life now that is more perfect, happy, and glorious—ten thousand times—than the best and happiest life on earth. The godly person receives spiritual life before in his conversion, but on the day of his death, he receives the life of glory. He is transformed into the glorious image and likeness of Christ. They have the perfection of holiness. The image of God is completed, and all sin wholly and perfectly abolished. Sin is a kind of death that cleaves to the soul. The remains of that in a godly man are reminders of death. But when a godly man departs this life, he is delivered from all remains of death. He is then delivered from the body of his death. Holiness, which is life that is given him but as a spark, shall be a flame then and shall make the soul to shine forth as the sun in the kingdom of God.

2. A godly person on the day of his death enters into a better world than on the day of his birth. 'Tis on the day of one's birth that one first comes into the world, comes abroad from being shut up in the womb into the world. But the soul of a godly man on the day of his death enters upon a state of more glorious liberty. It is like one escaped from prison. He is released from the body from where it was confined and kept in prison under the chains of sin and the flesh. It escapes from this world that is a loathsome dungeon in comparison to that more

glorious world that it enters into. The day of a godly man's death is the day wherein his soul is born into that glorious world.

The world that a man comes into on the day of his birth is a world of low, earthly, and mean enjoyment. But the world that the soul of a godly man is born into on the day of his death is a world of spiritual and divine enjoyments. This is a world of fading, vanishing pleasures, but that is a world of substantial, durable joys and delights. There are pleasures forevermore.

This world that men come into on the day of their birth is a world of sin and vanity and trouble. But the world that a godly man enters into on the day of his death is a world of perfection and holiness, of light and joy without any mixture of sin and sorrow. This earth is a valley of tears, but that is Mount Zion, when they sing a new and everlasting song. Where all tears are wiped from their eyes, and "sorrow and sighing shall flee away" (Isa. 35:10), where there is "no more death, neither sorrow, nor crying, neither shall there be any more pain: for the former things are passed away" (Rev. 21:4).

When a godly man dies, he enters into a world that has better inhabitants, and where there is better company than the world that he entered into on the day of his birth. This world that persons enter into on the day of their birth is a world that is full of wicked men, those whose hearts are full of hateful lusts and vile and unlovely dispositions, whereby they make one another miserable. But a godly man, on the day of his death, goes into a world where the inhabitants of which are all righteous and have no lusts in their hearts. They are all most excellent and lovely and full of love as what reigns in their hearts. They are united in the dearest friendship and with whom the departed saints converse in the most pleasant manner, without any to spoil or mar their conversation.

On the day of a person's birth, he is born into a world that is under a curse and has no guard against it; but on the day of his death, he enters into a world that is blessed of God, where there is no curse, but only joy and happiness, a world that is blessed continually with the glorious presence of God and the perfect manifestation and full enjoyment of God's love. 'Tis a world that is filled with the boundless love of God which doth as a river of life satisfy all the inhabitants thereof.

3. A godly person on the day of his death is brought to behold a more pleasant and glorious light than he was on the day of his birth. 'Tis on the day of a man's birth that he first beholds the light. He comes then to see the light of the sunlight, and it's a thing sweet to men. "Truly the light is sweet, and a pleasant thing it is for the eyes to behold the sun" (Eccl. 11:7). A man on the day of his death closes his eyes forever on this light. A veil of thick darkness is then drawn over his eyes, but the godly man loses not by this but greatly gains. Though he closes his eyes on the light of the sun, he opens them in the midst of the light of God's glory, who is the Father of lights, who hath clothed the sun with light in comparison of which the light of the sun is a dark shade. He sees the light of the Sun of Righteousness of him who is the brightness of his Father. He sees no more of the light of this lower world, but he is blessed with the light of the heaven of heavens where they have "no need of the sun, neither of the moon" (Rev. 21:23), nor of the light of a candle, "for the Lord God giveth them light" (Rev. 22:5), "and the Lamb is the light thereof" (Rev. 21:23).

This is a world where we may see the sun, that glorious body, but the godly man on the day of his death enters where he may behold an infinitely more glorious one. He may behold God. Matthew 5:8, "Blessed are the pure in heart: for they shall see God." The light of the sun discovers many pleasant objects to us. It discovers to us the faces of men, the faces of our friends, and the face of the earth with the trees and fields and many bountiful appearances that are the works of nature. But in the light of glory, the saints shall behold infinitely more glorious and ravishing objects with which that world abounds in comparison of which all these things that our eyes behold in this world are but dirt and dung.

4. The godly person on the day of his death is received by a better parent than persons are received by on the day of their birth. Persons are joyfully received on the day of their birth by their earthly parents, but death snatches them from them and from all earthly friends. A godly person on the day of his death leaves them in sackcloth and tears but is received into the arms of a heavenly Father. They are welcomed into his immediate and glorious presence and to the full enjoyment of his love to be in heaven forever. They will be in his family to dwell with his children and eat and drink at his table with them. They will partake with Jesus Christ his Son and with the glorified saints and angels, his dear children in the palace of his glory.

5. The pious soul on the day of his death is received to a better inheritance than on the day of his birth. A person on the day of his birth may be heir to a great estate. He may on the day of his birth come to be an heir of large earthly possessions. Death takes persons away from all their earthly possessions. If they have been in comfortable circumstances, or if they have been rich, death takes them away from all, but it translates them into better possessions, a more glorious inheritance. First Peter 1:4 says, "To an inheritance incorruptible, and undefiled, and that fadeth not away, reserved in heaven for you." They are then received to the possession of a kingdom, a crown of life, and to unspeakable and unsearchable riches and glory.

But a godly man on the day of his death is more joyfully welcomed into heaven than he is received by his earthly parents on the day of his birth. The birth of a person is looked upon as a joyful occasion by us. Children are often received into the world with joy and gladness by their friends but not with so much joy as the soul of a godly man is received into heaven on the day of his death. Indeed, there is oftentimes a great weeping among earthly friends on the day of a godly man's death, but there is joy among his heavenly friends when they meet him and welcome him to Mount Zion, the city of the living God.

Christ gives such a soul a joyful welcome to the place of his residence, and into his eternal presence, and into the arms of his dear love. The innumerable company of angels joyfully welcomes them and conducts them to the throne of glory. The saints who went to heaven before joyfully receive them and welcome them to their place to dwell with them. They rejoice that they are come to them. They rejoice to have their company and rejoice that they are come to join their society, to partake with them in their enjoyments and to join in their worship, singing joyful praises to God and to the Lamb. They congratulate them in their deliverance from an evil and sinful world, and from sorrow and affliction, and from the pains of death which they have just passed through, and coming to a state of eternal rest. If there be joy in heaven when one is converted and fitted for glory, so doubtless is there joy when they are received to glory. Thus, the day of a godly man's death is better than the day of his birth on the account of the glorious change made in his circumstances by death.

It is sometimes so on the account of the comfort and joy that attends the approach of death. It is not universally so that a godly man hath much comfort and joy at that time. 'Tis as God pleases to disperse to every man. He has reserved that thing in his own power, but yet this is true—that every godly man hath then a solid foundation for peace and joy. Even in the midst of the valley of the shadow of death, the godly man has cause to rejoice at the approaches of it, to bid it welcome, so for him to die is gain. And oftentimes God doth actively give much of the light of his presence that carries quite above all the fears of death. God sometimes gives such a sense of his love, such discoveries of being, such views of approaching glory and happiness that make the day of death a pleasant day. A pleasanter and more joyful day than a wedding day and sometimes the most pleasant day that ever he saw in his life (Ps. 37:3).

So it was with Stephen while they were stoning him to death. Though he died a violent death, yet the time of his death was a joyful time, a glorious time to him. He was filled with such joy that his face appeared as "the face of an angel" (Acts 6:15). And he cried out, "Behold, I see the heavens opened, and the Son of man standing on the right hand of God" (Acts 7:56).

APPLICATION

1. If it be so, then this should moderate the grief of those who have lost near and dear friends who were pious persons. The consideration of their joy should moderate your griefs, seeing that death was so joyful an occasion, the day of it so good a day to them. This should check immediate sorrow in you. If they were dear to you, then you are a well-wisher to them. You are disposed to rejoice at their welfare and to be glad at their prosperity. Will you then be overwhelmed in sorrow when they are in such a joyful and happy state?

If anyone here on earth who is very dear to us be in joyful circumstances and we meet them and see their prosperity and joy, our love and friendship to them will naturally dispose us to rejoice with them and not to sink with grief and sorrow. If we grieve, it will look more as if we were enemies than friends.

When persons lose dear friends, though those whom they have left are godly persons, they are ready to mourn as though some scornful thing had befallen the deceased. This is quite wrong and arises from insensibility and ignorance of what death is to them. Though their death may be sorrowful to you, yet you are to consider how joyful a thing it is to them. Though you mourn for your loss, you should rejoice at their gain.

If the pious relations you have lost be your children, you should consider that you rejoiced at their birth and therefore surely should not be sunk with grief at that which is much better to them than their birth. If they were your companions and their company was pleasant to you, you should consider that they are received to better company, and they stand in no need of your care or kindness. They are cared for by better friends. And though it is true you are parted from them and that is your loss, yet you are to consider that you yourself are also but on a journey. Whether they get to their journey's end to their Father's house a little before you, should you break your heart with grief further? How widely different is the case from what it would have been if your departed had left no comfortable hopes concerning their good estate. What cause have you to bless God for such a gracious and merciful a circumstance attending their departure?

2. The second use I would make of it is to persuade and urge persons to get into such a state that the day of their death may be so to them. Strive that you may be godly persons. That you may have your heart changed and nature savingly renewed. Then it will be thus with you—that the day of your death will be better than the day of your birth.

And here consider that you must die. There is no avoiding of that. Psalm 89:48 says, "What man is he that liveth, and shall not see death?" Every man is born to die. Ecclesiastes 3:2 says, "A time to be born, and a time to die." If you would give all the substance of your house, or if you had the wealthiest friends who were ready to give all they have in the world to save you from death, they could not do it. Psalm 49:6–7 tells us, "They that trust in their wealth, and boast themselves in the multitude of their riches; none of them can by any means redeem his brother, nor give to God a ransom for him."

If you were as powerful as a king and could command an army of many hundreds of thousands, or if you have the wisdom of Solomon, it would not save you or deliver you from death. You must know what that is that you have heard so much of, and seen so many instances of. You must know by experience what it is to die. You must be subject of all that belongs to death. All the change that it makes on the body, and your soul must pass from your body and go into an eternal and unalterable state.

3. How good it is not to have cause to be afraid of death. To be ready for it, let it come when and how it will. How much this adds to the comfort of life, to be able to think of death without misgivings of heart. They who haven't prepared for death have reason always to be in fear. The thoughts of death never can be comfortable for them. Men "through fear of death were all their lifetime subject to bondage" (Heb. 2:15).

Those who be not ready for death can never enjoy any rational quietness. He walks on snares or on slippery places, where he doesn't know every morning but that his feet will slip, and he shall fall and rise no more. He walks continually on the brink of hell and is hanging by a slender thread over the pit of hell. How uncomfortable it must be living in such discomfort. 'Tis enough to embitter every heart. A man in such circumstances can take no reasonable comfort in anything, for what comfort can a man have hanging over a fiery pit, though he be clothed in scarlet and have royal dainties? 'Tis better to live only on bread and water in safety.

But they who are ready for death need not fear. They may take the comfort of blessings of life which God gives them. Such may lie down safely. If death should by any means arrive before morning, they are ready for it. Oh how good it is to be able to look forward, to think of death and eternity with pleasure! Expecting the day of death as a better day than the day of one's birth. Isaiah 32:17 says, "And the work of righteousness shall be peace; and the effect of righteousness quietness and assurance for ever."

4. How vastly different from this is the day of the death of a wicked man. How miserable is such a day to such a one, the most awful day that ever he as yet had, though but the first of an infinite number of such days that are yet to come. This instead of being a better day than the day of his birth, it makes even the day of his birth miserable. It will make him to curse the day that he was born, for it had been good for such a person that he had not been born.

This day is a dreadful day to the wicked. A day of darkness and gloominess, a day of clouds and thick darkness. A day of death indeed worthy of the name of death. A day not only of temporal death but of the beginning of eternal death. A day wherein they will enter into the land of darkness as darkness itself, and the cloud of death and without any understanding and where light is as darkness. A day wherein they forever close their eyes on the light of the sun and not only so but never see any light or receive any comfort more.

A day wherein he is received into a world of misery not by friends but by carnal enemies, not with congratulations but to pain and injustices and torments and devoured by their merciless reign. All the awful outward appearances that attend death are but shadows of these unseen and amazing horrors and miseries that attend the death of a wicked man, which are but the sharing of eternal horrors. And sometimes the wicked have the beginning of these horrors while death is but in its approaches. Strong are the fears and the sense of wrath that they have while death stands by their bedsides staring them in the face. None can express the amazement that has sometimes been felt. Ecclesiastes 5:17 says, "All his days also he eateth in darkness, and he hath much sorrow and wrath with his sickness."

9

⊷⇒ ⇐⊷

Thy Name Is as Ointment
Poured Forth

Thy name is as ointment poured forth.
Song of Solomon 1:3

In this sermon that Edwards preached at Boston in 1733, he gives a
striking survey of the qualities, character, and nature of Christ as
Son of God and Redeemer.

As God come in the flesh, Christ was the most excellent person.
He shines, says Edwards, in the infinite holiness of the Godhead, and
he is clothed with all the majesty and glory of the Godhead. He is infinitely powerful, wise, holy, and gracious, and therefore Edwards urges
his readers to accept the gracious offer Christ makes, which is nothing other than an offering of himself to us. It is, says Edwards, nothing
more than this that Christ desires, that our hearts would be close with
him.

Edwards makes a very passionate plea in that Christ does not
merely offer himself but actually woos us to accept him. Christ seeks
to win and draw us, says Edwards, in such an endearing manner.

The sermon manuscript is the first example in this collection of
one of Edwards's oversize sermon manuscripts. It consists of seventeen leaves with no evidence of damage. The oversize sermons are
always a joy to read, since they are easy and pleasant on the eye.

Edwards's handwriting is usually so much more defined. There is very little reworking in this manuscript.

The name or title that is given to this song—the Song of Songs—confirms it to be more than a mere human song and that those things that are the subject of it are above torrent or tempest. We read in 1 Kings 4:32 that Solomon's songs were "a thousand and five," but this one song of his which is included in the canon of the Scriptures is distinguished from all the rest by the name of the Song of Songs as the most excellent of his songs, or more than all his other songs. The subject of it is transcendently of a more sublime and excellent nature than the rest, treating of the divine love, union, and communion of the most glorious lovers—Christ and his spiritual spouse of which a marriage union and conjugal love (which perhaps many of the rest of his songs treated of) is but a shadow.

The song begins with the spouse expressing her songs of the excellency of Christ, her longing desires after him and her delight in him. His excellency and her complacence in him are bountifully and lively set forth in this expression that I have now to insist on: "Thy name is as ointment poured forth." Such was her sense of his loveliness and so great was her delight in him that she loved his very name. It was precious to her. The very mentioning of it was to her like the pouring forth of some fragrant ointment.

Perfumed ointment was a thing very much valued among the Israelites of old, both to common and sacred purposes. It was made use of by divine direction as a suitable type of the graces of the Holy Spirit. There was a holy anointing oil appointed of God for this purpose that was of such an extraordinary fragrancy being compounded by divine art that any were forbidden to imitate it upon pain of being cut off from among his people.

Possibly special respect may be had to this holy ointment. In the text the excellencies of Jesus Christ are often in that song compared to the very same spices with which that holy oil was perfumed. The name of Christ is most fitly compared to this most precious and holy anointed ointment. It represents that grace that he is full of and is the fountain of.

The name of Christ is compared to ointment poured forth because then it is under the greatest advantage to send forth its odors. The name of Christ filled the soul of the spouse with delight as the holy anointing oil, when poured forth, filled the sanctuary with its fragrancy.

DOCTRINE

Jesus Christ is a person transcendently excellent and lovely. Our Lord Jesus Christ is a most lovely person that may appear by the consideration of the following particulars:

1. Jesus Christ is a divine person. He is the natural Son of God, having the nature and likeness of his Father. All the Father's beauty and glory shines forth in his Son. Hebrews 1:3 says he is "the brightness of his glory, and the express image of his person." He is his perfect image, but that image is not perfect that does not fully come up to the original. He is possessed of the infinite power and wisdom of the Godhead. One of the names by which the prophet Isaiah said he should be called is "The mighty God" (Isa. 9:6). So he tells us in Revelation 1:8 that he is "the Almighty." He is often in Scripture called the wisdom of God in the abstract. He shines in the infinite holiness of the Godhead. He is called "the Holy One" in Acts 3:14 and "he that is holy" in Revelation 3:7.

He hath in his heart the fullness of the grace and love of God. The love of Christ in its breadth and length and depth and height passes knowledge. Christ is clothed with all the majesty and glory of the

Godhead. Psalm 45:3 says, "Gird thy sword upon thy thigh, O most mighty, with thy glory and thy majesty." Psalm 45:6 says, 'Thy throne, O God, is for ever and ever." The angels worshiping before him cover their faces and their feet and cry, "Holy, holy, holy, is the LORD of hosts: the whole earth is full of his glory" (Isa. 6:3). That was Christ whom they then adored, as we are informed in the New Testament (John 12:41). Christ as a divine person is possessed of all possible excellency. In order to conceive aright of Christ's divine excellency, we are not only to consider his several intimate perfections separately but together as illustrating one another and rendering each other more glorious. Thus, his wisdom renders his power more glorious.

If there could be any being that should be infinitely powerful and could do what he pleased without wisdom to direct his power, he could scarcely be said to be the more glorious for his power. They are not fit to have power who haven't wisdom to guide them in the exercise of it. For on the other hand, his power reflects glory in his wisdom. However wise he were, yet if he were weak and unable to put his wisdom into practice, the glory of his wisdom would not be manifested. So his infinite understanding and power receive glory from his holiness. The more powerful and the more knowing and crafty a wicked being is, the more hateful. That alone is a glorious power and knowledge that is a holy power and knowledge. So infinite holiness receives luster from infinite wisdom and strength. He who is of great understanding and ability and is withal of a holy and excellent disposition is deservedly more esteemed than a lower and lesser being with the same virtue of inclination and will.

Indeed, holiness is excellent in whatsoever subject it be found. It is beauty and excellency itself and renders excellent all who are possessed of it. And yet more excellent when joined with great abilities. Christ hath each of these perfections in an infinite degree. He is infinitely powerful, wise, and holy.

So the infinite grace, mercy, and love of Christ express glory to and receive glory from every other attribute. How glorious and wonderful to behold a person of infinite greatness and majesty and withal of infinite goodness and compassion to see him who is the great Creator and supreme Lord of heaven and earth full of compassion and tender pity and mercy towards the mean and unworthy. His almighty power, infinite self-sufficiency, and majesty renders his exceeding goodness to his creatures the more surprising. And how does his love and mercy endear his power and dominion to us if Christ were one who is infinitely great and powerful and of a cruel disposition? It would render him infinitely dreadful but not amiable. But in him infinite majesty and infinite love meet together. What renders the infinite grace and love of Christ perfectly lovely is that 'tis an infinitely holy mercy and love and that he never exercises it in a way inconsistent with the perfect holiness and justice of his nature. Upon the account of the divine excellencies of God the Father and infinitely delights in him, the eternal joy and happiness of the Father in his complacency in the Son. Proverbs 8:30 says, "Then I was by him, as one brought up."

2. Christ is a transcendently excellent and amiable person if we consider him with respect to those excellencies that he possesses in his common nature. He is endued with all these excellencies that the human nature is capable of—and that in their greatest perfection.

I don't mention these as any proper addition to the excellency of Christ. He possessed divine excellency which is infinite and can't be added to. The creature excellencies that Christ hath in his human nature are but a communication of them. I therefore mention them only as additional manifestations of the glory and amiableness of Christ.

Christ has no more excellency in his person since he was incarnate than before, yet there were new manifestations of his excellency. He became the more amiable to us. The greater the variety in which the beauty of Christ was manifested, the more is he recommended to the esteem and love of those who are of a finite comprehension. Christ had some excellencies in his human nature of a different denomination from any in his divine nature, such as humility and meekness and the like, though they are from the communication of the same light and holiness. 'Tis the same light reflected out as 'tis reflected. It appears in a manner agreeable to the nature and state of a creature. And 'tis this light as reflected from the created creature that falls infinitely short of the divine fountain. Yet the reflection shines not without its proper advantages as represented to one view and affection as the glory of Christ appears in the qualifications of his human nature. It appears to us in excellencies that are of one's own kind. Exalted in our own way and manner and so in some respects particularly fitted to invite our acquaintance and draw our affections. The glory of Christ as it appears in his divinity, though it be far brighter, yet doth it also more dazzle our eyes and exceed the strength and comprehension of our sight.

When he was upon earth, Christ manifested in the whole course of his life a superlative wisdom and excellency of spirit. He set an example of perfect obedience to God, though his commands (especially some of them), were attended with such exceeding difficulty. What an exalted heavenly mind appeared in him, how much above an affection of the wealth and glory of the world as one object. It was his manner at such times as when he saw the multitudes more than ordinarily affected with admiration of him on the account of miracles to withdraw himself from their applause into mountains and private places to converse with God, neglecting the praise and admiration of men. He was of a wonderfully meek and lowly heart, as appeared in his contentment with so mean an outward condition, contentedly living in the family of Joseph and Mary in obscurity for thirty years. His contentment in poverty and under so much contempt as he suffered from men during his public ministry.

His condescending behavior in response to the meanest persons upon all occasions. His being so much more pleased with Mary's sitting at his feet and hearing his word than of Martha's care and exercise that she might sumptuously sustain him. His washing his disciples' feet, how contrary would such an action have been to the pride of the great men of the world. His willingly submitting to shame and smiting, though he knew how honorable a person he was. What a quiet, meek, and gentle spirit was he of under all the provocations that were offered him. How remote from a wrathful, revengeful spirit, though he was so constantly reviled, confronted, and abused. We have no instance of his seeking revenge in his whole life. When his disciples once moved him to it, he rejected their notion and rebuked them (Luke 9:54–55).

When men reviled and shamefully treated him before his crucifixion, he reviled not again. When they were executing their malice upon him to the utmost, when they were nailing him to the cross, he received it all like the Lamb of God. No shadow or appearance of any desire of revenge. No direction to his disciples tending that way. Neither did anything drop from his mouth manifesting any revengeful thought or mediation of heart. He employed his tongue another way, praying for their forgiveness at a time when none could suppose he could be disposed to dissemble. When he was under the agonies of death, what a wonderful spirit of love appeared in him. How continually did he seek the good of them, how full of compassion was he towards them under their spiritual and temporal calamities.

How often do we read of Jesus being agonized and being moved with compassion and his weeping with those who wept. How constant and tender his love to his disciples. It appears particularly in his being so much concerned in instructions praying for comforting them just before his death when he had all the horrors of that just before his eyes. Though he knew how ill the disciples would treat him in the time of his distress, how they would all forsake him and flee. He was not unmindful of Peter, even when he stood bound at the judgment seat, but he was concerned to receive him though he had been denying him with oaths and curses. Nothing could make him forget his love to his dear disciples. And how much was his heart upon laying down his life for his people. He could not bear to hear anything said against it. How sharply did he rebuke Peter when Peter said, "Be it far from thee, Lord: this shall not be unto thee" (Matt. 16:22).

And how much more glorious and surprising do these qualifications appear when we consider that they are in so great a person, the eternal Son of God, the Lord of heaven and earth, when we thus see infinite greatness and glory and such humility, infinite majesty, and such wonderful meekness in the same person.

3. The excellencies of Christ as exhibited to our contemplation and affection have great advantage from the constitution of his person. The consideration of Christ being both God and man recommend all his excellencies to us. It is what tends to endear the divine and infinite majesty and holiness of Christ to us. Those are the attributes of One who is in our own nature, a person who is one of us, who is become our brother. It encourages to look upon these divine perfections, however high and great. Yet as what we have some near concern in and more of a right to because they are owned and possessed by the head of our nature. It is a consideration that tends to invite us to a more intimate acquaintance while Christ remained only in the divine nature. His awful majesty and infinite exaltation above us did forbid that near approach and intimate concern. But now God is come down to us in our own nature.

And on the other hand, how much more glorious and surprising the meekness and patience and love and other human excellencies of

Christ does appear when we consider that they are in so great a person as the eternal Son of God, the Lord of heaven and earth. When we thus see intimate greatness and glory and such humility and infinite majesty and such wonderful meekness in the same person.

And then these virtues of meekness and lowliness of heart are greatly honored by being in a person so great and exalted—a person who is the most high God. They are qualifications that many condemn as though they were a certain meanness of spirit. However becoming those of mean condition and depressed circumstances, yet below the high and great. But how much is their dignity vindicated in that they are the qualifications of a person who is the King of kings and Lord of lords. How doth this tend to make them appear noble and honorable.

4. The character that Christ sustains and his relation to us recommend his excellencies to our esteem and love. He is our Redeemer and Savior. The very end of his being as God-man as in such a constitution of his person that he might be our Redeemer. The consideration of this tends to endear the excellencies of both his divine and human nature to us. He is lovely as an infinitely wise, holy, and gracious person. But he is more lovely to us considered as an infinitely wise, holy, and gracious Redeemer.

When we consider these glorious and amiable perfections as in One who is ours and we his, it may surely well render these the more dear to us. There is no person in the world who stands in so endearing a relation to Christians as Christ. He is our friend and our nearest friend. John 15:15 says, "I call you not servants . . . but I have called you friends." He is our brother. Hebrews 2:11 says, "He is not ashamed to call them brethren." He is our Father (Heb. 2:13). But that relation which our spiritual union with Christ is most frequently compared to is a husband or spouse. There is no relation that implies nearness and dearness but what is made use of in Scripture to represent our relation to Christ. The nearest earthly relations are but shadows of it and fall vastly short of fully representing the intimacy and excellency of it. We may well have the more complacence in his glory and beauty on this account.

5. The benefit we have by our Lord's perfections tends to endear them to us. They are amiable in themselves absolutely considered but more so to us as they are exercised for our benefit. Thus his divine power has been exercised to conquer our enemies and spoil principalities and powers for our sakes. His infinite wisdom has been chiefly manifested in the confluence and management of the affair of our redemption. "Wherein he hath abounded toward us in all wisdom and prudence" (Eph. 1:8). So the principal manifestations of his holiness have been in the same work. The holiness of Christ doth most gloriously appear in his love to his Father in that when he had set his heart on sinners and would redeem them, he chose rather to come down from heaven and humble himself even to death and spill his infinitely precious blood. Then that redemption should be inconsistent with the honor of God's majesty and authority.

His love and grace in its most glorious exercises are for our good. The infinite grace of his divine nature—that infinite ocean of love that is in his heart—was never manifested in any other way, in any comparison as it hath been in his coming down from heaven and laying down his life for us. It hath pleased him to distinguish us from all other creatures and even from the blessed angels of heaven in the exercises of this attribute.

The meekness of Christ was exercised towards men like ourselves and under like provocations as we have often been guilty of. His humility appeared in his contentment in the poverty and contempt which he suffered for our sakes and in his condescending treatment of us. These things may well endear these qualifications to us.

APPLICATION

The use that I would make of what has been said is to move and persuade to an acceptance of the gracious offer that Christ makes of himself to us. This transcendently lovely and excellent person offers himself to us. We have an opportunity to obtain a special interest in him. If we do but accept him, if our hearts close with him, he desires no more. He doesn't offer to sell himself to us for our righteousness or anything that we can do for him, a grace to give to him. He offers himself freely. If our souls embrace the offer, if we entirely close with him and receive him as the supreme object of our esteem and love. Receiving and giving ourselves to him heartily, consenting that he should be ours as our portion and ourselves to be entirely and eternally his. He demands no more if we thus accept him then he with all his glories and excellencies shall be ours. How glorious is the opportunity of being so nearly related and becoming so intimately united to such a person that he thenceforward should be ours and we his.

Christ doesn't merely offer himself to us, but he woos us and condescends to be importunate with us to accept him. He doesn't merely command but applies himself to us in a more endearing manner in a way that has the greatest tendency to win and draw us. But this exhortation may be enforced by the consideration of the circumstances of the offer he made of himself to us.

1. As a Savior he stood ready to undertake for us to save us from eternal ruin, to stand between us and wrath, to provide for us favor and acceptance with God, and to bestow eternal life upon us. The consideration of his superlative excellency may well influence us to accept him for our Savior and encourage us to trust in him as such. It shows his sufficiency for that work. The excellency of his person gives value to his blood, hence has its atoning nature that 'tis the blood of an infinitely exultant person. This gives value to his obedience in the Father's account and renders it a sweet savor to him. If we have so

excellent a person for our mediator and intercessor with God, we need not fear our acceptance with him. For upon the account of this his excellency, he is infinitely beloved of God, and the Father is infinitely well-pleased in him and always hears and accepts him. That voice from heaven at Christ's baptism and transfiguration said, "This is my beloved Son, in whom I am well pleased" (Matt. 3:17; 17:5). This may well encourage us to hear and trust in him.

2. Christ offers himself to us as a friend and patron with all his loveliness to our full enjoyment. If we accept him here, we will be with him as his dear friends, and we shall 'ere long be where he is and shall behold his glory and most intimately and freely converse with him.

When the saints get to heaven, they shall not merely see Christ and have to do with him as subjects and servants with a glorious and gracious Lord and sovereign, but Christ will converse with them as friends and brethren. This we may learn from the manner of Christ's conversing with his disciples here on earth, though he was their supreme Lord and did not refuse—yea, required—their supreme respect and adoration. Yet he did not treat them as earthly sovereigns are wont to do their subjects. He did not keep them at an awful distance but all along conversed with them with the most friendly familiarity as with brethren or a father amongst a company of children. So he did with the Twelve, and so he did with Mary and Martha and Lazarus.

He told his disciples that he did not call them servants, but he called them friends (John 15:15). So neither will he call his disciples servants but friends in heaven. Though Christ be in a state of exaltation at the right hand of God and appears in an immense height of glory, yet this won't hinder his conversing with his saints in a most familiar manner. He won't treat his disciples with greater distance for his being in a state of exaltation but will rather take them into a state of exaltation with him. This will be the improvement that Christ will make of his own glory to make his beloved friends partakers with him to glorify them in his glory. As Christ says to his Father in John 17:22–23, "And the glory which thou gavest me I have given them; that they may be one, even as we are one: I in them, and thou in me, that they may be made perfect in one; and that the world may know that thou hast sent me, and hast loved them, as thou hast loved me."

We are to consider that though Christ be greatly exalted, yet he is exalted not as a private person for himself only but as his people's head. He is exalted in their name and upon their account as their representative as the firstfruits. He is not exalted who be at a greater distance from them but that they may be exalted with him. The exaltation and honor of the head is not to make a greater distance between the head and the members, but they have the same relation, and under that they had before the members are honored with the head.

When believers get to heaven, Christ will conform them to himself the glory which the Father hath given him. He will give them this glory as he is set down on the Father's throne. They shall sit down with him on his throne and shall in their measure be made like him.

When he was going to heaven, Christ comforted his disciples with this—that after a while he would come and take them to himself that they might be with him again. And we are not to suppose that when the disciples got to heaven, though they found their Lord in a state of exaltation, yet that they found him any more shy or keeping a greater distance than he used to do. No, doubtless, he embraced them as friends. He welcomed them home to their and his Father's house and to their and his glory. They who had been his friends here in this world, who had been together here, and had together partook of sorrows and troubles, now he welcomed them to rest and partake of glory with him. He took them and led them into his chamber and showed them all his glory as he prayed, "Father, I will that they also, whom thou hast given me, be with me where I am; that they may behold my

glory, which thou hast given me" (John 17:24). The manner of exposition is to be noted: "I will that they also, whom thou hast given me, be
with me. I don't only pray that they would glorify me personally, but
the glory that the Father gave," as Christ had prayed in the beginning.

This is one end of Christ taking on him men's nature that his
people might be under advantage for a more familiar conversation
with him than the infinite distance of the divine nature would allow of.
Upon this account the church longed for Christ's incarnation. Song of
Solomon 8:1 says, "O that thou wert as my brother, that sucked the
breasts of my mother! when I should find thee without, I would kiss
thee; yea, I should not be despised."

One design of God in the gospel is to bring us to make God the
object of our undivided respect that he may engross our regard every
way. That whatever natural inclination there is in our souls, he may be
the center of it and that God may be all in all. There is a natural inclination in the creature not only to the adoration of a glorious Lord and
sovereign but to complacence in someone as a friend to love and
delight in, one that may be conversed with as a companion and does
not destroy nature and holiness or weaken this inclination of our
nature. But God hath so continued in the gospel that a divine person
may be the object even of this inclination of our nature. In order hereto
is come down to us and has taken our nature and become one of us and
calls himself our friend, our brother and companion. Psalm 122:8 says,
"For my brethren and companions' sakes, I will now say, Peace be
within thee."

The saints' conversation with Christ in heaven shall not only be as
intimate as but shall in many respects be much more intimate, for in
heaven that union will be perfected which is but begun in this world.
And while the fruits are here, there is a great deal that remains of sin
and darkness to separate and disunite them. But then all obstacles of
a close union and most intimate communion will be removed. This is

not a time for that full acquaintance and those manifestations of love which Christ designs towards his people hereafter.

When the saints shall see Christ's divine glory and exaltation in heaven, this will indeed possess their hearts with the greater admiration and adoring respect. But it will not keep them at a distance but will form only to heighten their surprise when they find Christ condescending to treat them in such a familiar manner.

So if we accept Christ, we shall hereafter so be admitted to him that there shall be nothing to hinder the fullest enjoyment of him to the satisfying of the utmost encouragement of our souls. And this shall be our entertainment to all eternity. There never shall be any end of this happiness nor anything to molest or interrupt our enjoyment of it. In offering himself to us, he doth naturally offer us the full enjoyment of God the Father also.

3. In being united to Christ, we shall have a more glorious union with and enjoyment of God the Father than otherwise could be. For hereby our relation to God becomes much nearer. We shall be the children of God in a higher manner than otherwise we could be for being members of God's own natural Son. We shall in a sort be partakers of his relation to the Father or his communion with him in his Sonship. We shall not only be the sons of God by regeneration but a kind of participation of the Sonship of the eternal Son. This seems to be intended. Galatians 4:4–6 says, "God sent forth his Son, made of a woman, made under the law, to redeem them that were under the law, that we might receive the adoption of sons. And because ye are sons, God hath sent forth the Spirit of his Son into your hearts, crying, Abba, Father." The church is the daughter of God not only as he hath begotten her by his Word and Spirit but as she is the spouse of his eternal Son. So we being members of the Son are partakers in our nature of the Father's love to the Son and complacence in him. John 17:23 says, "I in them, and thou in me . . . thou . . . hast loved them, as thou hast loved me."

Verse 26 says, "That the love wherewith thou hast loved me may be in them." John 16:27 says, "The Father himself loveth you, because ye have loved me, and have believed that I came out from God."

So we shall be one, according to our being partakers of the Son's enjoyment of God. We shall have his joy fulfilled in ourselves (John 17:13). By this means we shall come to a more intimate and full enjoyment of God the Father than otherwise could have been. There is doubtless an intimate intimacy between the Father and the Son. The former being in him shall partake with him in it and of the blessedness of it. So is the affair of our redemption ordered that thereby we are brought to an infinitely more exalted kind of union with God and enjoyment of him, both the Father and the Son, than otherwise could have been. Christ being united to the human nature, we have advantage for a more full enjoyment of him than we could possibly have had if he had remained only in the divine nature. So again, we being united to a divine person can have a more intimate union and intercourse with God the Father who is only in the divine nature than otherwise could be.

Christ, who is a divine person, by taking on him our nature, descends from the infinite distance and height above us and is brought nigh to us. We have advantage for the full enjoyment of him. On the other hand, we by being in Christ a divine person do ascend up to God through the infinite distance and love and have lovely advantage for the full advantage of him also. This was the design of Christ to bring it to pass—that he and his Father and his people to the most intimate union and communion. John 17:21–23 says, "That they all may be one; as thou, Father, art in me, and I in thee, that they also may be one in us: that the world may believe that thou hast sent me. And the glory which thou gavest me I have given them; that they may be one, even as we are one: I in them, and thou in me, that they may be made perfect in one."

Christ has brought it to pass that those whom the Father has given him should be brought into the household of God. He and his Father and his people should be one society, one family, and the church should be admitted into the society of the blessed Trinity.

10

That at a Time When a People Are Called for a General Humiliation, It Becomes Each One to Mourn for His Own Iniquity (Sermon 1)

But they that escape of them shall escape, and shall be on the mountains like doves of the valleys, all of them mourning, every one for his iniquity.

EZEKIEL 7:16

This sermon on Ezekiel 7:16 is the first of two that Edwards preached at an unknown date on what he notes was a day of public humiliation.

He begins this call to mourning for sin by making it clear that just as individuals are guilty for their own sin, so they should mourn specifically and individually for their sin. But Edwards adds that such mourning is not just for the punishment of that iniquity. There is a great difference, says Edwards, between being grieved that one must be condemned and damned, and being grieved because one has done evil. It is the latter, explains Edwards, that is properly called mourning.

Edwards concludes this first sermon with a challenging plea to his hearers to examine themselves seriously whether they have themselves been a cause of the spread or promotion of sin among others throughout the land.

The first sermon manuscript from this two-sermon unit, like the second, is another example of an oversize manuscript. The nineteen leaves are very easy to read, and it has little in the way of corrections.

God never punishes any man except it be for his own sin, and he suffers for no other guilt but what is upon his own soul. And although there is such a thing as being partakers of other men's sins and so of the same punishment, yet men partake of them no other way than by making of them their own, either by promoting, assisting, or consenting. We are guilty of Adam's transgression, not as it is the sin of Adam but as it is our own. He stood as our common head and representative. Our own souls by this means became contaminated with guilt and filthiness. Jeremiah 31:30 says, "But every one shall die for his own iniquity: every man that eateth the sour grape, his teeth shall be set on edge." Ezekiel 18:20 says, "The soul that sinneth, it shall die. The son shall not bear the iniquity of the father, neither shall the father bear the iniquity of the son: the righteousness of the righteous shall be upon him, and the wickedness of the wicked shall be upon him."

So it is with respect to God's public judgments on a people or land. Men are punished for none but their own sins. They partake of common judgments only as they partake of common sins either as they have added to the scope by their own sins or have promoted and some way encouraged and not done their utmost to prevent by their prayers and endeavors the sins of others and of the land.

God is wont therefore frequently at such times as he rises up to take vengeance on a people, to deliver the righteous from the common calamity, either by taking of them away from the evil to come, by receiving out of a sinful and troublesome world into a better, or by distinguishing by preserving of them in the midst of it. As for the righteous, they are not afraid of evil tidings. Their heart is fixed on trusting in God. Thus when God was revealing to his prophet what dreadful judgments should come on the land of Israel, he bids him go and tell the righteous that nevertheless it should be well with him. Isaiah 3:10 says, "Say ye to the righteous, that it shall be well with him: for they shall eat the fruit of their doings."

God imputes to none the guilt of any but their own sins and makes them partakers of common judgments for any but their own iniquity. So it becomes everyone in a time of humiliation to mourn each man for his iniquity, as we find of those who escaped of the children of Israel from God's destroying judgments did. They were upon the mountains "like doves of the valleys, all of them mourning, every one for his iniquity." Here we may observe:

1. What is the occasion of this mourning? For this we must look into the foregoing verses. There we find it was God's public judgment upon the land and people of Israel, not so much for God's judgments upon them in particular for those were some that escaped. But they that escape of them shall escape. But it was God's manifestation of his anger against the public and their nation in general. Of these judgments and destruction speaks all the foregoing part of the chapter. Ezekiel 7:2–3 says, "Also, thou son of man, thus saith the Lord GOD unto the land of Israel; An end, the end is come upon the four corners of the land. Now is the end come upon thee, and I will send mine anger upon thee, and will judge thee according to thy ways, and will recompense upon thee all thine abominations."

We have the manner of Israel's foretold destruction described in verse 15: "The sword is without, and the pestilence and the famine within: he that is in the field shall die with the sword; and he that is in the city, famine and pestilence shall devour him." And now come the words of our text, "But they that escape of them shall escape, and shall be on the mountains like doves of the valleys, all of them mourning, every one for his iniquity."

2. What was the generality of this mourning? Note that all of them were mourning. Not only the wicked kings and rulers who had a chief in the wickedness of the people and so a chief hand in pulling down the judgments of heaven on the land. Not only those who had been more naturally wicked—but all of them.

3. What was the object of their mourning or matter of their repentance? Their own particular sins. The calamity was general upon the nation, but their repentance is particular. They do not so much run out against others, or if they were only to blame, as the chief procurer of this destruction to their land, but everyone mourns for his iniquity.

DOCTRINE

At a time when a people are called to a general humiliation, it becomes each one to mourn for his own iniquity. There are various ways wherein a people are called to a general humiliation by the general abounding of sin by general declension: When God in his providence testifies his displeasure, when we are particularly called in providence to call earnestly upon God for such and such public mercies, and when we are called thereto by those to whom it appertains to appoint days of general humiliation as there is occasion. All these ways except the last were the children of Israel called to that general humiliation we read of in this portion of Scripture. In all those ways are we this day called to humble ourselves before God.

In explaining of the doctrine, we shall speak to these two things: What is intended in the doctrine by mourning for our iniquity, and why it becomes each particular person in times of public humiliation to mourn for his own iniquity.

What is intended in the doctrine of mourning for our own iniquity? We shall first tell what is not and what is intended by it.

1. By mourning for our own iniquity is not intended only a mourning for the punishment of our iniquity. The expression clearly contains more in it than this. Mourning for the evil that is brought upon us for sin cannot properly be called a mourning for sin. There is a punishment, an evil that is affixed unto sin that sin naturally and necessarily brings upon the mind. Such is the disturbing of the peace and calm of the mind, trouble of conscience and so many sins, ruin of our good name, ruin of health, shortening life, and destruction of our temporal welfare. There are some sins that bring a man to piece of bread if lived in others that make the name to stink in the nostrils of mankind. A mourning for those things is not a mourning for sin.

There are other miseries that are brought on sinners more directly by the appointment of God as a punishment of their iniquity. God sometimes signally punishes men's sins in this world. But the punishment that is appointed for the workers of iniquity in the future world is that which is the proper punishment of the wicked that is indissolubly connected with obstinate sinning. The mourning for those is not what is called in the Word of God mourning for sin. Whether those evils this punishment is full or feared, the devils mourn in this sense, and the damned souls their weeping and wailing and gnashing of teeth is on the account of the punishment of their sin.

Their mourning and sorrow is incomparably deeper than ever is felt by mortals on earth. Yet none will say that they properly mourn for sin. This would very improperly be called mourning for sin, for 'tis not a mourning for. 'Tis another manner of thing that is the object of this mourning. There is a great difference between being grieved that one must be condemned and damned, and being grieved because one has done evil, which alone is properly called mourning for sin. For all men in the world, whether good or bad, love pleasure and hate pain. Therefore, all will be grieved when they must lose the one and bear the other that yet may as much set for and as strongly inclined to sin as any.

There are doubtless many who never mourn for in any other but this exceeding improper sense. They look upon themselves as true penitents. Some of those mourners whom God will comfort have been frightened with hell and the thoughts of death and judgment. On the account of this, their fear and danger are sorry for what they have done. They are sorry they have exposed themselves to such miseries. Especially is this way often the case with those who are on a deathbed, when the terrors of death take hold upon them and the dreadfulness of eternal misery appears in lively colors to them. Then indeed they mourn for what they have done and accuse themselves with folly, whereas if they know they should escape misery, they would be easy and unconcerned about their sin.

2. By mourning for our iniquity is not intended only a mourning for some of our iniquity. By mourning for sin is intended a mourning for sin in general and cannot be supposed only to intend sorrow for a part, that we mourn for some particular sins that we have been guilty of and retain other sins in our hearts, affections, and practice. He who loves some sins as much as he is grieved for others cannot be said any more properly to mourn for sin than to rejoice in it.

'Tis true indeed that no man in the world can mourn particularly for every sin committed. They are so many in number that they cannot be numbered, nor is it possible any should remember all the sins ever they committed. But they may have such a repentance and hatred to their sin in general that they may go other than to the very nature of it.

They may sincerely mourn for all that can be remembered of whatever kind. On the contrary, there are some who are sorry only for such and such actions that perhaps have been most detrimental to them or are most heinous, still being as much friends as ever to other sins and lusts. But no such partial repentance is what is intended in the text or doctrine, for mourning for our own iniquity.

3. Positively, men may be said to mourn for their own iniquity, when the iniquity of their actions is the object of their mourning; when they mourn for that in their iniquity which makes it to be iniquity, that turpitude and filthiness which is in the action. The mourning for this is naturally implied in the expression "mourning for sin."

Now in those who mourn for their actions on the account of the misery that ensures this is not the object or matter of their mourning, not the evil of sin but the evil of punishment. They do indeed, and so do the damned mourn that ever they did the actions, but 'tis because of their consequences. But the true mourner is grieved because he sees a baseness in his own actions, in their nature that is most arduous to him and which he mourns that ever he practiced. It grieves him that ever he practiced things that showed such base ingratitude. Such abominable injustice makes things in their own nature so exceeding odious, unworthy, and detestable, so contrary to true excellency and what is really lovely. Others may mourn for their self-destroying actions, but such as those only mourn for their iniquity.

4. Those mourn for sin in a proper sense who mourn for the disobedience of their actions. Evil actions may be considered various ways, either as actions of an ill tendency in their own nature, or as actions of ill consequence, or they may be looked upon as irrational actions or as sin that is disobedient to God. He who truly mourns for sin mourns for this in them—disobedience to God. For actions are sin no otherwise than as they are contrary to God's law. He who mourns

for his evil actions under any other consideration cannot be said to mourn for sin.

The true mourners for sin, beholding God's excellency as with joy and pleasure with grief, do turn their eyes towards that which is against him, that they themselves have been the authors of. Psalm 51:4 says, "Against thee, thee only, have I sinned, and done this evil in thy sight."

We are come now in the second place to show why it becomes each particular person in times of general humiliation to mourn for his own iniquity. Not but that it also becomes us at such times to mourn for the sins of others, for the sins of those we are concerned with, for the sins of the town or society to which we belong, to mourn for the sins of the land and for that iniquity, vice, and impiety that abounds in the world. 'Tis the property of the true lovers of God to lament the sins that are committed by others and to be grieved at the heart for the dishonor and abuse that is done to their God and Redeemer. Psalm 119:136 says, "Rivers of water run down mine eyes, because they keep not thy law."

And thus it becomes us to do in times of general humiliation and especially to mourn for those sins that are the abounding iniquities of the land. But most of all doth it become us at such times to look into our hearts and examine our ways and to mourn for our own iniquity. These are the sins that we have most especial reason to lament because 'tis ourselves who have been the author of them. The guilt of these appertains to our own souls 'til we turn from them by repentance.

1. By our sins we have contributed to the guilt of the land. When a people are called to humble themselves before God for their sin as the sins of a nation or country. Surely 'tis everyone should take care that he laments particularly that part of it which he himself has been guilty of.

'Tis but mockery to God to pretend to keep a day of humiliation for the sins that abound in a land and not be humbled for what we ourselves have contributed thereto and to bewail our own part. It ought to be a most humbling consideration to us that we have added to the score and ourselves have helped to procure the anger of God against that public society of which we are a part. 'Tis partly on the account of our sins that God is frowning upon us and that he hides his face from us or rather is coming forth in his providences against us. The anger of God is more fierce, the thunder of his wrath more dreadful, and God's judgments the more grievous for our sins. When we see God coming forth against us and manifesting his displeasure, certainly we ought to meet him, prostrating ourselves in the dust with tears of repentance, the deepest humiliation, and most humble confessions of those sins of our own which have partly incensed him.

2. In times of general humiliation, every particular person ought to mourn for his own iniquities. All those sins that bring guilt and the judgments of God on a people or land are seated in particular persons. The contrary notion and a whole world is made up of particular persons. So all the sin that is in the world is committed by particular persons. The sins of one or two particular persons have sometimes brought such guilt on a whole nation that on the account thereof they have been beaten down before their enemies, and very awful judgments have been brought on the whole by their means. We have a remarkable instance in Achan for whose sake Israel could not stand before their enemies. We find this account in the seventh chapter of Joshua. He is therefore called the "troubler of Israel" (1 Chron. 2:7).

All the troubles that are brought upon our Israel are for the sins of some as others. Some undoubtedly are the "troublers" of our Israel. Alas, how little reason have we to clear ourselves as if we, as if our sins, had contributed nothing to the troubles of the land. We have much more reason to reflect with bitterness on our own ways than to charge these and those, making ourselves innocent. The children of Israel did not thus act as doves of the valleys, mourning every man for his own iniquity. We have in some measure been the troublers of Israel. We have therefore great reason to turn our eye upon ourselves and look on our own ways with blushing and the greatest grief.

If everyone contents himself with only a general and external humiliation, who shall mourn in particular if everyone says that his sins add but a small matter to the sin of the land and so neglect particular repentance. None of the iniquity of the land will be truly lamented, which brings me to the third reason:

3. Why everyone on such occasions should mourn for his own iniquity. This is the only way whereby God's displeasure can be removed from the public. If all the guilt of all the sins of the public is in particular persons, how can it be removed but by a particular repentance?

'Tis not a show of bewailing the sins or saying before God that we are a declined and backslidden people. 'Tis not a show of lamentation for the dullness and deadness of times or the prevailing of iniquity in the land. 'Tis not only a lamenting of the decay of religion in general that removes the tokens of God's displeasure against us. Persons may seem to do thus and yet be chief troublers of Israel. A person may do this and yet have great part of the guilt of those sins which he seems to lament, seated in his own soul not regarded.

It becomes us rather to reflect on what we have done to lament and sigh for our own transgressions. This is what God expects and which alone will cause him to take away his judgment from us. If we were ever brought to this and not only to make an external show of celebrating days of humiliation but to have the chief work of the day within ourselves between God and our own souls and were brought to lie in the dust and to abhor ourselves for our own ill deservings whereby we have in some measure hastened and aggravated God's judgments. We might hope to see those clouds which seem to be hanging over us scattered, and God unveiling his face and the light of his countenance beginning to shine forth upon us.

4. We ought to mourn particularly everyone for his own sins because by them we have promoted the sins of others and have been made partakers of their iniquities. We pretend to mourn and be humbled for the sins of the public society we belong to. But we ourselves in part have been the occasion of them and have not only contributed to the sin and guilt of the land inasmuch as our own sin being cast into the scale has made the weight heavier otherwise than it would have been. We have been the occasion of the sins of other men being greater than otherwise they would have been.

Sin is a spreading poison. If one part of the body be infected with it, it will not be that alone. Other parts will not be free, but the whole body will suffer by it, especially those parts that are neighboring. 'Tis an infectious disease, a catching plague, that is most easily and quickly communicated from one to another. Galatians 5:9 says, "A little leaven leaveneth the whole lump."

1. We have been made partakers of other men's sins in that we have not done our utmost to prevent their sins or to bring them off from them. God has placed us in the midst of human society not for ourselves only, but also to promote the good of others, and most of all to promote their greatest good—even the good of their souls—and to do what we can to prevent their most dreadful misery, their spiritual and eternal death. Especially doth God expect of Christians who have little in comparison to do with any king but a future life that they do their utmost to promote each other's good as Christians, and that we pretend to be the followers of him who laid down his life that he might save men from sin and hell and bring men to holiness and heaven. We should do what in us lies to promote the same design and to be as secondary saviors, to save men from the same spiritual adversity.

The new commandment that Christ gave unto us was to love one another. One-half of the law is to love our neighbor as ourselves—that is, to endeavor to promote our neighbor's true interest as we do our own. By this we are obliged not only to endeavor to cleanse our own ways but to endeavor to prevent sin in our neighbors, or to bring them off from them. This is what God so much expects of us. If we neglect, he looks upon us as part guilty of their sin and of the blood of their souls which we did not endeavor to prevent. When our neighbor was perishing by us, we did not lend a hand to save him from ruin.

If we see a neighbor sinking and we willingly stand by and see him drown, shall we not justly in some measure be thought guilty of murder? Or if we should see a house take fire and willingly see it burn down when we could have quenched it, should we not in some part be guilty of destroying the owner's substance? Or if we should know of a treasonable outing or plot against the king and did not do what we could to frustrate it, might we not justly be looked upon as a traitor?

For if we see souls running to everlasting ruin and sinking into the pit of hell and don't endeavor to do our utmost to stop them, shall we not by God be thought partly guilty of their blood? Or if we stand still and see the enemies of God fighting against heaven and oppose them not, shall we not by God be looked on as guilty in some measure of their hostile acts?

We this day pretend to be humbled for the sin of the land, but we ought to consider whether or no there is not the more sin in the land through our neglect, and whether it has not been in our power to prevent much of it. Whether it is not probable that with the blessing of God we might have brought some, at least in some measure, off from their evil and perhaps been instruments of their saving conversion from sin to holiness, no doubt. But if one-half of the land or only those who make a profession of godliness had done this, sin would not abound amongst us as it now doth and God's frowns might have been stayed. The zeal of Phinehas, though but one man, turned away the wrath of God from the whole congregation, as we see in chapter 25 of Numbers, verses 6–11.

By standing by and seeing others go on in sin and not endeavoring to dissuade them from it and bring them off the practice by what means we can, we do really promote their sin and encourage and embolden them in their course. To hold our peace and to do nothing in such a case is to do a great deal. Thereby we manifest in part our consent and approbation, and they take it either that we do approve of their actions or at least are indifferent about it. And indeed to be still and inactive in such a case is a tacit approbation and does indeed show either that we have nothing as not very much against what we see done, and this is one way whereby we are made partakers of the sins of others and do promote them by our own sin.

2. Men by their own sin do promote the sins of others inasmuch as thereby they dishonor God and make others have a mean esteem of religion. Men are apt to judge of religion as any profession by those who profess it. If a people of any kind of profession are generally a mean object kind of people, men judge that profession as religion they are of to be accordingly mean and despicable. So if a people who profess the Christian religion are sinful and live odious lives, bystanders and spectators will pass sentence upon their religion as a mean and worthless profession. They will see that the professors of it are so bad in their lives and will be apt to judge that it is but a mere empty theme, a dream, the effect of the wild imagination of men, and nothing else will be confirmed in their unbelief of a future state and eternal judgment. "For do not we see" (they will say) "that these who say they do believe these things live no better than other men." They cannot believe that they themselves do really believe them, seeing they act no more under the influence of them, and if they don't believe them, who should?

An infidel, one who professed he did not believe the Christian religion to be true, being once asked how he could quiet his conscience in such a desperate state, made answer, "I rather wonder how you can quiet your consciences in such a common, careless course of life, believing as you do. If I believed such things as you do, I should think no care and diligence and holiness could be enough."

We in a Christian land say that those who are very profane and wicked are like heathen, but in Turkey they say that those who are very vicious are like Christians. So great a tendency have the sins of them who profess Christianity to beget in the minds of others unbelief, a mean opinion of Christ and Christianity. Romans 2:23 says, "Thou that makest thy boast of the law, through breaking the law dishonorest thou God?" Wicked men hereby get a great confirmedness in their way, go on with less remorse of conscience.

We ought to consider therefore especially on occasions of general humiliation whether we have not this way promoted the sin of those with whom we have been conversant. Have we not by this means kept persons in a state of stupidity or cast a damp upon the hearts of those who have been in some measure convinced and have been hopefully sitting not in religion? Have we not been a means of quenching the smoking flax? Are there not fewer religious persons in the land by our means? Are not those who are godly less lively and those who are wicked more confirmed by our sin? Ecclesiastes 9:18 says, "One sinner destroyeth much good."

3. Men by their own sins do promote the sins of others by the evil example of them. Any common degree of observation is sufficient to teach us what a mighty power and influence example has upon men. Nothing is more common than for me to follow others to hell for example and company sake. Evil examples are some of the chief of the devil's charms whereby he draws and allures men to the bottomless pit. And what reason have we to lament it before God? Our ways have

been no more pure in the sight of men. Everyone should mourn that those things that have appeared in them have given Satan an advantage in some measure over the souls of others.

11

That at a Time When a
People Are Called for a
General Humiliation, It
Becomes Each One to Mourn
for His Own Iniquity
(Sermon 2)

But they that escape of them shall escape, and shall be on the mountains
like doves of the valleys, all of them mourning, every one for his iniquity.

EZEKIEL 7:16

This is Edwards's second sermon on this special day of mourning
for sin. Building on the foundation he laid in his first message,
Edwards now proceeds to show the seriousness of making a show of
humiliation while remaining in known sin. Nothing, says Edwards, is
more provoking to God than hypocrisy. From this, Edwards moves on
to a detailed account of the nature of true mourning.

The manuscript of this sermon consists of another sixteen oversize leaves that are easy to transcribe. Again, there are almost no
corrections.

T his text sets before us an example of that which is the very thing that wants to be done in the land. 'Tis what God is waiting for, in the expecting of which he withholds his hand and keeps back his thunder and doth not stir up all his wrath. 'Tis not the external solemnizing of days of testing that he is waiting for, but that each one should be mourning before him for their own iniquity. If this were done, we might hope to see happy times to our land. If it were generally done in the world, there would ensue glorious things throughout the earth. If once a people could be persuaded of this, the point would be gained. With an eye to this we have already insisted on those words from this doctrine.

DOCTRINE

When a people are called to a general humiliation, it becomes each one to mourn for his own iniquity. And first we observed what is in a proper sense to mourn for our own iniquity. We observed that mourning for the punishment of our iniquity, or the mourning for only part of our iniquity, is not what can properly be called a mourning for our own sin, but that we do truly mourn for our own iniquity.

We showed why it became each person in times wherein God calls of general humiliation to mourn for his own sin because thereby we contribute to the guilt of the land. We also showed that all the sin of the land and world is seated in the souls of particular persons because this is the only way to obtain a removal of the tokens of God's displeasure. Men by their own sin have promoted and been made partakers of the sins of others, they do not do their utmost to prevent and bring them off from their sin, they make others have a mean esteem of God and religion, and others' sins are promoted by their evil example.

We now proceed to make improvement of this doctrine.

1. Use of instruction. Inference is it so that it becomes everyone when God calls for general humiliation to mourn for his own iniquity, then undoubtedly secret confessions and supplications do become us at such times. We ought at such times much to lament our sins publicly, and it becomes us to be particular in the kinds, circumstances, and aggravations of those sins that are public and general, and which all are in some degree guilty of, for the lost cannot clear themselves. It becomes us also to be particular and earnest in our joint supplication, for the smiles of heaven upon us. But yet that particular confession of our personal sin can be done alone in secret. Those public confessions that suit the sins of some will not particularly suit the ways of all.

Since it becomes all, therefore, when God frowns upon a land to retire from the world and prostrate their souls before him who fear in secret, there they may with the greatest freedom open their hearts and spread their sin and guilt, their own iniquities before him whom they have offended. There we may with the utmost freedom confess to God the circumstances of our sins before him who sits on a mercy seat. He is the Lord God gracious and merciful, forgiving iniquities, transgressions, and sins.

Hence we learn the cause why God's hand is stretched out still against this land. Notwithstanding our yearly returns of days of humiliation, may not God say of us in general that we draw nigh unto him with our lips while our hearts are far from him? Wherefore God is declaring that he does not accept our public pretences. The heavens, instead of clearing, rather seem in some respects to grow thicker and blacker, and God is shaking his rod over us with a more threatening hand.

Neither have we only God's threatenings, but God makes us in many regards actually to feel his displeasure. 'Tis because God has not yet seen us as doves in the valleys mourning for our own iniquity. How few true mourners for sin are to be found amongst us? Has not the number of them rather decreased than increased? There are many who will speak of the sins of the country with a seeming lamentation, but how few of those truly and chiefly lament their own transgression.

2. Use of examination. Whether or no, we are true mourners for our own iniquity. There are many—yea, 'tis evident there are very many—who can in no respect be called mourners for their sin who have no manner of sense, either of the evil or so much as the danger of their sins are concerned, neither about their nature, nor even of their sin. They have neither that mourning that arises from remorse of conscience nor that which arises from a real sensibleness of the odiousness of their ways. Let us in the first place examine whether we are not some of these.

But if we have a sorrow or at least a concern about our actions, let us see of what kind it is. Is it not only a mourning for the punishment or feared event of sin, or is it properly a mourning for the sin itself because of a turpitude that we see therein that fills us with abhorrence? Is it the disobedience of the actions that we mourn for, or is it a partial repentance that we experience? Or is it of all manner of sin that we have been guilty of, sins of heart and life, original and actual sin, omissions and commissions?

3. Use of exhortation. To exhort all to a particular mourning for their own iniquity at this day when God is manifesting his displeasure against the land. We have shown the reasonableness of this already inasmuch by our sins we have contributed to the guilt of the land. We have helped to pull down the judgment of God on the land. All the sin and guilt which is in the whole land is seated in particular persons, and we have no reason to be clearing of ourselves before God. Let every one of us consider how we have promoted the sins of others and so have been a sort of spiritual murderers, either in being active in promoting the death or carelessness about the preservation of the life of the soul. Yea, in some measure we have been murderers of our land

inasmuch as we have not done our past in healing its wounds and deadly diseases, and have not done our part to prevent sin, and so to prevent God's judgments. But we have rather by our own sins increased the disease and stirred up God's wrath.

But here we shall offer something further to the consideration of everyone to move him to this duty.

Let it be considered that except we mourn for our own iniquities, we shall but the more anger God by our pretences of public humiliations. 'Twill be but mere mockery to pretend to humiliation for the sins of the land and nation if we all the while hold our own sin as a sweet morsel under our tongues and hug it as a dear friend in our bosom. Mourning for sins begins at home. He who truly mourns for the sins of others will most certainly mourn for those that he himself has been guilty of. 'Tis impossible anyone should be truly grieved that God is dishonored in the world and if so much contempt is cast upon his holy laws and that Jesus Christ is so much slighted and holiness no more practiced, when at the same time he is not grieved that he himself has dishonored God and contemned the same law and has slighted the same Lord Jesus Christ and has himself gone contrary to holiness.

Everyone therefore that doesn't find the greatest mourning for his own sin may be assured that he is not truly grieved. Whatsoever grief he may pretend for the sins of the times for the errors in points of doctrine or worship for pride and covetousness. Although there are many who pretend to be mourners for these things, who will seem to sigh to think what the land is come to, yet none of these are true mourners for these things but only those who mourn chiefly for their own sin. The true mourner is indeed heartily grieved at the overflowing of iniquity in the world and to see how others slight the commands of his Father and God. But when he comes to consider how he himself has dishonored this God and Savior who is so dear to him, it causes far greater grief and fetches from him the deepest sigh.

This is the temper of true penitents. They not only truly lament the sins of others, but when they see those sins in others that do so grieve them, it puts them in mind of their own iniquities, the reflection on which causes the most deep humiliation and abasement. Except we mourn thus, God will not accept our fastings and public days of humiliation, but his anger thereby will be increased and incensed. Instead of procuring a removal of heaven's frowns, we shall by our fasting make them more dreadful. By our external shows of humiliation, we shall but make work for humiliation and repentance and may expect that God, when he comes to reckon with us, will punish us for this with the rest that we have so mocked in our pretences of general and public repentance.

Nothing is more provoking to God than the hypocritical performance of the parts of divine worship. Isaiah 1:13 says, "Bring no more vain oblations; incense is an abomination unto me; the new moons and sabbaths, the calling of assemblies, I cannot away with; it is iniquity, even the solemn meeting."

Let it be considered that except we do thus, we may expect that God will execute judgments upon us. 'Tis very evident to anyone who has his eyes open that iniquity very much abounds in the world and so much in this country that it is truly worthy of wonder that God has not yet made us to drink more deeply of the cup of his wrath. But God's Spirit "shall not always strive with man, for that he also is flesh" (Gen. 6:3). God is in heaven and we are upon earth and we are but worms. And God will not always bear to be disobeyed and rebelled against by such. He is a jealous God and will vindicate his own honor. Worms shall not always swell with enmity and venom against God unpunished.

The reason why God has not yet come forth against us to our ruin is because for this—to see everyone mourning for his iniquity. For this doubtless God has kept back vengeance. He is yet striving with us to bring us to this. We shall enjoy divine cultivation, house, his Word, his ordinances, and ministers and liberties continued to us, but we have no reason to expect that it will be so always. The axe has a long time lain at the root of the tree, and we cannot expect that it will lie still always if we continue fruitless—a bringing forth of wild grapes. Justice has said already concerning us, "Behold, these three years I come seeking fruit on this fig tree, and find none: cut it down; why cumbereth it the ground?" And mercy has made answer, "Let it alone this year also, till I shall dig about it, and dung it" (Luke 13:7–8). But if nonetheless it continues barren, mercy will not prevent its being cut down.

God bore a long time with the old world. Doubtless a long time before God commanded Noah to build the ark and for 120 years afterwards striving with them by the preaching of Noah. But when no means would reclaim, he finally overthrows them in a dreadful manner by opening the floodgates of heaven and breaking up the fountains of the great deep and only eight persons were saved. First Peter 3:20 says, "Which sometime were disobedient, when once the longsuffering of God waited in the days of Noah, while the ark was a preparing, wherein few, that is, eight souls were saved by water."

How long also did God bear with the ten tribes, using all manner of means with them but at last was provoked totally to overthrow them and remove them out of his sight, they still remaining impenitent (2 Kings 17:13–18). He did so with the tribe of Judah and the city of Jerusalem, after he had for some hundreds of years been luring them by his prophets, and they still remaining obstinate and inflexible. God gave them up into the hand of the king of Babylon. The people of Israel were God's peculiar people above all other people on the face of the earth, and the city of Jerusalem was the city of God's special residence and manifestation of his presence and was called the holy city. And the same city and same people were again overthrown in a more dreadful manner after Christ's time by the Romans.

And Jesus Christ himself often foretold it. The nation had got to a dreadful degree of wickedness in Christ's time for which cause he called them a wicked and perverse generation and a generation of vipers. But yet God bore with them a long time. Christ himself strove with them by his preaching and mighty works. Weeping over Jerusalem, he declared that he often would have gathered her children as a hen doth her chickens under her wings but yet God bore with them.

About forty years after that, he then brought that dreadful destruction upon them, and tribulation so great as is quite unparalleled by any that ever happened to any city or people whatever according to what Christ foretold in Matthew 24:21: "For then shall be great tribulation, such as was not from the beginning of the world to this time, no, nor ever shall be." Ever since they have remained dispersed as vagabonds, all over the face of the earth, as we see them at this day.

We likewise may justly expect many heavy judgments of God against us except we prevent it by timely repentance. Let everyone therefore who has any love of the land be thereby moved to the duty we are now urged to, nor let any think that they themselves shall escape the common judgment if they continue in impenitence.

That we each person may be moved to mourn for his own iniquity. Let it be considered that they who do not thus have no reason to hope that they shall be interested in public blessings and deliverances. If God has a design of mercy on the land in general, such as those who don't mourn for their sin can't expect that they shall have a part for though they have had a part in the sin. Yet they had none in the repentance and therefore cannot expect to have the part of penitents.

If God works a reformation in the land in general to make them fit for the reception of his benefits, those who yet continue insensible of their sin may expect to be overthrown alone, and that when others are blessed they shall be cursed. When others enjoy smiles, they may expect frowns. Isaiah 65:13–14 says, "Therefore thus saith the Lord GOD, Behold, my servants shall eat, but ye shall be hungry: behold, my servants shall drink, but ye shall be thirsty: behold, my servants shall rejoice, but ye shall be ashamed: behold, my servants shall sing for joy of heart, but ye shall cry for sorrow of heart, and shall howl for vexation of spirit."

Let it be considered that all those who truly mourn for their own iniquity may depend upon it that they shall be delivered from common calamities. They shall either be delivered by God from those things which are calamities to others, or God will so order them that they shall not be calamities to them. In both these ways God properly delivers his people from common calamities. God can either keep pains and losses and temporal adversities from them or cause that although they happen to them they shall not hurt them. Here is one of those ways God will certainly secure those who are his. He will either keep them out of the fire or, if they are cast in, will cause that they shall not be burned, though it be as hot as Nebuchadnezzar's. Isaiah 43:2 says, "When thou passest through the waters, I will be with thee; and through the rivers, they shall not overflow thee: when thou walkest through the fire, thou shalt not be burned; neither shall the flame kindle upon thee." In this spiritual sense, Mark 16:18 may also be interpreted: "They shall take up serpents; and if they drink any deadly thing, it shall not hurt them."

God is wont in times of common calamity to hide the righteous, as in his "pavilion" (Ps. 27:5). He is wont to be a shelter to them in the midst of a storm and preserve them from the rain by overshadowing them with his wings, as the dove overshadows her young. While others are exposed to the dire storm of wrath, they are hid by God. He takes care to hide them in a safe place where no evil shall come nigh them. Isaiah 26:20 says, "Come, my people, enter thou into thy chambers, and shut thy doors about thee: hide thyself as it were for a little moment, until the indignation be overpast. For, behold, the LORD cometh out of his place to punish the inhabitants of the earth for their iniquity: the earth also shall disclose her blood, and shall no more cover her slain."

This distinguishing of true penitents from others is represented by setting a mark or seal upon them. Such a mark was typified by the mark of the houses of the children of Israel in Egypt—the striking of their blood upon their doorposts, that God might pass over those houses upon which he saw this mark, and might not slay the firstborn therein, as in other houses of Egypt.

We have showed that none do truly mourn for the sins of a nation or people, but those who mourn for their own iniquities. Therefore, the fourth verse of the ninth chapter of Ezekiel is pertinent to our present purpose: "And the LORD said unto him, Go through the midst of the city, through the midst of Jerusalem, and set a mark upon the foreheads of the men that sigh and that cry for all the abominations that be done in the midst thereof." Verse 6 says, "Slay utterly old and young, both maids, and little children, and women: but come not near any man upon whom is the mark." Under the New Testament dispensation, God is wont thus to distinguish those who fear him as well as under the old. Revelation 7:3 says, "Hurt not the earth, neither the sea, nor the trees, till we have sealed the servants of our God in their foreheads."

God often distinguishes the righteous by delivering them from the temporal judgments which others are involved in. Thus he delivered only Noah and his family of the whole world. Thus God delivered Lot. The angels could do nothing 'til he was got far enough from the city. This was more common under the Old Testament, but is not very common under the New. Thus Christ took care for the deliverance of

Christians from the common destruction of Jerusalem. Matthew 24:16 says, "Then let them which be in Judaea flee into the mountains."

Let us consider what special cause God in his dispensations has given us of mourning for our own iniquities at this time. God in his temporal judgments against us doubtless intends to put us in mind of ill deserving what God has given us to know from one time to another. How easily he can cut us short of our hopes and disappoint our expectations and deprive us of those blessings which we take with our eyes and think to grasp in our hands. He has shown how grievously he can affect the whole land by that which one would look upon as a very inconsiderable matter. He can exceeding afflict many thousands by those who are as nothing in respect of number, that God's hand might be the more seen therein. Deuteronomy 32:30 says, "How should one chase a thousand, and two put ten thousand to flight, except their Rock had sold them, and the LORD had shut them up?" Other tokens of God's displeasure in his rebukes with respect to our temporal interests have we had as everyone's thoughts may suggest to him.

What special cause have we to be humbled for our own iniquities on the account of God's spiritual judgments which are far the most dreadful judgments because they immediately respect our eternal welfare which is infinitely more important than our temporal? The greatest judgment that can be inflicted on a people is the taking away of his Holy Spirit. This is far greater than the withholding of the dew and rain and a temporal famine, a judgment that commonly precedes the overthrow of a people. Those accounts which we have of the destruction of Jerusalem by the Romans—that dreadful desolation that Christ foretold—tell us that a little while before it was taken there was a voice heard in the Holy of Holies in the temple saying, "Come, let us go hence."

How much the Holy Spirit has left us of this land is declared by that special great dullness with respect to religion amongst professors and others that little concern there is about things pertaining to another world that increase vice and profaneness, the reign and prevalency of worldly mindedness and the shock that the Christian doctrine and worship have received. This is the rod of God which has already made us smart and more dreadfully threatens and calls aloud unto us to mourn for our own iniquity.

In so doing, let us follow these directions:

1. Let us particularly recollect our sins. Let us not content ourselves with general reflections and mourning for sin in general without looking back particularly upon the various stages of our lives. Let us go back as far as our memories will lead us and trace our own footsteps over again and follow ourselves in our thoughts in all the way that we have gone. Jeremiah 2:23 says, "See thy way in the valley, know what thou hast done." Let us observe narrowly all the bypaths where we have turned aside, all the places where we have turned to the right hand or to the left. Let us mark where in the course of our lives we went out of the way after some of Satan's shows where we followed him and in what parts of our life we hearkened to his whispers. Let us go over all that way of sin that we have traveled again in our thoughts, viewing the foolish and sinful steps that we have taken with tears and bitter lamentations. Let us be as particular in our reviews as we can and willingly let no sin or wandering escape our reflection and repentance.

Let us recollect our sins committed more immediately against God as acts of contempt of him or anything whereby he has made himself known. Our misimprovements of sabbaths, our slight and disobedience to his Word, our abuse of God's ordinances and our opportunities.

Let us also reflect particularly on our sins that have caused injustice, uncharitableness, contention, evil-speaking. Let us reflect on those sins which do most directly reflect ourselves, our pride, our intemperance or impatience. Let none willingly escape.

2. Let us recollect the aggravations of our sins. Let us behold our own sin in its own proper hue and not paint and mask it over as we have done. Let us behold our sins on every side and discover all the turpitude and odiousness which is in them as we are viewing our own footsteps and the path that we have gone in. Let us see when and where we sinned against mercies and where we turned aside clear, plain convictions and the particular calls of God to us. Let us see where we refused to hearken to the invitations of heaven but have gone contrary to them. Where we went counter to warnings of our danger. Let us view all that ingratitude, presumption, and folly with which our actions have been mixed.

3. Let our reflections be accompanied with the humblest confessions while we are viewing our works and their aggravations. Let us spread them before God and acknowledge the ill desert of them.

4. Let our sins be accompanied with thorough reformation. This is that which God chiefly looks at and is the better half of repentance without which God will not accept our confessions and our fasting and external humiliation nor will he hear our supplication. Isaiah 1:15–17 says, "And when ye spread forth your hands, I will hide mine eyes from you: yea, when ye make many prayers, I will not hear: your hands are full of blood. Wash you, make you clean; put away the evil of your doings from before mine eyes; cease to do evil. Learn to do well; seek judgment, relieve the oppressed, judge the fatherless, plead for the widow." Isaiah 58:5–7 says: "Is it such a fast that I have chosen? a day for a man to afflict his soul? is it to bow down his head as a bulrush, and to spread sackcloth and ashes under him? wilt thou call this a fast, and an acceptable day to the Lord? Is not this the fast that I have chosen? to loose the bands of wickedness, to undo the heavy burdens, and to let the oppressed go free, and that ye break every yoke? Is it not to deal thy bread to the hungry, and that thou bring the poor that are cast out to thy house? when thou seest the naked, that

thou cover him; and that thou hide not thyself from thine own flesh?" This was the way the men of Nineveh turned away God's wrath. Jonah 3:8 says, "But let man and beast be covered with sackcloth, and cry mightily unto God: yea, let them turn every one from his evil way, and from the violence that is in their hands."

12

*Those Sinners Who Are
Saved, It Is God Who Saves
Them*

O Israel, thou hast destroyed thyself; but in me is thine help.
HOSEA 13:9

In this undated sermon from Hosea, Edwards begins by recounting that he has already explained the verse previously and showed how the words came in. So now he will concentrate on preaching that God is here teaching Israel that even though they were the means of their own destruction, that does in no way mean that they could be the means of their own salvation. Hence the doctrine as it is given in the sermon's title.

Edwards then spends some time explaining why only God could bring about salvation. An infinite price had to be paid for the greatness of that which was injured, which is nothing other than God's infinite majesty. He then explains why God so acted to bring about salvation. God gave a Redeemer, not through any need God had of men, or of their love or service, nor was it their prayers or cries that moved him. He did all he did in salvation of himself. He was moved to it, he says, purely of his own good pleasure.

But Edwards also wants it to be understood that God is giving a Redeemer. That Redeemer is God himself. And just as God is the author of salvation, so he is also the author of all the means for the applying of that redemption. These include the Scriptures, the ministry, and election.

The sermon manuscript is an oversize original consisting of sixteen leaves, with little evidence of changes. In the body of the sermon there is some evidence of water damage, but none of the words are affected. The application consists of six pages.

We have already explained this verse and have shown how the words come in. We shall only here observe that God in the words teaches Israel that they were the means of their destruction but they could not be the means of their own salvation. When they were well, they were able to destroy themselves; but when they are destroyed, they are not able to help themselves.

There are two things supplied in the latter clause. First, that God only can help them, and second, that he stands ready to help them though they are foolishly the means of their own destruction. But as we showed from the former clause, those who are destroyed destroy themselves. So now from the latter clause we intend by the help of God to speak from this.

DOCTRINE

Those sinners who are saved, it is God who saves them. This we shall show with respect to all the particulars of a sinner's salvation. Everything that is done from first to last in order of his being saved.

1. 'Tis God who does all that is done to purchase the sinner's salvation. The sinner was in such a condition that he could not be saved without a good deal being done to make way for his salvation. The

sinner is fallen from God, is become a rebel against him, and is become subject to the curse of the immutable law of God. Some wonderful thing must be done if ever there is a way made, a door open, so that there should be any opportunity for the sinner's salvation. The majesty and honor of God and his holy law must be vindicated. And this can't be done without the offering of a price equivalent to the greatness of that which was injured, which is the majesty of God. Since the majesty of God is infinite, so an infinite price must be offered to satisfy for the injury done to that majesty, of which price God alone can be the author. Only he who is infinitely rich can afford an infinite price.

The sinner can pay no such price for himself. If he offers thousands of lambs and ten thousands of rivers of all the dearest things he has in the world, he offers that which is not in his own right. Even if it were, it is nothing compared with an infinite price. He has no such tendency as retrieves the honor of God's majesty and authority. If he should offer his righteousness, he offers what he cannot, for that is the very thing that he lost by sin. If he could offer any, he gives no more than God's just due and his doing his duty at one time is far from satisfying for his not doing of it at another. And if he could offer more than was due, it would yet be infinitely less than the price required.

And if he offers to suffer or should actually suffer to make satisfaction to suffer, 'tis the very thing that is required, but it is that he should suffer forever. If he has suffered for a time, there is an eternity of suffering yet behind. If it be attended that his temporal suffering does pay part of the debt, yet there is never the less behind. If he suffers ten years, yet his future eternity is as great as it was before, and he is under obligation to suffer to all eternity. So that the sinner can do nothing towards paying this price. But 'tis God alone who can bring it forth out of the infinite treasures of his sufficiency. He is the author of the purchase of salvation.

He gives a Redeemer to purchase it by his obedience and death. It was not any need that God had of men or of their love or service that moved him to it. He doth this of himself. It was not the prayers or cries of sinners that moved him to it, but he was moved to it purely of his own good pleasure. He gave this not only unrewarded and unmerited but unasked for.

When the condition of sinners was so helpless and desperate so that nothing else but such a Redeemer could possibly deliver him, God gave his Son. He from eternity entered into a covenant with him that he should redeem them, that he should take upon him their nature and become a servant in their stead and suffer for them. He was willing to part with him for this salvation. Him whom he loved infinitely, he gave to suffer reproach, pain, and a cursed death for them.

The Redeemer actually paid the ransom. 'Tis God only that gives the Redeemer, and the Redeemer is himself—is God—whom the Father gave and who gave himself. This he also did purely of himself. Though we read that he was sent by the Father and that he received commandment of the Father, yet the Father did not command him to undertake it. But when he had of his own accord undertaken it in the covenant of redemption, he thereby became a mediator and as such he was subject to God and was commanded by him. Christ freely gave himself. He did step in and speak for men and afford to undertake for them out of love and pity to them. So great a love had he to them that this moved him to undertake for them and to offer himself.

He took not on him the nature of angels, but his delights were with the sons of men. He was not moved by any respect of advantage from men or because man was worthy that he should do this for, but it was their great unworthiness that both made it necessary that he should undertake and that moved God's pity.

'Tis Christ wholly and only that makes satisfaction. Angels don't make any nor can they make any if they should do or suffer anything that they are able. Men are not able to pay the price themselves nor any part of it. They can do nothing. Even if they could do a thousand times more than they do, they could do nothing that could atone for the least sin or any way oblige God to save them in whole or in part. Men cannot atone or purchase one for another. A pious and gracious father can't by his tears or prayers or obedience make any atonement for the sins of a child or purchase any grace for the child. Neither can one dear friend offer anything that is worthy to be accepted as a price for another friend. 'Tis Christ alone who is God, who can purchase remission of sins and salvation. Thus 'tis God who does all that is done to purchase a sinner's salvation. That person himself who lays down the price is God.

2. God is the author of all the means for the applying of Christ's redemption. He is the author of the Word, that great instrument of men's salvation. 'Tis God who has given us that gift, that precious treasure, the Bible. All Scripture is given by inspiration of the Holy Ghost. If God had not given us his Word, mankind would have been in a miserable condition, would have been under a necessity of perishing. Men never would have been able to come to the knowledge of the mind and will of God, except God himself had revealed it. It never could have been known what we must do in order to obtain the pardon of our sins and salvation. The light of nature was not able to discover it. How could men by the light of nature know the incarnation and death of the Son of God and that his death and obedience should be accepted for sinners and that by believing in him we become partakers of his obedience and death?

God also is the author of all the ordinances of the gospel by means of which he communicates grace. 'Tis he who appointed prayer and the preaching of the Word and sabbaths and public assemblies and sacraments and church discipline. These are very necessary in order to the salvation of men's souls. You may easily conceive what a sorrowful case religion would be in if there were no sabbaths and no public assemblies, no public ministry and no discipline. Religion would soon run to utter ruin.

'Tis God who has appointed the ministry of the gospel. 'Tis he who appointed that order of men to explain, to reprove, to rebuke, to exhort and to warn, to counsel and to direct souls in their various difficulties. To be the mouth of God to the people and of the people to God and to administer the sacraments.

'Tis God who causes the gospel to come to some particular parts of the world when others are lost in darkness. So God anciently chose out the nation of the Jews and separated them from all the nations in the world. Now under the New Testament dispensation, the church is abundantly more enlarged and is not any longer confined to any one particular nation. Yet the gospel doesn't reach to all nations. Some are chosen nations, others are reprobate nations. They live in utter darkness and go down to destruction. God is wholly arbitrary in this matter. He sends the gospel to what nations he pleases. We know that the gospel came forth first from the land of Canaan where Christ and his apostles dwelt. God has so ordered it that it reach quite to us who live on the opposite side of the globe, when many countries that are very near never were gospelized. All those parts of the world are at this day regions of darkness. Where God has any of his elect there he orders that the gospel shall come.

'Tis God who bestows the special advantages men are under for their salvation, such as a pious education, the living amongst a religious people, or living under a powerful ministry. If men have special advantages from their natural abilities or good natural dispositions from their circumstances and manner of life so they shall be less in the way of temptation than many others, 'tis all from God. He who disposes all things by his providence makes some men to differ from others by their special advantages.

3. 'Tis God also who marks all that 'tis necessary upon the heart in order to bestow salvation. He is not only the author of the purchase of salvation and is the author of all the outward means of salvation and all the advantages men are under for the obtaining. But he works all that is wrought within themselves, who tends that way before conviction. 'Tis he who works conviction in men. 'Tis evidently from something else than themselves that some men who have the same outward means are greatly awakened and made sensible of the dangerous condition that they are in and are exceedingly concerned what they shall do to be saved. Others, though they are told never so much of hell and of the uncertainty of life, are little or nothing concerned about it. Except God is pleased to do it, those who are now unawakened never will be awakened except God pleases. They intend to be awakened hereafter, but it is a great question whether they will be or no for they will not be 'til God is pleased to awaken them.

So 'tis God who makes men see the plague of their own hearts and makes them sensible that they can't be their own Savior. This imagination strongly possesses the hearts of most natural men that they must save themselves. God brings some off from it and makes them see what poor, miserable, wretched, blind, and naked creatures they are.

It is also God only who works grace in the heart. He infuses a principle of life. A dead corpse can as soon infuse a principle of life into itself, as a dead soul to live of himself as God's second creation. He exerted a mighty power in creating man as body and soul at first, and he exerts as mighty a power in creating of him appears. The sinner can as soon create a world as he can renew himself unto holiness.

And as God works grace, so he confirms it. He continues to work it on the preservation of the world. So is the preservation of grace in the heart. He keeps man from falling from grace. If God should withdraw his continued operation, godly men would fall from grace. Thus

God works all that is wrought in the heart that is needful in order to salvation, both before conversion, in conversion, and after conversion. Men can't work them in themselves, neither can ministers work them in men, nor can angels work them in men. They can't work conversion, nor can they preserve a saint when he is converted, nor do they convict and awaken men before conversion any other way than as God's servants and messengers.

'Tis God who gives light in the understanding. 'Tis he who teaches and instructs the soul. He teaches men the danger of sin and the evil of their hearts and makes them to know God and Jesus Christ. 'Tis he who works in them a right inclination of will, so that the inclination of the soul shall be towards God and Jesus Christ. He also works holy affection, gives holy fear, love and hope and joy. And he works a power and ability to act to exert holy actions. Philippians 2:13 says, "God worketh in you both to will and to do of his own good pleasure."

4. All that men do that any way tends to their salvation is of God. All man's good purposes and resolutions which they take up are from God. Men sometimes purpose and resolve that they will break off their sins and set themselves to seek God. The reason why they purpose so is because God stirs them up to it. And if men perform their purposes and resolutions, that is also from God. Many men have purposes that hereafter they will leave their vices and seek God. But multitudes never perform those purposes of theirs, and 'tis of God when they do perform them. If he is pleased to assist and strengthen and stir them up, they will do it; otherwise, they will be as far from it as ever they were.

'Tis of God that men strive when they seek and are earnestly engaged. There are many who seek who don't strive but go on in a careless, cold, dull way of seeking. There are some few who are earnestly engaged, but 'tis because God has mercy upon them. 'Tis

God enables them to be earnest in prayer and in resisting their sins and corruptions and in using other appointed means.

'Tis of God that men take a suitable method in seeking of him that they don't seek him in a wrong way. 'Tis he who gives them direction either mediately or immediately. If they read in the Bible and there find direction thereby, that surely is from God. If they are directed by ministers, they are God's messengers. 'Tis God who in the first place directs them that they may know how to direct others.

If men persevere in seeking of God 'til they find him, that is of God. Many who seek him do not hold out; they return as the dog to his vomit. Many are discouraged, and many are drawn off by temptations, and many take up with a false hope and so grow self-righteous and secure. But 'tis God who makes men to follow on to seek him with the same steady resolution that they never will leave seeking him 'til they find him.

'Tis God who excites and enables men to do all they do in order to their salvation after a principle of grace is infused. 'Tis God who gives them to lay hold on Jesus Christ and to embrace him as offered in the gospel. 'Tis God who makes them rise up and open the door and let him into the heart and makes them willingly yield themselves unto him to be his. 'Tis the Father who draws man and makes him run into the arms of his grace and love. He does this by shining into the heart and making a discovery of the sufficiency and excellency of Jesus.

And 'tis of God that Christians are enabled to live a holy life, which is necessary to eternal life as it is the way to it. The godly man can't exert one holy action without God. Much less can he perseveringly live a holy life.

5. 'Tis also God who fulfills and completes their salvation. After all those things are done that we have mentioned, there still remains the end of them, which is the actual bestowment of eternal life. God is the author of the means and the end after salvation is purchased by the

paying down a sufficient price. After means of grace are instituted and after grace is actually infused and men have believed in Christ—yea, after they have lived a holy life—they can't attain the end of these things themselves. They can't of themselves attain unto glory.

'Tis God who is with them when they die and gives them victory over death. He delivers them from the power of the grave. He receives their souls and perfects the work of sanctification. He takes away all remaining corruption, makes them to be without spot or wrinkle or any such thing. He fills the souls brimful of holiness so that there shall never more be any manner of evil inclination. All the inclination of the soul shall be to love God, to praise him, and to praise and glorify and enjoy Jesus Christ. He then makes the soul appear with a marvelous beauty, puts a glory upon it, and makes it shine as the sun. He then will wonderfully perfect the natural faculties of the soul. He will exceedingly enlarge the understanding and increase the soul's precepts and activity and deliver from all natural infirmities that our minds are subject to in this world.

God then will fill the soul brimful of pleasure and joy by giving the enjoyment of himself and of Jesus Christ and the enjoyment of the company of heaven. And 'tis God who will raise the body at the last day and will restore it to the soul, not as it is now but a blessed and glorious habitation, an incorruptible and spiritual body that shall be delivered from all manner of infirmity or weakness and shall be strong and active and adorned with an unfading beauty and glory forever. And soul and body shall be advanced to the highest honor, beauty, and pleasure and shall without interruption enjoy it forever and ever.

Thus God is the sole author of the salvation of those who are saved, even from the very first beginning of it in the eternal covenant of redemption, to the end and consummation of it in the eternal glory of the saints.

APPLICATION

Reproof is of use to those who think to be in part their own Savior. There are many who are sensible that they are in some measure destroyed, though they are not sensible that they are utterly destroyed or are they sensible that they have ruined themselves. That think to help themselves. They don't say that in God only but in myself is my help, and they imagine that they shall be their own saviors.

There are those who think to make some atonement for their past sins, by their reformation and good behavior for the future. They think then that they have committed many sins in times past, yet they are now heartily sorry for it, and they have left it off and intend to be very careful for the future, and they think that surely that may be accepted. They think that they have no other than some sins and infirmities with those that are common to all mankind. Therefore, if they amend their practices and are sorry for their sins, they think that God should forgive them. Some godly men have so much of this disposition that they are ready to magnify their own righteousness and so make light of their sins. They are ready to complain if God hides his face from them and brings afflictions upon them, as if they were hardly dealt with, and they are ready to find fault that God does not take so much notice of their holy walk as they expected he would.

Such are guilty of making themselves in part their own saviors. But this is the work of Christ Jesus. His greatest work is to make atonement for sin. Therefore, such put themselves in Christ's stead and assume his glory to themselves.

Some make themselves their own saviors by thinking to move God by their religious behavior to give them conversion. They think that by their righteousness they offer a price that God may well afford to give them grace for. There are many who read and pray with the very thought that by continuing to do so with earnestness and diligence, they shall incline the heart of God to them and make him propitious to them. They do it with the very same view that the heathen of old used to offer their sacrifices. They thought that the gods wanted sacrifices and were refreshed and satisfied by the fumes of them. So they conceive that they do God good by their prayers and reading and keeping the sabbath and the like. Since they don't expect to be saved without being converted, they hope that the pains they take and the righteousness they perform will have this power with God to incline him to give them conversion.

By this also they take Christ's work into their own hands. But Christ purchased conversion as well as other parts of salvation. Therefore, when they imagine that they can purchase salvation, they put themselves in Christ's stead.

Some people think by their own strength to work in themselves repentance of sin and love to God. They be not sensible how depraved their hearts are and how destitute of any foundation to work upon when they would work repentance and love to God in their hearts. They don't see why they can't come to love God if they labor and strive after it as well as to love other things. Let such as do this consider:

1. That it is absurd to suppose that he who is wholly destroyed is able to help himself. He who is wholly ruined is ruined of all things whereby he finds relief. If there be any relief still left with him, then for that reason he is not wholly ruined. Man may be greatly hurt, exceedingly damaged, and yet he may have relief left in his own power—but not he who is destroyed. We are taught in the former part of the verse that sinners have destroyed themselves. Therefore, we may as well suppose that nothing can be the efficient cause of something as that the sinner can be the efficient cause of his own salvation.

2. Consider that if you could do as you think to do for yourself, you could do a greater thing than the angels can do. The angels are mighty in strength. One of them is probably stronger than many thousands of men. We read that there was an angel that smote of the camp of the

Assyrians one hundred fourscore and five thousand in one night. But yet the angels are none of them so great as sinners think to do—that is, to be their own savior. This work was thought too great for the angels. There was none but an infinite and divine person who was able to do it.

You must have more righteousness than the angels. If the righteousness of one of the angels was given to you, it would not be sufficient to atone for one of your sins nor to merit the least favor for you. The angels by all their strength can't convert a soul. None of them can bring a soul truly to repent of sin and to love God as many men hope to do.

3. If you could do as you hope to do, you would be able to do that which is one of the greatest works of God himself. 'Tis one of the most glorious works of God to make a sinful soul holy, and it is exceedingly magnified in the Scriptures. 'Tis a greater work than Christ's miracles which he wrought. Greater than healing the sick, casting out devils, or opening the eyes of the blind. Yea, a more glorious work than raising the dead. John 14:12 says, "Verily, verily, I say unto you, He that believeth on me, the works that I do shall he do also; and greater works than these shall he do; because I go unto my Father." Christ did not mean that his disciples should be able to do greater miracles than he did, but that they should be means of the converting of souls which was a greater work than his miracles.

Yea, this work of regeneration is compared to the creation of heaven. Later this very thing is called the creating of a new heaven and a new earth. Isaiah 65:17–18 says, "For, behold, I create new heavens and a new earth: and the former shall not be remembered, nor come into mind. But be ye glad and rejoice for ever in that which I create: for, behold, I create Jerusalem a rejoicing, and her people a joy." The creation here spoken of is the same sort of creation as that spoken of in 2 Corinthians 5:17: "If any man be in Christ, he is a new creature: old things are passed away; behold all things are become new."

Therefore, what a vanity it is for anyone to imagine that he can work holiness in his own heart or that he can bring himself to love. If we should see a man standing over a dead corpse and endeavoring to raise it to life or if we should see anyone trying to create a world, it would be a ridiculous sight. But these things are no more beyond us than the making of ourselves holy.

Sinners who are saved are saved by God. Those who are partakers of salvation give God the glory of their salvation. Those who were nothing surely did nothing but extol the name of God, who has wrought such wonders for you. Praise God for the purchase of your salvation, for the salvation of all was not purchased. God chose you and left others. God the Father covenanted with the Son from all eternity to redeem you when he said nothing of others.

Therefore, glorify God the Father who gave his Son for you, and love and praise the Son who gave his life and his blood for you. Give God the praise for all the means and advantages you have been under, that you have lived where you might read the Bible when you pleased, and lived where you might weekly hear the gospel preached. Praise God that before you were stirred up to seek salvation, God made you earnest in seeking and did not suffer you to be discouraged nor to leave off seeking before you found him. Praise God that he was pleased actually to do that wonderful work for you—even the converting of your soul—and that he turned you from darkness to light and from the power of Satan unto God.

Consider how much God and Jesus Christ deserve to be loved by you for these things. Hereafter you will see better than you do now when you come to see what is the completing and perfection of salvation. Your salvation was procured at infinite cost. It cost God an infinite price to redeem your soul. It was accomplished by infinite power, by the same power that made the world. Therefore, love God who did so much and expended so much for your salvation.

13

All Mankind of All Nations, White and Black, Young and Old, Is Going in One or the Other of These Paths, Either in the Way That Leads to Life or the Way That Leads to Destruction

Enter ye in at the strait gate: for wide is the gate, and broad is the way, that leadeth to destruction, and many there be which go in thereat: because strait is the gate, and narrow is the way, which leadeth unto life, and few there be that find it.

MATTHEW 7:13–14

T his is an early example of a sermon Edwards preached to the Indians at Stockbridge after leaving his ministry at Northampton. And with his particular hearers in mind, Edwards's doctrine seems carefully chosen. All mankind, with no distinction of color, is on one of two paths in life—one that leads to life and the other that leads to destruction and misery.

Edwards reinforces this a little way into his message when he states that there are many nations in the world with different languages and many different customs, but all share one thing in common—their inclination to sin.

Edwards concludes with a practical list of the kind of people the godly should not be. Those, for example, who don't pray to God in secret; those husbands who are cross to their wives; and wives who don't honor their husbands; and those who are capable of reading the Bible and praying in their families, and yet do not do those things.

The original sermon manuscript of eight leaves is written not in paragraph form but in separate sentences, more as notes. At times the writing is somewhat more difficult to read than other oversize sermons, perhaps because of the speed with which Edwards wrote this manuscript.

There are two ways that men walk in. One is the way that leads to life and happiness. The other is the way that leads to destruction and misery. So there are two gates or doors that all men enter into. One lets into heaven, to eternal life and joy; the other lets into hell, a world of darkness and fire.

All mankind of all nations, white and black, young and old, are going in one or the other of these paths, either in the way that leads to life or the way that leads to destruction. There are many thousands of people who die every day and go into another world. They all go either to heaven or to hell. None go to any other place than one of these two.

Christ tells us in the text that the door and path that leads to life and happiness is small and narrow and that therefore but few enter into this door and few go in that narrow path.

But the gate is wide and the way broad that leads to death and that many there are that go in through it. Here I will do three things: (1) show who they are that go in the way to destruction, (2) show that this way is a broad way, and (3) show that many go in this way.

1. All are going in the way of destruction who are heathen and who worship the sun and moon and who worship the devil and don't worship the true God who made the world and Jesus Christ his Son. Also going in the way of destruction are those who don't worship God according to the Scriptures, such as those who try to get to heaven by worshiping the virgin Mary or worshiping dead saints and the images of Christ.

Also headed for destruction are those who hear the gospel preached and never receive instruction, who will not believe the Bible is the Word of God, or who deny the Christian religion to be the true religion. They live under the light of the gospel and go to meeting, but yet the light does not shine into their hearts. They are blind and don't see the glory and loveliness of God and Christ. They hear the Word of God and don't do the things which God says but live wicked lives. These are they who from time to time get too much drink.

Yea, they who steal and cheat and all they who lie are going in the way of destruction. They turn from their sins and do well for a while and then turn back again and get drunk and grow as bad as ever. They never have been convinced of sin to see what wicked, miserable creatures they are, and how they deserve to go to hell.

They are beasts. They pray and take pains in religion and are proud of their goodness. They make up for their sins and desire that God should make much of them. They don't see what poor creatures see and can't help themselves. They stand in need of Jesus Christ to help them and wash them from their sins in his blood.

Though they do many things in religion, yet 'tis nothing but an outside show. Their hearts are not in it. They never give their hearts to God. They never have their eyes opened to see the excellency of Christ and never in their hearts come to him to save them. They never truly repented of their sins and mourned and had their hearts broken for their sins.

2. Thus I have told you who they are who go in the way that tends to destruction. I now come to show what it means by the way being a broad way. The meaning is that men can go in it without taking any pains. We need not take any pains to go in it at a wide gate or to get along in a broad way because there is room enough. We have no need to strive and take pains to get along.

'Tis hard to walk in the way of religion and holiness, but 'tis easy to go in a way of wickedness. 'Tis what all men are inclined to naturally forge in this way to destruction. It appears to the wicked inclination of the heart. 'Tis like stones rolling down hill.

3. There are many who go in this broad way. All men all over the world are wholly inclined to sin and wickedness. There are many nations in the world that have different languages and a great many different customs, but all are alike in this respect: all are inclined to sin. And the world is everywhere full of wickedness. Some go on in one way of wickedness and others in another and some in a great many paths of wickedness.

All men are going to another world. Thousands are dying every day, and most of them are going to hell. They go along apace in the roadway that leads to hell, thousands and ten thousands of them crowding and pushing one another along towards hell. Most of this world are marked as awfully going along in the broad way that leads to destruction, just as the waters of a great river are continually going down to the sea. And as thousands die every day, so they go through the wide gate into hell just as the waters enter the sea at the wide mouth of a great river.

Now therefore I counsel you all to take heed that you don't go in the broad way that leads to destruction. If you are going in that way, stop and turn about and turn your feet into the other way that leads to life. Though it be easy to go in it and you love to go in it, yet consider where it leads—down into everlasting fire. They who go down in this way and go in at the broad gate into hell never come out again.

'Tis easy to go to hell, but 'tis not easy to bear the torments of it after you get there. If you are going on in this way, you don't know how near you may be to the end of it. It may be you may dip into hell before next year, or before next month, or before tomorrow morning. 'Tis easy to go downhill and hard going uphill, but you had better go uphill to heaven than downhill to hell. It won't be the easier because a great many are going there, tormenting one another like hands of fire to burn one another. Therefore, don't live in those ways of wickedness that I have told you about—all of which lead to death.

Don't only forsake some ways of sin, but forsake all sin whatsoever. Don't only forsake them for a while, but forsake forever and ever and never return to them anymore. And don't only do well outwardly, but give your hearts to God and Christ. Take your hearts off from the things of this world, and set your hearts chiefly on the next.

Some people hate their neighbors and are hateful and will take revenge upon those who have loved them as well as those who displease them. They will fight with their neighbors and are of a contentious, quarrelsome spirit. They will swear and curse and use bad language. They are lascivious and will act and talk lasciviously. They slander against others and talk false therein against them and delight to talk against them and won't let them speak for themselves. Their manner is to use quarreling, reproachful, scaldy language.

They don't strictly keep the sabbath; they will hunt or work or ply upon the sabbath day. They won't go to meeting and attend the Word of God in his house. They be not concerned for the good of their souls. They mind the things of this world more than the things of another. They don't pray to God in secret. They can read in the Bible and pray in their families and yet take no care in those things. They are covetous and won't pity the poor and won't put themselves out of their way to help their neighbors in distress. Some husbands are cross with their wives, and some wives don't honor their husbands. Some parents don't take care for the good of their children's souls to instruct them and give them good counsel and pray for them. Some children don't love and honor and obey their fathers and mothers.

Some people will do wicked things in the dark, or in secret places where men don't see them. They are lazy and slothful in religion and won't take a great deal of pains in their duty and serving of God and trying to obtain salvation. They do well in some things but yet don't forsake all their wickedness. They have some sin that they love dearly and will not let go. Some sin is like a sweet morsel that they hold in their mouths and will not spit out.

14

*So None Ought to Come into
the Christian Church but
Good Men*

Again, the kingdom of heaven is like unto a net, that was cast into the
sea, and gathered of every kind: which when it was full, they drew to
shore, and sat down, and gathered the good into vessels, but cast the bad
away. So shall it be at the end of the world: the angels shall come forth,
and sever the wicked from among the just, and shall cast them into the
furnace of fire: there shall be wailing and gnashing of teeth.

MATTHEW 13:47–50

This sermon is another example of one of Edwards's sermons to
the Indians at Stockbridge, preached in January 1751.

Edwards begins by describing briefly what the kingdom of Christ
is, and he makes an interesting analogy. Just as King George's people
are George's kingdom—they being that part of the world that he rules
over—so the people of Christ are the kingdom of Christ because they
are that part of the world that belongs to Christ.

This sermon is a clear presentation of the separation that will take
place at the judgment. God, who has allowed the righteous and the
unrighteous to dwell together, will gather his elect and cast away
the wicked. The picture that Edwards uses is that of the fisherman's

net catching both good and bad fish, but eventually there will be separation.

The nature of Edwards's application is even more challenging. He exhorts his hearers to make certain—if they have been already gathered in the net of the gospel—that they know themselves to be good fish and that their hearts are right with God. He then tells them, it is the case with them as it is among the English and others, that there are many more bad than good, and even though men might be deceived, God will not be.

This oversize manuscript consists of seven leaves. The body of the sermon begins with long, complete sentences, but after the application starts, then the work consists much more of brief jottings.

By the kingdom of heaven sometimes is meant heaven and the state of happiness in another world. Here is meant the Christian church or the whole company of Christians all over the world. As King George's people are his kingdom, they being that part of the world that he rules over, so the people of Christ are the kingdom of Christ because they are that part of the world who belongs to Christ and who have Christ for their king.

'Tis called the kingdom of heaven because Christ the King is from heaven and the laws of his kingdom are all from heaven. The new heart and new nature that his people have given them is holy and heavenly, and the country they are to live in forever with Christ their King in heaven.

'Tis said that the kingdom of heaven is like a net that was cast into the sea. The sea is the whole world of mankind just as a net that is cast into the sea doesn't take all the fish in the sea but only goes round and fences in a few. So the kingdom of Christ doesn't take all the world but only a part. The people of Christ are separate from the rest of the world, a peculiar people to him to be Christ's part. As the net cast into the sea separates the fish that are of it from all the rest in the sea, that they may belong to the fisherman and be his part of the fish of the sea while the rest are set alone and not meddled with.

The fishermen who cast the net are ministers of the gospel whom Christ appointed to gather men into his church. Several of Christ's disciples were fishermen. This was their trade they got their living by. And when Christ called them to follow him and to be his disciples and minister, he told them that they should no longer catch fish, but he would make them fishers of men to catch men.

When a fisherman casts a net into the sea, what he aims at is only good fish that are good for food. He doesn't desire to catch any but good fish, but yet the net will gather every sort—good and bad. So none ought to come into the Christian church but good men. But because ministers can't know men's hearts, every sort will come in— good and bad. As there will be some bad fish in the net, so there will be some bad men in the kingdom of Christ.

When their net was full, the fishermen drew the fish out of the sea. The fish after they were in the net were but a short time in the sea. They were soon drawn to the shore. So the professors of religion will be but a short time in this world. They will soon be taken away out of this world into the other world.

While the fish were in the net in the sea, it could not be seen what the fish were—whether good or bad. But when they were drawn to shore, then it could be seen plainly what they were, and the bad could easily be distinguished from the good.

So while we can't certainly say what professors of the Christian religion in this world oftentimes be—whether good or bad men— when these men are taken out of the world when this world comes to an end, then it will be seen.

When the fish were in the sea, good and bad were mixed together, but when they were drawn to the shore, they were separated. So in this world good men and bad are mixed together. But God will by no means suffer the wicked and the righteous always to dwell together but will certainly separate them in another world. 'Tis said that the good were gathered into vessels. They were prepared and kept as those who were prized and made much of. So God will save his saints and make much of them as precious to him and as those whom he dearly loves.

But the bad fish were cast away as those that were good for nothing. So in another world God will cast away wicked men. He will have no regard to them. He will take no care of them but will dispose and hate them. If they have been never so great and rich men and have been never so much honored in this world, yet God will throw them away and trample them underfoot.

So shall it be, says Christ, at the end of the world. The angels shall come forth and sever the wicked from among the just. Many are separated before the end of the world. When men die, they go into another world where the good are separated from the bad. But yet many are left in that world where good and bad are mixed together 'til the end of the world. But at the end of the world all shall be separated. Then all the wicked shall be severed from amongst the just. When Christ appears coming in the clouds of heaven, it will soon be seen what men be. The difference between good and bad will positively be seen.

Christ will then send his angels to separate them, on his right hand and left. 'Tis said the wicked, after they are taken forever from among the just, shall be cast into a furnace of fire. After the day of judgment, not only will the souls of men be punished, but their bodies—which shall be raised from the dead—shall be thrown into eternal fire.

The fire shall be exceedingly great and dreadful because it will be the fire that God will kindle by his great power and fierceness of his great wrath for the wickedness of men and therefore doubtless vastly more terrible than any fire in this world.

'Tis said there shall be weeping and gnashing of teeth. They will wail because there will be many dreadful things and what they cannot bear. And also because they never shall have any hope of being delivered but will know that there will be no end to their misery.

APPLICATION

Now I come to apply these things to your serious consideration. You have had the gospel preached to you. The net has been let down, and many of you have been gathered in it and brought in among the people of Christ into the kingdom of Christ. But remember, they who are gathered in the net are not all good. The net gathers of every kind, both bad and good. So 'tis to be found that you who are called Christians are not all good.

'Tis to be found with you as 'tis amongst the English and others who are called Christians. There are many more bad than good. Men can't certainly know how many of you are good and how many are bad, but God knows. You may deceive men with a good outside when your hearts are rotten, but you can't deceive God.

And remember that although good and bad are mixed together in this world—they live together in the same houses, they come to meeting together, and they may sit down at the sacrament together—but they won't be mixed together always. The time will soon come when God will show the great difference by opening the hearts of men that all the world may see what they be.

When Christ comes at the end of the world, they and the wicked shall be separated from among the just. Then many of them who used to come to meeting together and used to eat and drink together and used to go hunting together shall be separated one from another, never to be together anymore.

Christ says that in that day two shall be grinding at a mill. One shall be taken and one left. Many parents shall be separated from their children. Brethren and sisters. Many husbands from their wives and wives from their husbands. One shall be set on the right hand of God and the other on the left. One with glorious angels, others with devils. One shining forth as the sun, the other appearing hateful and dreadful in the image of the devil. To the one Christ will say, "Come, ye blessed" (Matt. 25:34), and to the other, "Depart . . . into everlasting fire" (Matt. 25:41).

The one shall go into everlasting life, the other into everlasting burning in a furnace of fire that never shall be quenched. Then shall that be supported which God says in Isaiah 65:13, "Behold, my servants shall rejoice." Remember what Christ says, "Strait is the gate, and narrow is the way" (Matt. 7:14). There are many who will come in that day and say, "Lord, Lord, have we not prophesied in thy name?" (Matt. 7:22). But he shall say, "Depart from me" (Matt. 7:23).

Therefore, take heed to yourselves that you be not at last like some of the bad fish which shall be cast away. See to it that your hearts are right with God. Don't keep an outward show but get a clean heart, a holy heart that hates all sin and loves Christ and loves all the people of Christ and loves all the ways of God. Unless you have a new heart, you never will be good; and don't think it enough only that you may be good in some things, for if you don't have right hearts, you will live wickedly in other things. This is the reason that some men reform their lives for a little while only and then turn again. Their hearts were never changed.

15

※⊃ ⊂※

What Is Meant by Believing in Christ?

And he said unto them, Go ye into all the world, and preach the gospel to
every creature. He that believeth and is baptized shall be saved.

MARK 16:15–16

This is a further example of a sermon Edwards preached to the
Indians, but this is a sermon he preached twice. The first occasion
when Edwards delivered it was to the Stockbridge Indians in the same
month as the previous example; the reproaching, Edwards notes, was
to the Mohawks in February 1752.

Edwards begins this message with a brief summary of the history
of God's relationship with man from before the time of the flood to the
coming of Christ, which, says Edwards, was 1,740 years earlier when
Christ first came and preached the gospel. Before the gospel was thus
preached, says Edwards, the English were ignorant and dark, just like
the Indians were before the English came to them.

A very clear exposition follows on what it means to truly believe
on Christ for salvation. Damnation, with all that this involves, will be
the consequence of not thus believing and so being saved. There shall
be no end of their misery, warns Edwards, even after thousands of
years. In fact, it will be just beginning.

The sermon manuscript is another oversize original of sixteen leaves, written in individual sentences rather than paragraph structure. Much of the sermon looks hurriedly written, with some evidence of corrections.

Before Christ came, there was but one nation that worshiped the true God, which was the nation of the Jews. All other nations in the world worshiped idols, the sun, moon and stars, images, and the devil. The nations of the world first of all worshiped the true God who made heaven and earth and continued to do so for some time after the flood. But in two or three hundred years after the flood, they began by degrees to grow more wicked and to forget the true God. The devil drew them away to worship other things that weren't gods.

And then God called Abraham and separated him from the rest of the world that he might keep up the knowledge of him and of the true religion in his posterity. And after this all the world besides the Jews who were Abraham's posterity fell away to the worship of idols and had wholly left the true religion. And so all continued worshiping idols for about 1,500 years 'til Christ came, which was 1,740 years ago when first he came and preached the gospel to the Jews only and so continued 'til the Jews put him to death.

But after he rose from the dead, he told his disciples, "Go out into all the world and not only preach the gospel to the Jews but preach and teach all nations and preach the gospel to every creature," as we are told in the text.

Because they had been the people of God for so long, the Jews were proud of their advantages and thought that no other people could be saved but them. But Christ has died that all who believed, of whatever nation, should be saved and that he who believed not should be damned.

And so we have an account how the disciples afterwards went all about the world preaching the gospel to all nations. By degrees, a great many nations threw away their idols and turned to the Christian religion. So that in about three hundred years after Christ, a great part of the world became Christians. There was the greatest change and alteration in the world that ever was.

Christ was the Light of the world. The preaching of the gospel was like the rising of the sun in the morning that shone away all darkness and filled the world with light. Before this the English were ignorant and dark just like the Indians were before the English came here. Christ in the text tells his disciples what they must preach to all nations and how all men of all nations might come to be saved. He tells them that they who believe in him shall be saved and they who don't believe shall be damned.

This forenoon I shall speak from these words, "He that believeth shall be saved." And I shall do two things. I shall first show what it means by believing in Christ, and then I will show how this believing in Christ is the way to be saved.

1. What is meant by believing in Christ? For a man to believe in Christ is to come to him with all the heart. To take him for his Savior and give himself to him, to be one of his people and to have all his dependence on Christ to make him happy. There are a great many who are called Christians who are baptized and keep sabbath days and go to meeting who don't truly believe in Christ.

There are a great many who own the Christian religion and say they believe in God and that Christ is the Son of God and Savior of sinners, but they don't truly believe in Christ. They who are wicked men, who walk in wicked ways—let them say what they will—they don't truly believe in the Lord Jesus Christ. Such are those who don't believe in Christ with all their hearts. They in their hearts don't come to Christ to be his people and to take him for their Savior. They who truly believe in Christ, they know Christ. God opens their eyes to see how great and how glorious he is and how good and how lovely he is. If a man be blind and doesn't see how excellent Christ is, he will never come to him and accept him as a Savior with all his heart.

They who truly believe in Christ see the excellency of the great things that the Word of God teaches about Christ and the way of any saved by him. They are fully convinced by the Word of God. They who truly believe in Christ see what wicked, miserable creatures they be, and so they see their need of a Savior to deliver from their misery. They who don't know their misery and don't see their need of Christ won't come to him with all their hearts. If a sick man who is likely to die does not know that he is dangerously sick and thinks he is pretty well, he won't go with all his heart to the physician to save him.

They who believe in Christ see that they can't help themselves, that if Christ doesn't save them they must perish. And they see how exceeding sinful they be all their lives and that they deserve to be damned. They who don't see how wicked they be and how they deserve to perish can't come with all their hearts to Christ to save them. They who truly believe in Christ see that he is able to save him, that there is enough in him for us. When they see how great and glorious he is, this will convince them that for so glorious a person to die, he is great enough to answer for all their sins. And they see that his love and mercy and pity is enough for such poor, wicked, miserable creatures as they are.

They who truly believe in Christ see how lovely he is, and they love him with all their hearts. They who don't love Christ never will come to him with all their hearts to save them. They who do truly believe in Christ give themselves to him to be his people. They give their hearts to him. They are made willing to give up themselves to him wholly in soul and body forever.

They who do truly believe in Christ in their hearts forsake all for Christ, forsake all their sins, forsake the world, and are willing to leave all for Christ. They who truly believe in Christ are willing to forsake father and mother, wife and children, brothers and sisters, houses and lands—yea, and their own sins—rather than to forsake Christ.

2. I come now to show how that thus believing in Christ is the only way to be saved by Christ. All who are saved are saved for Christ's sake alone. God saves them wholly on Christ's account. But God won't save any for Christ's sake whose hearts don't come to him for salvation. We can never pay God for the sins we have committed against him by anything we can do. Christ has done it for us. Therefore, our hearts must go to Christ for salvation, and we must go nowhere else.

Christ has suffered for us and has satisfied for our sin and has paid down a sufficient price for ourselves. He has done all there is. There is nothing for us to do now but believe in Christ and with all our hearts to come to him for salvation.

If Adam had never fallen, he would have had eternal life on his own account and on his own goodness. But now since we have fallen and lost our goodness, we are saved only for Christ's sake. We are not saved for our goodness. You must never expect to be saved for your good deeds, for your goodness can never pay for your badness.

It makes God very angry when such wicked creatures as we are expect to be paid for our goodness. If men do never so much in religion, if they read the Bible, pray never so much, come to meeting, if honest, if they give to the poor, they must not think that these things pay for their sins and that God will save them for these.

We must see our own vileness and wickedness and lie down in the dust before God. We deserve nothing but to be cast into hell. And we must come to Christ and trust in him only and not in our own righteousness for salvation. We can't be saved without being good, but 'tis not because our goodness is sufficient to do anything for itself. But 'tis because all whose hearts come to Christ will be good, and if men be not good, their hearts never will come to Christ.

Christ has paid for all our sins and has done enough for ourselves without anything of ours. Yet God won't save any for Christ's sake but such as belong to Christ. God does not look on any as belonging to Christ whose hearts don't come to him. They whose hearts come to Christ are joined to Christ. They belong to him and therefore are saved for his sake. They who believe in Christ, their hearts are joined to Christ. So with certainty they are called members of his body. Christ is the head and they are the members. And sometimes in the Bible, Christ is compared to a tree and they who believe on him to the branches. And sometimes Christ is called the husband, and the soul of a believer is called his wife. As the heart of a wife is joined to her husband, so is the believer's heart joined to Christ.

The great reason why God is willing to save God's own is not because of their goodness or for anything they do. They are sinful, unworthy creatures. He saves us because we are joined to Christ. All who are joined to Christ, God will save them for Christ's sake, for God always loves Christ. He has done enough and suffered enough for their salvation. This is the great difference between the way of getting eternal life which purposed to Adam before the Fall and that which is now. If Adam had never sinned, he will have been made happy for his own goodness. But now we can be saved only by believing in Christ.

Mark 16:16 says, "He that believeth not shall be damned." I shared in the forenoon how all who believe in Christ shall be saved. I would now show how they who don't believe shall be damned. I told you in the forenoon what it was for a man to believe in Christ. How it is come to him with all the heart, to have him for his Savior and to give himself to be his, to be one of his disciples, and to look to him for all his happiness.

They who don't thus come to Christ can never be saved. Not one man can ever be saved in any other way. Now I will show what it is to be damned and give the reasons why many men don't believe in Christ.

1. To be damned is to be deprived of all good and to suffer misery to all eternity, the fruit of the wrath of God for sin. They who are damned are lost. God throws them away and never will take any care of them or show them any mercy. They shall be separated from God.

They who are saved shall come near to God to dwell with him. But they who are damned shall be driven away from him. God will love those who are saved. But they who are damned, God will be angry with them and hate them and be their enemy forever.

They shall have no part with the saints in heaven. They shall see them at a great distance but shall never come nigh to them. They shall be deprived of all the good things of this world, and they shall have no good things in another world, so that they shall have nothing. They shall be wholly deprived of all good. They shall wish and long for many things, but they shall have nothing. They shall have perfect darkness and not the least beam of light. And they shall suffer all misery. They shall be filled full of misery. They shall be like a cup thrown all over and the next that is filled as full as it can hold.

When they die, the soul goes out of the body. God will send no angels to take care of it, and he will let the devils take it. The devils will fly upon it like hungry lions and wolves and shall carry the soul down into hell. There the soul shall be cast into a great fire and shall be tormented continually without any rest day or night. The fire is not like our fires in this world. Those fires are fires fired by men, but that fire will be the fire of the wrath of the great God. And at the end of the world, the dead body shall be raised, and the soul shall be joined to it again, and then the body and soul both shall be cast into a great fire along with the devils. There shall be no end of their misery. After thousands of years, it will be but just beginning and no nearer to an end.

God will have no pity upon them. If they pray to him, he won't hear their prayers. He won't hear their cries and shrieks.

Now in this world God stands ready to pity sinners if they will hearken to him and come to Christ. But if they won't hearken, he will not pity them in another world. They shall have no way to escape or find no way out, nor will they find any to help them. They shall have no friends. God won't be their friend, and Christ will not be their friend, nor the angels nor good men, those who were their friends in this world. The devils will be there and serpents to torment them. Others who be in hell along with them will hate them, torment one another, those who used to be their friends in this world. So they will have no hope. When they think of eternity before them, they shall have no hope—and oh, how that will break their hearts!

2. Consider the reasons why every man who does not believe in Christ shall be damned. All men have sinned and deserve to be damned. All men are naturally full of sin. And there are no saviors of sinners, no way of salvation but by Christ. And therefore all they who don't belong to Christ must be damned. But none belong to Christ but they who are joined to him. But none are joined to Christ but only they whose hearts come to Christ and so believe in him. They who don't believe in Christ can't be saved by Christ because they must have him for their Savior.

If they are baptized and go to meeting and seem to show respect to Christ, yet God looks at the heart. He sees that and he sees that their hearts despise Christ, and therefore God doesn't look upon them as belonging to Christ. God doesn't count them the people of Christ, nor have they any part in him. If they have no part in Christ, nothing that they can do—none of their goodness—can save them. 'Tis Christ's death and his goodness that satisfies for sin and buys heaven and not their goodness.

APPLICATION

Now therefore, let everyone look into and search his own heart and see whether he does truly believe in the Lord Jesus Christ. Don't think it enough that you come to meeting, that you are honest, that you keep the sabbath days, that you don't get drunk. You must do these things, must keep the sabbath, but these things alone won't do. You must give your whole heart to Christ.

Have your eyes ever been opened to see the glorious excellency of Jesus Christ? Has the light of the Word of God ever shined into your hearts so that to see the excellency of that Word that teaches Christ and the way of salvation by him? Has that Word of Christ been sweeter to you than the honey on the honeycomb?

Is the Word of Christ sweet food to your soul that puts new life into you and is better than silver or gold? Do you see your need you have of Christ? Do you see what poor, wicked, miserable creatures you are? Do you see that all your goodness, all your prayers, and all that you do is not worthy to be accepted of God and can never pay for your sins? Is your heart broken for your sin, and do you see what a filthy, vile, abominable creature you are?

Do you see that you don't deserve any mercy, that you deserve to be cast into hell forever for your wickedness? Do you see that you are like a poor, little infant who can't help yourself? Does your whole heart go to Christ and him alone as your Savior? Do you give your heart to Christ, and are you willing with all your heart to give yourself to Christ to be his people forever and ever? Are you willing to forsake all for Jesus Christ? The Scriptures say that he who believes in Christ is like a man who sells all for one pearl of great price (Matt. 13:46). Are you willing to forsake all your sins, forsake all the world for Christ?

I advise all poor sinners to come to Christ for salvation and to give themselves with all their hearts to him. You are poor, miserable creatures. You are in danger of going to hell and stand in great need of

Christ. There is no other way for you to be saved. God never provided any other Savior but he. You must come to Christ; you can't do without him. If you don't come to him, you must be damned forever and ever.

You have a last opportunity that many others don't. You have the gospel preached to you. You are instructed in the way of salvation by him, and many others have no such privilege. Christ in his Word calls you to come to him. He invites, he bids you come and welcome. If you are a great sinner, a wicked person, if you have done wickedness in these times, yet Christ is ready to receive you if you will come to him. Christ calls all men and women, young and old and little children. All are invited to look to him that they may be saved.

Christ gave direction to preach the gospel to every creature under heaven. Christ has provided a great feast, set his door wide open, and says, "Whosoever will may come." You may come and eat without money, come for nothing. Christ has paid the price, and you may come for nothing. Nothing is required of you for your own eternal beings and having all the glory of heaven but only to come to Christ with all your heart. You may have Christ for your Savior and may have all heaven only if you will give Christ your heart. Christ stands at the door and knocks. If you will open the door, he will come in, and he will give himself to you and all that he has.

Now is your opportunity while life lasts. Christ never will invite you and offer himself to you anymore after you are dead. The Scriptures say if you won't hear now while Christ calls to you, he won't hear you when you call to him in your misery. But he will laugh at your calamity and mock you when you are in great distress.

Christ this day calls and invites you. I am his servant, and I invite you to come to him. Make haste, delay not. Give your heart to Christ, and he will save you from hell, and all heaven will be yours.

16

---✦✦---

When the Spirit of God Has Been Remarkably Poured Out on a People, a Thorough Reformation of Those Things That Before Were Amiss Amongst Them Ought to Be the Effect of It

Many of them also which used curious arts brought their books together,
and burned them before all men: and they counted the price of them, and
found it fifty thousand pieces of silver.

ACTS 19:19

This sermon from Acts 19 was preached by Edwards on April 1, 1736, a day set aside as a fast day. It was an encouragement to seek seriously for the pouring out of the Spirit both on the land and the people and to understand that when he does come, he not only awakens and converts the unconverted, but he renews and confirms grace on the converted.

For the background Edwards uses the miracle of the burning of books on magic that took place in Ephesus. This was a sure sign that the Spirit had been poured out and that real and visible reformation would occur.

In his application of the doctrine, Edwards applies it to the local town. He testifies that the townspeople are experiencing a remarkable outpouring of the Spirit, but he exhorts the people to live in such a way that they do not quench what God was doing. He also includes a lengthy appeal to the young people to avoid all evil.

The last point he makes is interesting. He criticizes a practice that he says has been found among them in times past but which should not be so now since God has so remarkably poured out his Spirit among them. This was the practice of sleeping during the meeting.

The sermon manuscript is a typical duodecimal booklet, consisting of forty-two leaves with little or no evidence of damage or reworking. The application consists of twenty-two leaves.

We have here in the context an account of an extraordinary, daring act of the Spirit on the city of Ephesus. It was a very great city and one of the chief cities in that part of the world. In the beginning of the chapter, we have an account of Paul's coming to Ephesus. When he came, he seems to have found but few Christians there. It is said that he found certain disciples who had been baptized unto John's baptism—in number, above twelve. After he had conferred with those persons, Paul went into the synagogue of the Jews that was in the city and spoke boldly for about the space of three months, disputing and persuading the things concerning the kingdom of God.

But Paul had but little success here amongst the Jews, whom the apostles everywhere found the most backward of any people upon earth to receive the gospel. The Jews at Ephesus, instead of believing, were hardened and spoke evil of the Way before the multitudes. Instead of receiving the gospel themselves, they refused it and labored also to prejudice others against it. Whereupon Paul left the synagogue and went amongst them no more and separated the Christians from them and returned to another place—the school of one Tyrannus—and preached the gospel to the Gentiles who assembled there. And there the apostle Paul had better success than he had in the synagogues amongst the Jews, so that he continued residing there for two years together.

He had not been long preaching there in that school before there began to be an extraordinary pouring out of the Spirit of God with his preaching. Multitudes of people from all parts of the city—and not only so but the country round about—came to hear him, as stated in Acts 19:10. And there was extraordinary assistance given to Paul so that he was enabled to confirm what he preached with many and very great miracles (vv. 11–12). And God gave an extraordinary attestation to Paul by many visitations and remarkably bearing testimony in his words against some of the Jews who endeavored to rival Paul in his works and miracles.

The effect of these things upon the people through the pouring out of God's Spirit was very extraordinary. This seems to be one of the most remarkable instances of the pouring out of the Spirit of God that we have anywhere in the Scriptures.

We have an account of some remarkable effects of it in the text and foregoing verses in the remarkable evidence as there was of the people's repentance. Ephesus was a heathen city. There were some Jews living in it, yet most of the inhabitants were heathen. And the heathen world of that day was exceedingly full not only of idolatry but of all manner of vice and immorality and especially in great and populous cities such as Ephesus. But when the gospel came to be preached and to prevail amongst them, it had a wonderful effect in bringing of them in great multitudes to repent of their wickedness. The evidences of their repentance here taken notice of are two—confessing and forsaking. We have an account of their confessing in the verse preceding the text, "And many that believed" (v. 18). And in the text we have an account of their forsaking concerning which we here observe:

1. They forsook using curious arts and magic arts. The heathen world before the gospel took place was exceedingly addicted to sorcery and divination. So it was in Egypt and the Chaldean Empire. As we read of the magicians and astrologers and sorcerers and soothsayers in Babylon and Chaldea, so it was also in the Roman Empire that flourished at this time.

The devil was the god of the heathen world. They were given up to him, and many of these pagan people had an immediate intercourse with the devil in the use of magical and diabolical arts. But these arts they now forsook on Paul's preaching of the gospel to them. They had now done with this wickedness that had been practiced so long amongst them and was looked upon as no wickedness before but was thought among the heathen a credible and honorable practice.

2. We may observe the thoroughness of their reformation manifested by their burning their magical books. It might have been possible for them to reform their conjuring without burning their books. They could have refrained from using their books and not have burned them. They could have sold them to others, who would have been glad of them. But they had such an indignation against the practice and such an abhorrence of their former wickedness that they would not suffer the books to exist. They were very cheerful in burning of them. They publicly took more delight in burning them than ever they had done before in using them.

3. Notice how openly they did it. They did not burn them secretly, but they brought their books together and burned them before all men that they might bear a testimony against their same wickedness and against themselves in the most open manner possible. They who do sin and openly repent will love to have their former wickedness

disgraced. They won't plead for it or hide it. They will not desire that anyone should think well of it but will desire no other than that it should be openly represented to the world as a thing to be abhorred and detested.

4. Notice the great numbers of those who thus forsook this wickedness. This is signified in two ways. It is expressed that they were many, and then the number appears by the price of the books that were burned—fifty thousand pieces of silver. This shows how great the pouring out of the Spirit there was and how extraordinary the effect as it follows in the next verse. For we are not to suppose that all or one quarter of them who were converted, or it may be not one in thirty ever had used this practice. But yet there were so many such converted who had used it. Besides those there were many persons and witches amongst them who were least likely to receive the gospel, for they were more especially under the devil's power. They probably got their living by their art, and they were under much greater temptation not to burn them than others were.

5. We may observe their denial of their worldly interest in thus forsaking their sin in burning that which was of so much cost. There appeared to be a spirit in them to make no account of their worldly interest in comparison of their duty. Such a spirit was there to prefer Christ to their worldly interest that there were fifty thousand souls at once for the sake of Christ. As was before observed, they might have sold those books and got all this money by it. As has also been already observed, many of them got their living by those curious arts. They were wont to use conjuring as a trade, as appears by the account we have of a damsel who used this art in Acts 16:16.

Besides the loss of the price of the books, they also lost the means of their gain and many of them of their livelihood. Yet so powerfully were they wrought upon by the Spirit of God that this was no hindrance to their forsaking their wicked practices and their embracing of the gospel. They cheerfully sold all for the pearl of great price (Matt. 13:45–46).

DOCTRINE

When the Spirit of God has been remarkably poured out on a people, a thorough reform of those things that before were amiss amongst them ought to be the effect of it. This leads me to two propositions.

1. Before the Spirit of God is poured out on a people, there will be many things found amiss amongst them. Man is an exceeding corrupt and perverse creature, prone and bent to evil. If God lets men alone, they will run into all evil. Towns and societies of men will be corrupted with many evil things. Not only will a great deal of corruption and wickedness prevail in men's hearts, but many evil ways will be prevalent amongst them. There will be many things wherein such a people do greatly fail of their duty. Only then will there be many things wanting that God justly expects and requires of them.

And there will be many corrupt practices that will be prevalent among them that are to the dishonor of God and contrary to the rules of Christianity and that are unbecoming of a Christian people. Many things render us unlovely and are dishonorable and disgraceful to a people and render them uncomfortable one to another. Many evil things tend as well to their own temporal as well as spiritual calamity.

There will be things that are public and that will be done by them as a people that are evil and corrupt practices. These will become common and grow barefaced. Wickedness will in many instances be countenanced and not suitably opposed or frowned upon. If they are a professing people, yet if they are destitute of the Spirit of God amongst them, their profession of Christianity won't prevent it. If they enjoy never so great light and external means and there be many faithful endeavors used by ministers, if the Spirit of God be withheld, all won't prevent there being many corruptions prevailing amongst them.

2. When the Spirit of God has been remarkably poured out on a people, a thorough reformation of those things ought to be the effect of it for the following reasons:

Reason 1. This is one end of God's pouring out his Spirit on a people to reform them. Ezekiel 36:25 says, "Then will I sprinkle clean water upon you, and ye shall be clean: from all your filthiness, and from all your idols, will I cleanse you." Isaiah 4:3–4 says, "And it shall come to pass, that he that is left in Zion, and he that remaineth in Jerusalem, shall be called holy, even every one that is written among the living in Jerusalem: When the Lord shall have washed away the filth of the daughters of Zion, and shall have purged the blood of Jerusalem from the midst thereof by the spirit of judgment, and by the spirit of burning."

Reason 2. 'Tis what the pouring out of the Spirit on a people has a natural tendency to. This is evident from the nature of the Spirit of God who is a Holy Spirit and therefore an enemy to all wickedness. It is an enemy to it as fire is to filthiness and therefore is called a Spirit of burning. The Spirit is said to purge away the filth of the daughter of Zion in that text just mentioned. And it always has in a greater or lesser degree this effect, as is evident by what we see and find by experience. It has a tendency to this in three ways—by its awakening and its converting and also by its confirming influences.

1. By its awakening influences. When the Spirit of God is poured out on a people, sinners are awakened. The effect of awakenings, if they are to any considerable degree, is reformation. When sinners are awakened, they are made sensible of the dangerous nature of sin and the guilt that it brings and the wrath that it exposes to. Therefore, they dare not commit sin as they used to. While those awakenings last, they will be afraid to go on in their former sinful practices.

2. The Spirit tends to it by its converting influences. It brings men not to a partial but thorough reformation, not only to reform or abstain

from sin for a while, but to reform forever, everlastingly to back off from their old wicked ways. Many and probably the greater part of those who brought their magical books together and burned them that we have an account of in the text were savingly converted and forever forsook their curious arts. Some men are reformed who are not converted, but none are converted without being reformed. Men under awakenings are afraid of their former evil ways. But none who are converted hate their former evil ways and therefore forever forsake them.

3. The Spirit of God, when poured out, also tends to reformation in its confirming influences on those who were converted before. When the Spirit of God is poured out on a people, it is not only on the unconverted to awaken and convert them but also on the converted to renew and confirm grace on them and to enliven the exercises of it. When it is not a time of the pouring out of the Spirit of God on a people, very commonly 'tis a droll and dead time with the godly as well as others. They have not the zeal against sin, don't oppose prevailing acts, nor exert themselves for the renewal of those things that are amiss among a people as they have a spirit to do when they are more enlivened.

They are dull and sluggish. Sin and Satan prevail, and they have not the heart to make any thorough opposition as they ought to do by reproving sin by being a testimony against it and using means to remove it. But when the Spirit of God is poured out upon a people, it stirs them up to be more thorough and disposes them to exert themselves more against it.

Reason 3. Why such a reformation of a people ought to be the effect of a pouring out of the Spirit upon them is that hereby such a pouring out of the Spirit redounds to the glory of God. Herein appears the excellent effect of the pouring out of the Spirit. The pouring out of the Spirit being to the glory of God depends on the effect of it. In being efficacious, it is glorious. This effect arising from the pouring out of the Spirit on a people redounds to God's glory in two ways:

1. From the excellency of the effect. When anything proves efficacious among a people to reform to make them forsake their former evil ways and brings them to walk morally and religiously, and all orders of persons, all societies and companies accordingly act and behave regularly, this is an excellent effect. All will acknowledge the desirableness and excellency of the effects. Every man's conscience testifies that these things are to be approved of and that such a people are much to be commended above other people. There is that natural light on every man that will force him to acknowledge such things to be praiseworthy. Romans 14:17–18 says, "For the kingdom of God is not meat and drink; but righteousness, and peace, and joy in the Holy Ghost. For he that in these things serveth Christ is acceptable to God, and approved of men."

Such a people as walk regularly are more honorable in the eye of the world than other people, for "righteousness exalteth a nation: but sin is a reproach to any people" (Prov. 14:34). The world, though wicked, will yet give testimony that such a people are a more wise people than other people. Deuteronomy 4:5–6 says, "Behold, I have taught you statutes and judgments, even as the LORD my God commanded me, that ye should do so in the land whither ye go to possess it. Keep therefore and do them; for this is your wisdom and your understanding in the sight of the nations, which shall hear all these statutes, and say, Surely this great nation is a wise and understanding people." This is an excellent effect, both as it renders any society or community of persons lovely and also as it renders them happy. It tends surely to their temporal peace and quietness and renders men useful and comfortable one to another.

2. This is a visible effect. The external reformation of a people, though it be an excellent effect of the pouring out of the Spirit, yet is

not the most excellent effect. The effects that are wrought on the hearts of a people in thoroughly changing them and adorning the mind with Christian grace is a more excellent effect. But yet the reformation of a people is an effect of the pouring out of the Spirit that is in some respects peculiarly to the glory of God because it is visible. 'Tis that which the world can see. 'Tis obvious to all the observations of all beholding. The effect that is wrought on the heart is not visible to the world, for we be not able to see the hearts of others. But when the pouring out of the Spirit of God is followed with a remarkable reformation of a people, that is what appears to the world. Hereby all men may see what an effect the Spirit of God has had. The root is out of sight, but the fruit can be seen. Men have no other way to judge but by what is seen. Therefore, 'tis this way chiefly that God's declarative glory is promoted amongst men who are bystanders by the pouring out of the Spirit on a people. 'Tis this way chiefly that God's glory in such a work appears to the world because this is the effect they can see.

The declarative glory of God consists in showing and making known his glory, but God's glory in such a work can be made known and manifested no other way than by something that can be seen. Therefore, Christ gives that direction to the disciples in Matthew 5:16, "Let your light so shine before men." The light that is under a bushel and can't be seen is not to the glory of God amongst men. But in order to accomplish that, the light must shine before men.

The credit of the work that is wrought by the pouring out of the Spirit depends very much on the visible reformation of a people that tends to convince bystanders that it is the work of God. More than anything else, this tends to convince them that 'tis something more than finery and imagination, something else besides man's empty notions. 'Tis effectual that is a great effect to be seen, for they may observe that the people are quite changed. They are quite a different sort of people from what they used to be. They have forsaken their former evil practices. When men observe this, it will be natural for them thus to argue with themselves. Certainly there must be something of reality in this, or else it would never be attended with such an effect.

This work can't be of the devil that works reform in a people and makes them a much better people than they used to be. The devil does not delight in bringing men off from their sins, from their vices and rendering a people as happy people. He loves to make them wicked and miserable. Certainly therefore, this must be the work of God and so such a work of God redounds to the glory of God abroad in the world.

Reason 4. Gratitude obliges a people who have received such a mercy to their utmost to improve it this way. When God pours out his Spirit on a people, he bestows on them the greatest mercy that ever is bestowed on any people. 'Tis the greatest blessing that they can receive. 'Tis a greater mercy than if God should feed them with the finest of the wheat and should cause them to wash their slops in butter and should cause the rock to pour them out rivers of oil. 'Tis a greater blessing than if God should shower silver and gold and pearls out of heaven on a people. And therefore such a mercy lays a people under the greatest possible obligation to thankfulness to God and to show gratitude to him in all proper ways and especially in laboring to do that which shall be pleasing unto him. So that it will be very ungrateful if they don't forsake those things that have been heretofore food, things that are displeasing to God. They are a people distinguished by God's favor to them so they may distinguish themselves by a desire to serve him and give everything to please and honor him.

Reason 5. When a people improve the pouring out of the Spirit that way, that is the way to have such a mercy continued. This is the way to have the Spirit of God still poured upon them and to have God continually dwelling among them. This is the way to have the work of conversion still carried on amongst them. 'Tis the way to have those who are converted to have most of the presence of God continued to them, to live in the enjoyment of much light and comfort. A right improvement of any mercy is the likeliest way for the continuance of that mercy, and there is no more likely way to be deprived of it than to neglect or abuse it. If a people don't reform those things that were amiss amongst them, it will be no wonder if God withdraws from them, for God is of purer eyes than to behold evil and to commit loathsome iniquity. Evil shall not dwell with him. If we would have God amongst us, we must cast away all our idols and must remove all leaven out of our houses.

Christ will walk in that garden where there are pleasant fruits. But if we suffer to grow in our garden any root of bitterness or poisonous herbs and don't weed them out and purge them away, it will be no wonder if Christ has no delight to walk in it. The prevalency of any immorality or evil way will have a tendency to prevent the Spirit among that people. It will have not only a moral but also a natural tendency to deaden religion, for any sinful way, if continued in, hardens the hearts of a people.

Reason 6. The making such an improvement of the pouring out tends to the propagation of such a mercy. The more it has this effect, the more literally it will be that a religious concern will be propagated to other people round about. For as has been already observed, this work very much tends to convince them of the reality of the work of the Spirit. It will tend to stop the mouths of objections. By this the greatness of the work of God was visible to the heathen in Ephesus when they saw that it had such a remarkable effect upon men as to cause them in such multitudes to forsake their wickedness, that magicians forsake their curious arts and burn their books when they see them cheerfully deny themselves of their worldly interest. And such things as these were what had a main influence in the conversion of the heathen world to Christianity at and after the apostles' times, as ecclesiastical history informs us. They were impressed when they saw the remarkable effect the gospel had upon the Christians. What a great change it made in their lives. How those who before were naturally vicious became eminently of a strictly moral, harmless life and what self-denial Christians were ready to put themselves to for the sake of Christ. It was astonishing to them and convinced them that there was certainly something divine in the religion that they embraced which was prevalent to win over multitudes from among the heathen to embrace the gospel. This was one main means why the greater part of the Roman Empire, which contained the greater part of the then known world, in a little time renounced their heathenism that the whole world for so many years had lain in and embraced Christianity.

APPLICATION

I come now particularly to apply this doctrine to the case of this town. To exhort that those things may henceforward be performed that in times past have been found amiss amongst us. It has lately been with us as it was in Ephesus in that respect, that there has been a great and very wonderful pouring out of the Spirit of God amongst us and in that the Word of God has mightily grown and prevailed amongst us. Let it also be with us as it was with them that we thoroughly break off all our former evil ways. As has been observed, the pouring out of the Spirit naturally tends to this effect, and it has had that effect in a great measure amongst us. Many things that were formally found amiss amongst us have been in a great measure reformed and are for the present reformed. But let it be a thing that we are intent upon and that our hearts are engaged in, that this reformation may be thorough and universal and that it may be continued.

Let us not only reform some of those things that were found displeasing to God amongst us—but all. And let it not only be short restraint just while this remarkable pouring out of the Spirit is yet a new thing. But let it be a final breaking off of our known evil ways. Let us not return as the dog to our own vomit and as the pig that was washed to her wallowing in the mire. I would mention some things in particular.

1. Let the remarkable pouring out of the Spirit that has been amongst us be followed with a lasting reformation. A wicked spirit after the world, a worldly spirit is a very sinful spirit and very provoking to God. It is a spirit to set up the world against God and therefore 'tis called idolatry in Scripture, as Colossians 3:5 says, "Mortify therefore your members which are upon the earth; fornication, uncleanness, inordinate affection, evil concupiscence, and covetousness, which is idolatry." Ephesians 5:5 says, "For this ye know, that no whoremonger, nor unclean person, nor covetous man, who is an idolater, hath any inheritance in the kingdom of Christ and of God." Seeing God has been so liberally bestowing those things that are infinitely better amongst us, God may well expect that there hereafter appear a very great difference in us in this respect from what there used to be. There should in no wise be that inordinate spirit after evil and idolatry as there was before.

When there was a remarkable pouring out of the Spirit at Ephesus, it had this effect upon the people: It wonderfully weaned them from the world as evidently appeared by what we are told in the text. They for the sake of Christ burned up at once all their worldly possessions, as much as came to fifty thousand pieces of silver. Multitudes of them forever forsook those wicked acts that they used to depend upon for their worldly gain. And it was much taken notice of amongst us the last spring and the winter before, how much people's minds seemed to be taken off from the world, how they seemed to care but very little about it. There seemed to be no appearance of any wicked spirit after the world. It was generally observed with much approbation as a good token how greatly people's minds were taken up about things of greater importance. But if it was a thing to be approved of then, so it is now as much spiritual things are of as much greater importance than worldly things as they were then.

How will it look and how much to the dishonor of God and religion will it be if persons, while seeking an interest in Christ, will seem to have their minds very much taken off from the world? But when once they think they have made sure, they will run full speed into the world again. Let everyone look to himself, and consider whether he is not guilty. One would think that men could have no peace in their own minds in doing thus, it is so unsuitable and a thing of so bad an aspect. 'Tis in the mouths of every man how the town is growing worldly again. What a great difference there is in the town in this respect from what was the last year. All speak of it as a thing to be lamented. But whose fault is it? We can observe the error in others, but can we observe nothing in ourselves?

Let us, as becomes a people whom God has so dealt with as he has with us, keep the world in its place. Let our minds, our hearts, and our strength be taken up about something else, and let the world always be set on the lowest place. In that way we need not fear being punished, for Christ has promised us: "Seek ye first the kingdom . . . and all these things shall be added unto you" (Matt. 6:33).

2. Let there be no more of that party spirit appearing in the town that formerly has been found amongst us. 'Tis a thing well known that in times past the town has been divided into parties and that such a division long existed and that this has been the occasion of a great deal of strife and contention. A party spirit is what comprehends a spirit of pride, a spirit of malice and envy and contention and idolatry and many other vices. Innumerable are the mischiefs occasioned by it. When a town is divided into parties, one party will be jealous of another. Those who are of a different party won't be friendly one to another. It keeps persons at a distance in their affections and makes

men a kind of enemy one to another. They stand ready to think ill of what others say or do, and their hearts are prepared to oppose one another on all occasions, especially on public occasions, and commonly they are far from doing one another justice. There is nothing said or done by those of one party that will be taken well by the other party, though it be never so right.

Men's prejudice blinds their eyes and stops their ears so that they won't hear reason. Their being divided into parties is an occasion of these spirits being often lodged and used one against another. They are apt to be made angry by anything said or done by one of the opposite party, though it be but a little thing and not worth the taking notice of. And commonly they make it much their business to oppose one another. Justice and truth are oftentimes neglected in such cases.

Men can't impartially consider what is right and best for the public good, nor do they sincerely aim at it because their spirits are engaged in opposing one another. The thing they aim at is to get their wills one of another. And there is commonly in such cases a great deal of secret plotting and contriving to undermine one another. Thus there continually grows ill will and a spirit of hatred one against another, and they rejoice in one another's disappointments. And commonly there is a great deal of time spent in talking one against another, in backbiting one another when those who are of one party get together. Very often much of their conversation turns upon the faults and follies of the other party, and often ridicules their families and is much the source of debates, envyings, and wraths. These are common and a lively example of the case of a people divided into parties (2 Cor. 12:20).

But how unhappy is it when it is thus amongst a Christian people. How much provocation is there to God and how much do men wrong their own souls. James 3:16 says, "Where envying and strife is, there is confusion and every evil work." But I need not tell you that it has been very much thus in this town in times past. But since God has so wonderfully poured out his Spirit upon us, there has not been that appearance of a party spirit among us, but a spirit of peace and love has been visibly the effect of it, which is a blessed effect. Let us therefore take heed that there never be anymore an appearance of a party spirit amongst us as there has been. Let this happy effect of the pouring out of God's Spirit be continued amongst us. If we do not take great care, it will be apt to get in amongst us again.

There is the corruption in the heart that naturally tends and exposes to it. Good men have great need to watch themselves as well as others in this matter. Let me entreat all to watch over themselves, that we don't in the management of any of our public affairs get divided into parties with spirits edged one against another. And to avoid it we must bear one with another. We must bear with one another's infirmities. We must bear with one another's corruptions. We must condescend one to another. If every man will be stiff and will resolve to yield at all to his neighbor and violently to oppose everything that is done in public affairs.

If in the management of public affairs every man who is not suited or when things be not managed according to his judgment will try to make a party and to make a public stir, this will tend to confusion. For it never can be expected that everybody in a whole town will be of one mind on every public affair. Yet there is no necessity of making parties and raising tumults because of this. If we should go to fermenting a spirit of strife and division in the town concerning any of our public affairs, we should not take any course more enduring to the interest of religion amongst us. We should carefully avoid it both as we would regard the interest of religion and also as we would seek our own interest.

How much more comfortable living is it in a society that lives in love and peace than where there are brawls and perpetual contentions. We have tasted the sweetness of it of late since the Spirit of God has been poured out. Our experience may in some measure induce us to say as the psalmist does in Psalm 133:1, "Behold, how good and how pleasant it is for brethren to dwell together in unity." If we keep the unity of the Spirit in the bond of peace, this will be the way to have the Spirit of God continued amongst us. The Spirit of God is a spirit of love. This will be the way to have Christ who is the prince of peace delighting to dwell amongst us. "Live in peace," says the apostle Paul, "and the God of love and peace shall be with you" (2 Cor. 13:11).

When there is a spirit of division and contention raised in a town, it is commonly about some worldly thing. The world is the bone of contention and sometimes 'tis a little thing. 'Tis of very little importance. Let us consider whether a little of the world is worth the cost of the quenching the Spirit of God and ending the interest of religion in a town.

I hope there are many here who have the interest of religion at heart and that interest is alone their chief joy. This gives room to hope that my present exhortation will be heeded and conformed to.

Let the kingdom of Christ amongst us be steadfastly regarded by us above any other affair, either public or private. And let us follow peace one with another. If it be possible as much as in us lies, let us live peaceably with all men. And let us serve God together with one heart and one soul with hearty and sincere love one to another. Let nothing be done among us through strife or vainglory, looking every man not only on his own things but every man also on the things of others. Let all bitterness and wrath or anger and envy and evil speaking be put away from among us with all malice, with all lowliness and meekness, with longsuffering forbearing one another in love and let us not grieve the Holy Spirit of God whereby we are sealed to the day of redemption.

3. Let there henceforward be a thorough reformation of all licentious practices of young people in company. The land has got to a fearful position in this respect. Uncleanness abounds exceedingly in the land and goes on without change. There are many things that are customary in the land that do directly lead to all manner of wickedness. The youth of the land have made a strange progress of late in the liberties they take in company that are those things now commonly practiced by young people. Without doubt these tend to bring down the fierce wrath of God. Many of the young people in the country who die without doubt have a dreadful reckoning to pay in full for their licentiousness while they lived. The flames of their lust have enkindled fierce flames in hell to burn them to all eternity. And many young people get those wounds to their souls by their licentiousness while young. These they never get rid of, though they live to grow old. Their bones are full of the sins of their youth that lie down with them in the dust.

Lasciviousness is a thing that seems to have grown in the country much more than in proportion to other vices. This seems to be owing to certain customs that are commonly amongst young people and are countenanced and showed off and have practiced a long while as if they were innocent. Particularly I would mention one—young people who keep company spending their time in lying together on beds and very often for whole nights together. I know very well that this custom is very general in country towns in this land and has been so for a long time. For ministers to preach against such things commonly only raises laughter and is little regarded. But be that as it will, I will discharge a good conscience about it. The more general it is and the more it is allowed, the more is it to be lamented. And it may be one reason why it is grown so common and is looked upon no worse, is because it has not been duly testified against.

I think that this practice has been one great occasion of uncleanness being come to such a height in the country. There are such frequent breakings out of gross wickedness as there are, that needs no disputing about it to convince anyone who will allow serious thought about it. 'Tis a custom the greatest prevalency of which has a direct tendency to promote uncleanness. Therefore, it must be a pernicious custom that is condemned by an infinitely holy God at the day of judgment. It will be found another day that he who is of purer eyes than to behold evil has his holy wrath enkindled by such customs. He who pleads for such things now won't dare to hold up his head about such things when God appears.

If anyone inquires what hurt there is in it, I answer that 'tis a custom that exposes to wickedness and lays men open to temptation, and that is enough to condemn it. The Scripture warns us against all these things that tend to enkindle lust and lead to uncleanness. The wise man says with respect to this lust of uncleanness in Proverbs 6:27–28: "Can a man take fire in his bosom, and his clothes not be burned? Can one go upon hot coals, and his feet not be burned?" And if anyone says that he has practiced it often and never found it temptation to him, yet that won't justify the practice. For it has been so without doubt in thousands of instances, that what is no temptation to a person at one time has been a temptation that has overcome him at another. And will you therefore keep the custom 'til you are overcome? And if there be some instance of persons who never found it a sin to them, yet if we look on the practice in the general, it be a sin and in fact an occasion of a great deal of wickedness. It ought to be avoided by all who have the interest of nature at heart and would keep a good conscience before God.

'Tis a strange thing that such a custom should become so general and so countenanced in so great a part of this country that makes so light a profession of religion which would be looked upon injurious in other countries. The light of nature teaches other people the indecency and importunity of the practice.

And other practices and customs there are that are prevalent enough for the young people of the land which I forbear to mention. They tend to enkindle lust and without doubt enkindle the wrath of God. And such things are apt to increase and prevail. That to which persons are prompted by their evil inclinations, they are wont to be exceeding subtle in pleading for the lawfulness of. Hence young people are wont to quiet their consciences about many liberties they take. But let them remember that they never find it so easy to answer to an infinitely holy God when he shall call them to an account as they do to blind their own minds and quiet their own consciences for the present.

But licentiousness has got such footing amongst the young people in the land that there is no hope of it ever being routed out unless it be by a remarkable pouring out of the Spirit of God on the land. And therefore I thought myself called of God at this time to testify against such things, since there has been so lately so remarkable a pouring out of the Spirit of God on the town and on the young people in the town. I hope that there is now so much regard to religion in our youth that their ear would be open to such instruction. And let me now instruct our young people forever to break off such things. Let this pouring out be an occasion of a thorough reformation of such practices amongst us. All licentiousness in company is very vain and unprofitable. What is there got by it?

And if young people should abstain from such things, what would they lose by it? Though such things may gratify impure inclinations in young people, yet all licentiousness in an unmarried state does but mar the comfort and deaden the sweetness of a married life and doubtless very often brings a curse upon persons in a married state. God punishes them. Though they are converted and have savingly repented, yet God may and doubtless often does upset their sin with many bitter temporal afflictions after that. It may be that as long as they live, they will not feel the blessing of heaven upon them and their hearts as otherwise they would have.

I hope there are many of our young people who have repented of and abstained themselves for the liberties they formerly took. If it be so, I desire they would presently teach young people to rise up and instruct others, particularly their younger brothers and sisters who are beginning in company. Persons when very young are oftentimes ensnared in company ignorantly and for want of being well instructed in their duty and what they ought to avoid.

4. Another thing that I would exhort may be reformed amongst us is the neglect of family government. Family government is a thing that is exceedingly decayed in the country. I suppose there are many yet living amongst us who can give testimony to this by what they can remember of the state of family government formerly in the country and how much more strict orders were observed in families and how much greater authority parents generally maintained over their children formerly than is common now in the country. If parents have a disposition to establish government and strict order in their families, now is the time, since there has lately been such an extraordinary pouring out of the Spirit. They will find it abundantly easier at such a time than at other times. Children will more easily yield to their regulation. It will be more easy now to reform many ill practices in them than at another time. There are not those difficulties in the way now. Children have not so many ill examples set before them of irregular behavior as they have had in times past, and it may be they will have hereafter.

When irregularities are generally prevailing amongst children throughout a whole town, 'tis a difficult thing to reduce one family to good order alone. Therefore, let those who are disposed to establish good order and government in their families take this opportunity. The decay of family government in the land has been like the opening of a floodgate to disorder and vice to the rising generation and so a flood of corruption in the land. For family government is a principle restraint upon iniquity and corruption of young persons that God has appointed. Many heads of families have been guilty of Eli's sin. Their child can make themselves vile, and they did not restrain them, and 'tis well if they don't bring on themselves Eli's curse (1 Sam. 4:11–22).

Many parents by their carelessness and imprudent management lose all government over their children. There must be a steady hand of government if parents would have the government effectual. A rash and unsteady management confounds government. Some parents will at some times seem to be very resolute and even serious and at other times very indulgent, but government is not to be maintained by such means. And many lose their government by often threatening and seldom fulfilling, so that their command and threatenings come to be disregarded by the child. Parents should be careful how they threaten, but when they threaten, they should ordinarily fulfill the threatening if the crime threatened be committed.

The most effectual way to establish government over a child is to begin early. A child left to himself when little will never be subject to government. It ought to be a thing natural to a child to be subject to the parents' will. The child should not be able to remember when it was otherwise. A child should soon be made to know that he must be subject to the parents' command and then when government is once established, it should be carefully maintained by an ever-steady hand. And when it is well established, it should also be well improved. When a parent has once found the point that his child is in subjection to his government, when the ground is thus plowed, he may sow what he will upon it. He then has an advantage in his hands to train the child in the ways of nature and to establish good habits and to train up a child in the way that he should go that he shall not depart from it when he is old (Prov. 22:6).

5. Another thing I would exhort may be thoroughly reformed is negligence of paying debts. Has there not in times past been a just complaining in our streets by reason of their being so much of this neglect amongst us. How many creditors have suffered a great deal of wrong through persons neglecting to render them what was their due. If it is yet so amongst us after such a great outpouring, and so great a profession of religion amongst us, it will be very much to the dishonor of religion because this is a defect in moral honesty. For men to pretend to be converted and tell of great experiences, and yet not act like honest men is a great reproach to the profession they make.

6. The last thing I will mention is sleeping at meeting. This is a thing that has been found amongst us in times past, but it may well be expected that we should worship God with greater reverence and diligence since God has so remarkably poured out his Spirit amongst us. If there be many among us in our assembly who appear to be asleep in their seats in the time of divine service, this will be a thing that strangers will observe. When they come here, they will naturally take notice how people appear in their public worship, whether there seems to be an evident and remarkable difference between them and other people, whether they seem to give better attention or to attend with greater reverence and diligence. If they observe that we sleep at meeting as much as at other places, it will doubtless bring much to them in what they have heard of us.

Let me therefore entreat that this practice may be thoroughly reformed amongst us. I would desire that persons would avoid laying down their bodies in their seats in the midst of public worship. 'Tis a very indecent practice. It exposes persons to God's wrath and gives the congregation occasion to think they are asleep. Let neighbors show kindness to one another as to wake each other when asleep.

Since God has been so abundantly merciful to us, let us labor and worship him in the most decent and uncarnal manner and in the beauty of holiness.

17

━━⊷ ⊶━━

There Never Was Any Love That Could Be Paralleled with the Dying Love of Christ

For scarcely for a righteous man will one die: yet peradventure for a
good man some would even dare to die. But God commendeth his love
toward us, in that, while we were yet sinners, Christ died for us.

ROMANS 5:7–8

This sermon on Romans 5, preached in February 1752, was another message Edwards preached to the Stockbridge Indians. On the original manuscript, the editors involved in the Edwards project made two important notations. The first detailed that the sermon is probably defective at the end. The second unit consisted of only eight pages, and it also seemed to have no application. The second notation said that the above was correct. The sermon's application was actually identified in the sermon on 2 Corinthians 9:15, preached in May 1737.

As far as the subject of the sermon is concerned, Edwards gives several reasons why there is no love like the love of Christ. The first he gives is that of the distance in nature between the creation and the Creator. One of the comparisons Edwards uses is that there is a greater distance between the Son of God and men than there is between the earth and the highest star in the heavens; nor was there any love that fixed on an object so far from being capable of benefiting the lover; nor was there any love that fixed on an object whom the lover saw so far from being lovely; nor was there any love that fixed upon an object so far from loving the lover; nor was there any love that appeared in so great expressions; and lastly, never was there any love that was so beneficial to the beloved.

The sermon manuscript is a typical duodecimal booklet, consisting of thirty-two leaves. The sermon body concludes with the handwritten addition that this sermon was "copied out by Alex Grosart, New London, [18]54." Grosart traveled from Scotland in the nineteenth century and published a volume like this present one. It consisted of previously unpublished examples of Edwards's work. Even though Grosart had a copy of this sermon, it did not appear in that volume.

The comparison that is here made between the love of men one to another, and the dying love of God is a short digression from the argument that the apostle Paul is upon in the context. The apostle is treating of the good ground of the Christian's hope of the glory of God. In the beginning of the chapter, he describes the hope of a Christian by the greatness of the good that is the object of it and the joyfulness of it and the effectualness of it. It enables the Christian to glory in tribulation therefore being justified.

And he shows how the tribulation of a true Christian is a means of increasing and establishing hope—that a patient bearing of affliction gives that experience that greatly confirms hope. So that hope doesn't make us ashamed. Men are made ashamed by their hope in Scripture when their experience is not according to their hope. When it comes to it, they are disappointed of what they hoped for. But for Christians, when they are in tribulation and bear it with patience, their hope doesn't make them ashamed. They aren't disappointed. That is the reason that the apostle Paul gives because in that way of enduring the tribulation the love of God was shed abroad in their hearts by the Holy Ghost which was given to them.

God gives fresh supplies of grace to them who patiently bear tribulation. He pours forth the Holy Ghost upon them, which is the earnest of their future inheritance hoped for and is often mentioned as such.

And then the apostle Paul proceeds to show what reason Christians have to be assured that their hope of future glory shall not be disappointed. He uses this argument that Christ died for them even while ungodly, which was the greatest thing, Christ having done this even while under the guilt of sin. The apostle Paul argues that there is no doubt that guilt was removed by Christ's death. The salvation would be bestowed because it is not now so great a thing for God to bestow salvation after guilt is removed, as it is for Christ to die to remove that guilt.

To show how unparalleled the love of Christ is, the apostle in the first place declares the utmost extent of the love of men. "Scarcely for a righteous man will one die: yet peradventure for a good man some would even dare to die." By a good man here may be understood either a man with a qualification beyond righteousness. By a righteous man must be understood a man of moral justice, one who is willing not to wrong any man but to give everyone his due. And by a good man, a bountiful man, a man of a kind spirit, by goodness sometimes is meant holiness, godliness, and sometimes bounty and kindness as when we speak of the goodness of God.

If we understand it in this sense, the meaning of the apostle is this—that men will scarcely die for someone, though that other is a righteous man. He has always done fairly by him and never injured or did him any hurt. Yet possibly some would even die for one who not only never did them hurt but have been good to them. Those whom they have received a great deal of kindness from and lie under special obligation. And this is the utmost that men's love extends to, agreeable to what Christ says in John 15:13, "Greater love hath no man than this, that a man lay down his life for his friends."

Or else we may understand a righteous man and good in the text as synonymous terms and signifying the same thing and both in opposition to ungodly and sinners that it is here said that Christ died for. And so the word is changed from "righteous" to "good" only for sake of elegance of speech. And then the sense of the apostle is this—that none have scarcely ever gone so far as to lay down their lives for good and righteous men, let them be persons of never so good and excellent dispositions. But it may be sometimes the love of men has gone so far. But Christ died for those who were the reverse of righteous and good. He died for ungodly and sinners. The apostle herein takes notice of one instance wherein the love of Christ transcends all the love of men one to another.

DOCTRINE

There never was any love that could be as the dying love of Christ. It is that to which no love is to be compared, paralleled with the dying love of Christ. Never was any love of any other being, never the love of any creature to be compared with this love. The love of God in giving his Son to die, 'tis the love of the same being though not of the same person as it is equally great and wonderful. But we speak now of the love of other beings.

However great and wonderful the love of one creature to another has been in some instances, yet there has been no instance that has been any way to be compared with this. There is often a very strong affection in parents towards their children. There was a great love in

Jacob to Joseph. When he thought Joseph was dead, he rent his clothes and put sackcloth on his loins and mourned for his son many days. And when all his sons and his daughters rose up to comfort him, he refused to be comforted and said, "For I will go down into the grave unto my son mourning" (Gen. 37:35).

So very wonderful was the love of David to his son Absalom, though Absalom had been so wicked and rebellious, though he had murdered another of his sons, though he rebelled against his father and drove him away, though he set up himself to be king in his stead, though he went in to his father's concubines in the top of the house in the sight of the sun and in the sight of all eyes, and though he was then seeking his father's life when he himself was killed. Yet when David heard the news, he was deeply affected by it: "The king was much moved, and went up to the chamber over the gate, and wept: and as he went, thus he said, O my son Absalom, my son, my son Absalom! would God I had died for thee, O Absalom, my son, my son!" (2 Sam. 18:33).

So there sometimes is a very dear and strong affection in men or women towards those of the other sex. So very remarkable have been the instances of the love of friends of the same sex. We have a great instance of it between David and Jonathan. The soul of Jonathan was knit to the soul of David, and he loved him as his own soul. And David in his elegy testifies that his love was "passing the love of women" (2 Sam. 1:26). Jonathan's love was the more wonderful because the case between David and him was such as ordinarily causes hatred. David was his rival for the crown. The crown if it had descended hereditarily would have been Jonathan's, who was Saul's son. His father Saul hated David upon this account, but yet Jonathan thus exceedingly loved him.

And profane history gives us some such accounts of an exceeding dear love of two friends. Even so that they have greatly ventured their lives for them and lost their lives for the sake of their friend. And such instances as these are the highest that ever we read and hear of in men one towards another, agreeable to what Christ observes in John 15:13. But none of these are to be paralleled with the dying love of Jesus Christ. This love of Christ is unparalleled by any instance in the following respects.

1. Never was there love that fixed upon an object so much below the lover. Love is more remarkable and wonderful when there is every distance between the lover and the beloved. When the lover is greatly above the loved than when there is an equality amongst men. Generally those who are in condition greatly below them are neglected by them. They be not looked upon as worthy of their esteem or regard. Those who are little in comparison of them are little in their eyes, little in their thoughts. Those who are vastly below them, men look upon as inconsiderable whose friendship makes no addition to them. The love of men ordinarily seeks addition. Men set their love upon this or the other object and seek their friendship because they conceive that they shall be added to by their friendship. They neglect those who are greatly below them, as thinking that they are so little in comparison of them that they with them shall not be added to. Those men who are great in the world in high estate ordinarily neglect the mean and low. If they take notice of them, it is far from being in any such way as taking them into their friendship or setting their love upon them.

Men may sometimes set their hearts upon an object that is much below them but then 'tis because they think they see something in them that is not so much below. There is but one thing in any being that can influence him to set his love upon an object greatly below him and that is conceived of as such in all respects by the lover—and that is goodness, a man's good disposition. The heart of anyone who does so let him be who he will must abound with goodness.

If a great prince should love a poor man's child under some calamity and should pity it and lay himself out greatly for its relief and there should be all signs of its being only from mere goodness and compassion, would not this be looked upon as wonderful? But if it should be so that a noble prince should from goodness and benevolence exceedingly love and pity one far inferior, what is the superiority of one man above another to the superiority of the Son of God to us? The difference that may be between man and man may be great as to outward circumstances. There may be many accidental differences, but their nature is the same. A poor child has the same human nature as a prince. In many things there is an equality between a poor child and a prince. Yea, the child may be superior.

But Jesus Christ is infinitely above us in nature, he being of a divine nature. There is no distance of nature between man and man, but between God and man there is an infinite distance of nature—a greater distance than there is between the nature of men and the nature of worms. There is a greater distance between the Son of God and us than there is between the earth and the highest star in the heavens.

The Son of God was every way infinitely above us. Consider him with respect to his nature, with respect to his duration. Consider him with respect to all the properties of his nature, natural and moral excellencies. Consider with respect to honor and the respect of his Father. Consider him with respect to his dominion and sovereignty over the creatures. Consider him with respect to his works. He it is who has made the world; who has made sun, moon and stars; who made man; who made the highest heavens; and who made the angels of heaven. Consider him in his importance in the universality of things. He is the last end of all things. All things are made by him, and for him and by him all things consist. Consider him with respect to the honor and respect of the creatures. He is worshiped and adored by the angels of heaven and will be to all eternity.

Therefore, if we consider the dying love of Jesus Christ in this respect, there never was any love like unto it. Never was there any instance of such a stoop made by any lover. What are we, that one in such a height of glory and dignity should set his love upon us? Job 7:17 says, "What is man, that thou shouldest magnify him? and that thou shouldest set thine heart upon him?"

2. Never was there any instance of such love to those who were so far from being capable of benefiting the lover. There is amongst men but little disinterested love in those instances of great friendship that we have account of. In any story self-interest has some influence in the matter. The lover looks upon the beloved as one capable and fitted to contribute to his benefit. And a respect to himself is partly at least the spring of love and very commonly is the first mover.

Love in men ordinarily is from want, from the indigence of nature. It seeks that in others which it hath not in itself. The beloved is looked upon as one fitted to supply the wants and satisfy the cravings of its nature. But Jesus Christ is and always was above want. 'Tis impossible he should stand in need of anything. He had a fullness incapable of any addition. He possessed a treasure that could not be enlarged. He was from eternity perfectly happy in the enjoyment of the Father. Nothing that the creature can do can in the least add to his happiness. His blessedness is infinite and invariable.

Men are capable of benefiting one another. The case may be so that the meanest man, a little child, may benefit a prince. The case may be so that the greatest man in the world may stand in need of the help of a beggar. But our goodness extendeth not to Christ. If all the men in the world were never so united and so ardent in their love to Christ that they could add one mite unto him, it is as much impossible for us to add to the happiness of Jesus Christ as it is for us to add to the light of the sun and much further from being possible.

What need can one who infinitely enjoys God the Father and his love meet in him? What good can we do him? Christ is not dependent upon us or any creature. He gives unto all life and breath and all things. How can Christ be in any indigence or want of those whom he has created and who have their beings and their all from him? We can't give Jesus Christ anything that shall enrich him in any wise. We have no money, no price, no presents to offer him. Alas, we are poor beggars ourselves, and all we have we are dependent on his grace for.

Men's love generally is from want and because they be not sufficiently happy in themselves. But on the contrary, Christ's love is from fullness. Men's love seeks an addition to fill up their emptiness. But Christ's love is from his fullness and because he is so full that he overflows. Man's love adds something to himself, but Christ's love only seeks communication.

3. Never was there any who set his love upon those in whom he saw so much filthiness and deformity. Never any who loved those in whom they saw so little to attract their love. And so much to repel it and to procure hatred. Parents oftentimes have a natural affection to those children who are very unworthy and may love those who are undeserving from the natural propensity that is in men to love their own. Though ordinarily where there is a strong affection, men imagine they see that which is lovely, though indeed there be not anything.

When men love unless it be when they love from a principle of grace and from the influence of the Spirit of Christ upon their hearts to cause an imitation of him. I say otherwise when they love 'tis from something that they see that attracts their love—either some kindness or goodwill to them or something that is thought lovely, whether it is really so or no. But this is from the scantiness of that principle of love in their hearts.

There is such a fullness of love in the heart of Jesus Christ that it flows out towards those objects that have nothing to draw. The motive is within him. It seems it needs nothing to attract it. There is a sufficient spring in Christ's own heart to set it going. There is an overflowing benevolence that extends to those who have no beauty or excellency. Men, unless through the supernatural influence of the Spirit of Christ, have no notion of any such thing as being in love with those in whom they see nothing in the object to excite their love. But the dying love of Christ had no excellency to attract it. Man in his fallen state has nothing that is good in him. When he sinned, he lost all the beauty of his nature. Natural men may have somethings that appear amiable in the sight of men but nothing that is so in the sight of God, who sees things as they are.

Many of those things that are lovely in the sight of men are abominable in the sight of God (Luke 16:15). And as fallen man is destitute of all that was lovely, so he was full of all deformity. There is a filthy, a beastly, and a devilish nature that reigns in the hearts of natural men.

Jesus Christ, when he passed by us, saw us naked and loathesome. He might justly have turned away from us with abhorrence, have left us in our filth, stood at a distance from us as abominating to have anything to do with them who were so filthy. But it was otherwise; the time was a time of love. Instead of the lovely image of God, there was the foul image of Satan that appeared upon us. Corruption was our nature that was more odious in the eyes of Christ than the nature of a toad or serpent is to us. Natural men are like vipers. Their poison is as the poison of a serpent and as the venom of asps.

Men by sin became like a pig that delights to wallow in the mire. They are like a filthy worm that never feeds so sweetly as when feeding on carrion and never has its nature so suited as when crawling in the most abominable filth. In fallen men for whom Christ died, there were predominant all sensual and earthly disposition. A nature prone to sensual impurity and debased nature and yet a most abominable pride and haughtiness of spirit, an inclinedness to injustice and to those things that are in themselves most unreasonable.

And Christ saw all this deformity that was in their hearts. Men may set their love upon those who are very hateful because they are ignorant of them. They don't know what is in them. But Christ perfectly knew all our filthiness. The corruption of the heart of man was all naked and open to his view. And all the hateful actions of men—all their actual wickedness—was well known by him. Men may love those who are very wicked because they don't hate wickedness, but there is nothing so hateful to men as sin is to Christ. It is as contrary as possible to the divine nature, to the nature of the Son of God. Yet was Christ pleased to set his love upon them and to die for them.

4. Never was there anyone who set his love upon those who were so far from loving him and so unreasonably averse to him as Jesus Christ in his dying love to sinners. Men in their fallen state are the enemies of God and Jesus Christ. Nothing is more the nature or natural disposition of man as he is in a natural condition, than it is to hate God. He hates Christ and can do no other than hate him. Romans 8:7 says, "The carnal mind is enmity against God: for it is not subject to the law of God, neither indeed can be." Every natural man has a mortal enmity against Christ as well as the Jews who crucified him. And this Christ knew when he was pleased to set his love upon them.

This enmity is the more provoking because it was so infinitely unreasonable. We had no reason to have a spirit of enmity against Christ. He never had done us any wrong. On the contrary, all the blessings and benefits we receive are from him. Sinners have a spirit of enmity against him, though he is infinitely excellent and amiable. There are all possible lovely qualifications in him. Though he be the infinitely beloved of God, yet he is hated of men. Sinners had no delight in the excellency of Christ that God the Father so delights in.

Yea, that very excellency is what he is hated for. He is hated for his holiness.

Yea, such is the enmity that was in them so rooted and fixed and strong that Christ's dying love won't change them. This Christ knew when he set his love upon them and undertook to die for them. He knew that their enmity against him was such that they would have no gratitude. They would not be at all moved by his dying love. They would be so obstinate that they would not cast away their enmity 'til their wills were changed by his own mighty power.

And Christ knew that they had a spirit of contempt towards him, that they would slight and despise him. He knew that they had all such a spirit as the Jews and soldiers who spit upon him and mocked and derided him. He knew that they had such a spirit that when he was offered to them with all his benefits he should be slighted 'til their hearts were changed.

Never was any who loved those from whom they received such provoking wrongs and affronts as God did from sinners. They had disobeyed his commands, rebelled against him, cast his law behind their backs. Absalom had been guilty of exceeding great wrong to his father David but not equal to the wrong that sinners have done to God. Sinners violate infinitely greater obligations in sinning against God than Absalom did in sinning against his father. And then there was this difference: When he first set his love upon Absalom, David did not behold him with his unworthiness, as Christ did when he set his love on sinners: "For scarcely for a righteous man will one die: yet peradventure for a good man some would even dare to die. But God commendeth his love toward us, in that, while we were yet sinners, Christ died for us" (Rom. 5:7–8).

5. There never was any love that appeared in so great and wonderful expressions. Expressions of love are of three kinds: declarations, doings, and sufferings. The declarations of Christ's love

to his church in Scripture are wonderful, but deeds and sufferings are the principal expressions of love. And there is nothing in the declarations which Christ has made of his love in his Word, but the same is evident in what he has done and suffered for his people and that more abundantly.

What Christ has done for his people and the love which he has shown them is very wonderful. Never any who showed his love to another by doing so much for them as Christ has done. His love was such to his elect that he came down from heaven. He left the bosom of the Father. He laid aside his glory and came down to dwell on earth. He became incarnate. He took upon him another nature. It was a good thing for God to do, to take upon himself the nature of men. There never was so great and remarkable a thing done by any lover for his beloved.

It was a great thing that Christ should come to dwell amongst men—that he should so love us as to take up an abode amongst us for above thirty years as he did. But I shall not insist upon these things because the doctrine doesn't so immediately lead to the consideration of the doings of Christ for his people as his sufferings for the dying love of Christ that we are speaking of and will lay down this proposition.

There never was any in any other lover so great an expression of love as the sufferings of Christ. Expense and suffering for anyone is the greatest testimony of love. If one person bestows a great deal on another and does much for him, yet if it be without any kind of expense or suffering to self, it is not so great an expression of love, nor doth it show so great love. To be at any great expense of money or good for another—especially so as considerably to suffer in estate by it—is looked upon as a remarkable kindness to go through many hardships and endure great fatigues of body for another. To redeem one out of captivity and from any great calamity would also be looked upon as a kindness that laid a great obligation on the beloved. And 'tis a yet far greater expression of love if any should freely lose his life and be at the expense of his blood for them. Thus far perhaps, some earthly lovers have gone.

But there never was any who suffered so much for any earthly friend as Christ did. Whether we consider what he suffered outwardly or in his soul, there never was any instance of anyone who suffered so much outwardly for any man as Christ. History gives us accounts of some who have greatly ventured their lives in war for their dear friend and lost their lives. But whenever was it heard of that one man was willing to be put to a cruel, tormenting, lingering death for his neighbor and of his free will actually did it. But this Christ did. His death was a very cruel sort of death. Those lingering torments that Christ suffered would have overcome all merely human love. There never was any love of one man to another so strong that it would have been carried through such a kind of death.

Men in a pang of affection and pity might think that they were even willing to die for another, but Christ had purposed it of old. He came and was born into this world on purpose. Here he lived above thirty years in expectation of it, all the while looking and waiting 'til his time came that he should drink the bitter cup. So steady and strong was his love that he never repented it. And when death approached, though the expectation had the like effects upon him as the expectation of such a dreadful suffering would have had upon others in the same human nature, the thought of it was very terrible to him. Yet the terror did not overcome his love. And when he was actually feeling the pains of the cross, those strong pains—though they overcame his nature and killed him—yet they did not overcome his love.

His death, besides the painfulness of it, was attended with those circumstances that greatly aggravated the suffering. Christ suffered much outwardly just before his death. He was scourged and wounded with thorns and buffeted in the face by soldiers, treated most igno-miniously. He was spit upon and mocked and most contemptuously treated, and his death was most disgraceful. And besides what he suf-fered in his body, he suffered more in his soul. Sufferings of soul and body were united together. If he had suffered only in his body, his spirit might have helped him to support his outward pains, but he had darkness in his mind as well as pain in his body. He was smitten of God. God laid upon him the iniquities of us all.

How great his inward sufferings were we may conclude by the greatness of them before his crucifixion in his agony in the garden. We are none of us acquainted with such a degree of sorrow and anguish of spirit as shall cause such an effect. The trouble and sorrows of his soul were as much of the nature of the torments of hell as an innocent, holy person was capable of.

The sufferings of Christ were a greater expression and evidence of love for his being so great a person. If Christ had suffered no more than some other lovers have suffered for their friends, yet his suffer-ing would have been a more wonderful expression of love. 'Tis a greater thing for a person of such glory and dignity to suffer than for a lesser. 'Tis a greater thing for a person who is God to die than for a mere worm of the dust to die. 'Tis a more marvelous expression of love for a divine person to lay down his life and spill his blood. This is a greater expense than for a mere man. A mere man has not so great a price to expend his blood, is of small value in comparison of it.

If an earthly king should spill his blood for a poor man, it would be looked upon as a greater expense than if another poor man had done so, because his blood has more worth. Though this be indeed but a faint similitude to represent the difference between the value of the life and blood of the Son of God and that of mere man. If a mere man had suffered a hundred times so much as Christ did for the sake of some person whom he loved, it would not have been so great a thing, so wonderful a testimony of love, as for Christ to suffer as he did.

Who could have imagined that ever such a testimony should be given of God's love to a creature. Without doubt it was surprising to the angels when it was first revealed to them. It was a thing unknown and never would have been conceived of, had not God revealed it, that God, that a divine person should testify of his love by suffering, much less by such suffering. It was a more wonderful testimony of love that Christ should lay down his life for man, than if God had created a world for a particular man and had given it all to him.

But that we may be aware of how unparalleled this love to sinners appearing in this expression of it is, we should lay this and the former particulars together. We have observed already that never any set their love below him, but how much less was there ever any who set his love upon one so far below him to such a degree, did ever any after such a manner express his love to one so inferior to him. We observed before that there never was an instance of a lover who set his love upon one so far from benefiting him, but how much more beyond all parallel is it that Christ loved those who were so far from being capable of being any benefit to him, as to suffer so much for him!

So was there ever any like instance of any person being at such cost and expense for another out of love to him, who was so far from having anything in him lovely and than did so much deserve the hatred instead of the love of the lover? Was there ever any instance of a person's laying down his life and suffering so tormenting, lingering death for them who hated and were his enemies and had a natural aversion to him? If we put all things together and rightly consider them, the dying love of Christ will appear altogether matchless. As much as the heavens are above the earth.

And lastly, never was there any love that was so beneficial to the beloved. True love is fruitful. It always seeks the benefit and advantage of the beloved. And will procure it if there be opportunity. But there is no other instance of love that in this respect is to be equaled or compared with this. The love of men one to another in many instances may have been greatly to the advantage. Parents' love to their children may be very beneficial to them. Princes' love to their favorites may be an occasion of their advancement to honor and wealth. Men through their love to others may have brought out of low, miserable, and distressed circumstances, may be redeemed out of captivity, freed from cruel bondage and from a tormenting death, to the honor, health, and pleasure, but no such advantage that the dying love of Christ is of, to those who are the objects of it.

For by means of Christ's dying love, they are rescued from eternal destruction. They are saved out of the furnace of fire. The deliverance of Shadrach, Meshech, and Abednego out of Nebuchadnezzar's burning fiery furnace by the love of Christ, who himself came into that furnace to deliver them, is a type of his dying love whereby he delivers sinners from the furnace of hellfire (see Dan. 3:14–28). Sinners by means of the dying love of Christ are rescued out of the power of the devil, that roaring lion that seeks to devour souls as David delivered the lamb out of the mouth of the lion and the bear. They are rescued from a destruction a thousand times more dreadful than being torn in pieces by wild beasts and being devoured by serpents.

And by the dying love of Christ, those who are beloved by him are advanced to the greatest blessedness to the possession of a glorious kingdom, to the wearing of a crown of glory, to the seeing of God and fully enjoying of him to all eternity.

By the dying love of Christ, they are delivered from the foulest deformity and are now made and fashioned according to the image of God, having the brightness of God's holiness reflected from them. None knows the worth and sweetness of those things which Christ will give those for whom he died as tokens of his love. And what he has purchased by his death, the value of them is proportionable to the value of that price that was paid for them. The blood of Christ purchased things that can't be purchased for gold. Neither can silver be weighed for the price of them. And what makes the worth of them infinite is that they never will have an end. There will be no danger or possibility of losing them.

APPLICATION

The improvement I would make of this doctrine of the unparalleled love of Jesus Christ is to move and excite all who bear the name of Christians to love the Lord Jesus Christ. If the love of Christ is such that there never was any that could be paralleled with it, then if we don't love Christ, our ingratitude and baseness will be as unparalleled as his love. Such love as this should be enough to overpower and dissolve the most ungrateful and hard heart. Every particular that has been mentioned shows the unparalleled wonderfulness of the love of Christ to men, so it lays an unspeakable obligation upon us to love.

That one so great, so high, and so full and self-sufficient and happy and holy should set his love upon us so low and despicable, so impotent and unprofitable, so unlovely and deformed and who so injured and provoked him and who yet so hated him. That he should pity us under the calamities that were our just deserts that by our own wickedness and provocation had brought ourselves into, that such a thing should enter into his heart as being tormented to death for us. That we might be delivered from our just shame and from our distressed condition and might be brought to undeserved honor and blessedness in the enjoyment of him will surely be enough to move and draw our hearts, if we haven't hearts like the hearts of devils for ingratitude and baseness. But I will offer some things further in motive to this duty of loving the Lord Jesus Christ.

1. Let it be considered how much more cause we have to love Christ than he had to love us. We were under a necessity of his love that we could not do without if he had not loved men. It would have been better for them if they had never been born, but he was under no obligation to love us. He might have neglected—yea, he might have hated—us forever without being unjust, without the least disparagement to his holiness and divine glory. There was no reason why he should love us but his own mere good pleasure, but the case is not so with us. We are obliged in justice to love him by all the strongest bonds that can be.

Christ loved us when we were infinitely below him, and shall not we love him who is infinitely above us? Especially now he is come down from his height to us and equalized himself with us that we may be the more in the way of our love. It was a great humbling of himself for Christ to love such as we. It was descending from the highest height. But if we love Jesus Christ, we shall therein ascend our affections. We will be exalted to the most honorable object that possibly they can be fixed upon. It is a great honor that Christ does us that he is ready to accept our love. We were so little and inconsiderable that there was no proportion between us and the respect of Christ, for we were so small and so much below him. But the disproportion is as great but the right reverse with respect to our love and Christ—he is so much above it.

Christ loved us when he could receive no addition by us if we are added to him. He is not the greater or the better, for he is infinite and all-sufficient and can't be added to, though he is graciously pleased, having set his love upon us not to look upon himself complete. But if we love Jesus Christ, it will be on the contrary exceedingly. If we love him and he be ours, we shall not only be added to, but we shall be made. We shall come out of nothing into being. It will be a far greater exaltation than if we were from beggars turned to potent monarchs.

Christ loved us when we were utterly incapable of benefiting Christ. Our love could be no benefit to him. But 'tis the reverse with respect to us if we love Christ. He is so able to benefit us as he is able to do all things for us that we do or can need or desire. Christ stood in no need of us, but we do stand in necessity of Christ. There never was any who gained so much by their choice of the object of their love as men do when they choose Christ and set their love upon him.

Christ loved us when there was no loveliness to draw his love. There was nothing attractive to be seen in us. All was repulsive. We had nothing amiable or any way desirable in us. All was abominable to his pure eyes. But Christ has infinite loveliness to win and draw our love. He is the brightness of God's glory. He is the bright and morning star in the spiritual firmament. He is more excellent than the angels of heaven. He is amongst them for amiable and divine beauty, as the sun is among the stars. In beholding his beauty, the angels do day and night entertain and feast their souls and in celebrating of it do they continually employ their praises. Nor yet have the songs of angels ever declared all the excellency of Jesus Christ, for it is beyond their songs and beyond the thoughts of those bright intelligencies to reach it. That blessed society above has been continually employed in this work of meditating on and describing the beauty and amiableness of the Son of God, but they have never yet nor ever will comprehend it or fully declare it.

His excellency is such that beholding and enjoying of it will yield a soul-satisfying delight. There will be more delight and pleasure in one hour than this world with all that it has can afford in seventy years. Yea, if it won't afford more in a minute or second of time, it won't be from want of excellency or beauty but from want of power perfectly to behold it. It won't be from scantiness in the object but from the scantiness of the capacity of him who beholds and enjoys.

Christ set his love upon us who had never done anything to gain his love. We did not show any love to him, and indeed we had none but instead of that had enmity against him. But 'tis contrary with respect to us. He has done much for us. He has been merciful and gracious to us exceedingly. We never did anything for him. Yet he loved us, and he has done great and wonderful things for us.

2. Consider that from the greatness and wonderfulness of Christ's love we may be assured that our love will be accepted. There is this encouragement for us to make choice of Christ and set our love upon him, if Christ has so loved men as to suffer so much for them. There is no danger of their not being accepted in their love to him. It won't be looked upon by Christ as too much boldness for us to choose him for our beloved.

3. Christ is an importunate suitor for our love. Agreeable to his other condescension in dying for sinners, he also condescends to woo them, to invite them to come to him, and to yield their hearts to him. He knocks at the door of their hearts. Song of Solomon 5:2 says, "It is the voice of my beloved that knocketh, saying, Open to me . . . for my head is filled with dew, and my locks with the drops of the night." Revelation 3:20 says, "Behold, I stand at the door, and knock." Christ has sent forth his ministers for this purpose in his stead, to beseech men to close with him and yield to his suit. He invites those who thirst to come unto him and to receive the great blessings which he has purchased for them, to come buy wine and milk without money and without price, to come that their souls may delight themselves in fatness.

Thus Christ woos the hearts of sinners from sabbath to sabbath. He repeats his calls and invitations and the gifts of providence, which are means to allure them. Christ woos men by the blessings of his common providence, when he gives them outward comforts and enjoyments of one kind or other.

Hearken therefore unto Christ Jesus. It will be strange if all he does and all he says will have no impression upon you to draw your heart. When he calls, rise up and joyfully receive him. Don't let the door of your heart continue barred and your soul shut up against your Savior.

4. Consider that to live in love to the Lord Jesus Christ is the way to live the most pleasant life in the world. That will be the way to enjoy sweet communion with Jesus Christ. It is the most delightful entertainment to the soul to spiritually view the beauties and glories of such a beloved. It is a pleasant exercise to have the heart going forth in love to such a blessed one. And pleasant is it to receive the testimonies of his love. His love is better than wine. The King will bring those who love him into his chambers, and they shall be glad and rejoice in him and remember his love more than wine. Christ is the apple tree amongst the trees of the wood under whose shadow the saints may sit.

5. There is this encouragement also for us to set our love upon Christ—that if we do, he is willing to be enjoyed by us as fully as the soul can desire or is capable of. Amongst men, those who are great and noble, they are of the way of the mean and ordinary kind of people. There is scarcely any such thing as a peasant falling in love with a princess because he doesn't look upon such a thing as possible that he should ever come to the enjoyment of such as are so much above him.

But Christ, though he be so much higher than the highest, yet is willing to be freely and fully enjoyed by us poor, mortal men. He stands ready to honor us so much as to admit us into his society and conversation. To admit us to be his friends and companions and communicate himself freely and fully to us. There shall be no restraints, but those who love him may enjoy him in the utmost liberty and fullness. Christ came and took upon him our nature partly for this purpose—that he might be nearer to us and we might be under greater advantages most familiarly to enjoy. None can tell the intimacy with which believers enjoy Christ in the heavenly world.

18

In True Conversion Men's Bodies Are in Some Respect Changed as Well as Their Souls

And the very God of peace sanctify you wholly; and I pray God your whole spirit and soul and body be preserved blameless unto the coming of our Lord Jesus Christ.

1 THESSALONIANS 5:23

The thrust of this sermon, preached in July 1740, is that the Scriptures teach that not only the soul but also the body became the subject of corruption by the Fall. In a similar way, upon conversion, which is a restoration of that corruption, the body experiences change just as the soul does.

The sermon manuscript is a typical duodecimal booklet, consisting of twenty-four leaves with some evidence of damage. In the body of the sermon there is some evidence of deletions, additions, and corrections in Edwards's own hand, but nothing on the scale of a major rework of the sermon as a whole. The application consists of eight pages.

These words are a benediction that the apostle Paul gives the Christian Thessalonians with which he concludes many excellent precepts and counsels that he had given them in this benediction as may be observed.

1. Whom he wills the blessing from. The very God of peace, or as his words might have been rendered, the God of peace himself. The apostle had been earnestly exhorting them to holiness, urging of them in the foregoing verses to pray without ceasing, not to quench the Spirit, to hold fast that which was good and abstain from all appearance of evil. But he, though so great an apostle, could not make them holy. He could but counsel them and urge them to it, but God alone could make them holy. God is here spoken of as the God of peace, probably because of the holiness that the apostle had been exhorting them to esteem very much in love and peace. First Thessalonians 5:13 says, "And be at peace among yourselves." Verses 14–15 say, "Be patient toward all men. See that none render evil for evil towards any man; but ever follow that which is good, both among yourselves, and to all men." And when the apostle wishes them the blessing from the God of peace, it is with such emphasis: "the very God of peace" himself. It was a much greater thing for God to bless than for man, for whom he blesses is blessed indeed.

2. We observe the blessing itself that the apostle wishes to them, which is that they may be entirely holy or holy in every part.

The first part of the blessing is that they might be made holy. "The very God of peace sanctify you." That word *sanctify* as it is used in Scripture is of extensive signification. Sometimes it signifies making holy as persons. Or things may be sanctified or set apart to a holy use, whereby they may be said in a sense to become holy things. Thus God is said to have sanctified and hallowed the sabbath. He has set it apart for our holy use. So Moses is said to have sanctified Aaron and his sons when they were set apart to the priestly office. So the tabernacles and vessels thereof were set to be sanctified.

Sometimes by being sanctified is meant the same as being converted or saved from sin to holiness. So that to sanctify is meant the same thing as to make saints of them, as in Acts 26:18: "To open their eyes, and to turn them from darkness to light, and from the power of Satan unto God, that they may receive forgiveness of sins, and inheritance among them which are sanctified by faith that is in me." First Corinthians 1:2 says, "Unto the church of God which is at Corinth, to them that are sanctified in Christ Jesus, called to be saints." So the word seems most commonly to be used in this way in the New Testament. Sometimes the word signifies a carrying on the work of God in the heart, making holy in further degrees. So Christ prayed for his church in John 17:17: "Sanctify them through thy truth: thy word is truth." The word in the text probably is so used as to intend both those last two things, both making holy at once and making more holy by a progressive work of the Spirit. But if it be understood one only, it is most natural to understand of the former—making holy at conversion because the words that follow have respect to what is after conversion.

The second part of the blessing the apostle wishes them is that they may be kept holy as in the words, "Be preserved blameless unto the coming of our Lord Jesus Christ." And in both these—in both being made holy and kept holy—the apostle writes that they may be entirely holy, or holy in every part. This is expressed two ways: (1) By the use of the universal term, *wholly*, and (2) by mentioning their several parts.

There are three parts mentioned—the spirit, the soul, and the body. Here is a distinction made between the spirit and the soul, as there also is in Hebrews 4:12: "For the word of God is quick, and powerful, and sharper than any two-edged sword, piercing even to the dividing asunder of soul and spirit, and of the joints and marrow, and is a discerner of the thoughts and intents of the heart." By the spirit seems to be meant what belongs to the faculty of the will, including the tongue, the disposition and affections of the mind, as in Ephesians 4:23. Even as we now oftentimes use the word when we say such a one is of a good spirit or of an ill spirit. We mean of a good or ill disposition. By the soul is intended what appertains to the other faculty of the understanding, including the apprehension, thoughts, judgment, and reason.

But what I would more especially observe is that not only the two faculties of the mind are mentioned, but the body also is the subject of that holiness which men have blessing of God upon them in their being made holy and kept holy.

DOCTRINE

In true conversion men's bodies are in some respects changed as well as their souls. In speaking to this doctrine, I will mention some things that make the doctrine evident and show in what respect the body is changed in true conversion.

First, I would mention some things that make it evident that not only the soul but also the body is in some respect changed on conversion. The text is very full to the purpose, but the Scriptures supply us with other evidences of the same thing.

1. The Scriptures represent the body as well as the soul as being in some respect the subject of the corruption of nature by the Fall. When man fell, he became totally corrupt in every part, in body as well as soul. So the apostle Paul, speaking in the third chapter of Romans of that corruption that all wicked by nature are the subjects of and to show how they are totally corrupt, mentions the several parts or members of their body—their throats, tongues, lips, mouths, and feet: "Their throat is an open sepulcher; with their tongues they have used

deceit; the poison of asps is under their lips: whose mouth is full of cursing and bitterness: their feet are swift to shed blood" (Rom. 3:13–15). So wicked men's eyes are spoken of as full of sin. Second Peter 2:14 says, "Having eyes full of adultery, and that cannot cease from sin." So we read of an evil eye in Proverbs 23:6 and 28:22. So we read of the lust of the flesh and the lust of the eyes in 1 John 2:16. So also we read of an uncircumcised ear in Acts 7:51.

The apostle James speaks of the tongue as being a fire, a world of iniquity, the defiler of the whole body (James 3:6). The tongue, and the rest of the body, is spoken of being the subject of sinful defilement, as it also is in 1 Corinthians 3:16, where the apostle tells us that our bodies are the temple of God and means as we live we display this temple of God. And so we often read of wicked hands in Scripture (Acts 2:23) as well as unclean, impure hearts (Gen. 6:5).

Now sure it is so that our whole man, the body as well as the soul are changed by the Fall and become corrupt. Doubtless the whole is renewed in conversion, for conversion is a restoring of man from that corrupt state into which he fell or at least is the beginning of such a restoration. When a man is converted, the restoration is begun of all that was corrupted by the Fall.

2. Christ died that the body as well as the soul might be saved. Therefore, the salvation of both is begun when a man is brought home to Christ. In the state that man was brought to by Adam, so the body was brought as well as the soul. The body was liable to death as well as the soul. By Christ the body is saved and glorified, for by Christ comes the glorious reformation of the body: "For since by man came death, by man came also the resurrection of the dead. For as in Adam all die, even so in Christ shall all be made alive" (1 Cor. 15:21–22). And nothing of man is saved but by being brought home to Christ and united to him when union is begun in effectual calling or conversion. Then the body as well as the soul is redeemed. Therefore, the body is

then sanctified as well as the soul. The body is hereafter to be glorified as well as the soul. All that is the subject of glorification is also the subject of conversion and sanctification, but sanctification is the beginning of glorification. Grace is the dowry, the firstfruits of glory.

3. The Scriptures often represent the change that is wrought in conversion as being a renewing of the whole man. The old man is first to be put off and the new man put on, as stated in Colossians 3:9–10: "Ye have put off the old man with his deeds; and have put on the new man, which is renewed in knowledge after the image of him that created him." Here the conversion of man is plainly compared to the creation of man. When man was at first created in the image of God, it was not only a soul but a body that was created. All that was created at first when God created Adam is found in conversion, which is a new creation. That is said, for example, in 2 Corinthians 5:17: "Therefore if any man be in Christ, he is a new creature: old things are passed away; behold, all things are become new." In a sense his old body is passed away, and he possesses a new body as well as a new soul.

So the old man is said to be past and the new one put on in Ephesians 4:22–24. So in conversion the old man is said to be crucified with Christ (Rom. 6:6). And Christians, being called new creatures, plainly shows the same thing. When man is born, the whole man is the subject of what then comes to pass. The whole man receives being in the first conception and birth. And so is it in the new birth. The whole man is involved, so is he born again, and he becomes a newborn (1 Pet. 2:2).

4. Particular members of the body are spoken of in Scripture as being renewed in conversion as particularly. So that he is unconverted (Isa. 6:10). And God gives them clean hands as well as a pure heart (Ps. 24:4). And so in Christ's miracles, which were types of conversion. Christ sometimes restored wicked hands and healed defects of the tongue and of the feet, so that the lame leaped as a hart and the tongue

of the dumb sing whereby was signified into the world to renew those members of his body.

Now I will explain this matter and show in what respects the body is changed in conversion.

Negatively. I don't suppose there is any immediate change made in the constitution of the body. I don't know of any ground that we may have from any of these places of Scripture that have been mentioned, to suppose any such thing as that there is some immediate work of God upon the body in conversion altering the form of the body or changing the temperament of the blood or other juices of the body or anything of that nature. It seems to be a false notion that some have had of the corruption of nature, as though it originally consisted in a depraving of the constitution of the body. Adam, when he sinned, had the nature of his body poisoned by the forbidden fruit that he ate and thereby his bodily appetites that before were mediate became extreme, and so the body infected the soul and made that corrupted. It thus would be reasonable to suppose that the renewal of nature in creatures was also originally a work of God upon the body, satisfying the depravity and expelling the poison of that and so mediating the appetites of the body. For doubtless the restoration of nature in one sense began where the corruption of it began—in the Fall of man.

But the cause of the corruption of nature is quite contrary. It doesn't begin in the body and so proceed from thence to infect the soul, but it goes to the very root. It begins in the soul and from thence infects the body. And so it is in sanctification the immediate work of God in sanctifying and renewing the nature is upon the soul. There the renovation begins and goes from thence to the body. The renovation of the body in conversion does not at all consist of any work of God on the flesh or blood or constitution. There is no other alteration in the body in conversion than only what is the natural and necessary senses of the influence and gracious act which the soul has over the body. All

Scripture tells us that the depraving and renewing of the nature of man begins with the heart and proceeds from thence to the members of the body, to the eyes and the mouth and the hands and onwards.

Affirmatively. The change that is made in the body is in the appetites and acts of the body. They change the influence of the new dispositions of the soul.

1. Those appetites of the body that before governed and bore rule are now restored and kept under. They are new and bright and subject to the Spirit and to the love of God. 'Tis by what is said of the appetites of the body that sin is said to reign in our mortal bodies before conversion. Romans 6:12 says, "Let not sin therefore reign in your mortal body, that ye should obey it in the lusts thereof." After conversion are those faculties kept under, as the apostle says of himself in 1 Corinthians 9:27: "But I keep under my body, and bring it into subjection: lest that by any means, when I have preached to others, I myself should be a castaway." And the convert doesn't only restore the appetites' faculties of the body by voluntarily appeasing and denying those appetites. But also those appetites are lessened and brought lower by his appetites' being infused into the soul.

'Tis the nature of man that the more one desires or inclination prevails and swallows up the more, the more the heart is taken off from other inclinations. The soul can't have several inclinations of a very diverse, very intense nature, and at least they can't be in vehement act at the same time. That which is very vehement employs and takes up the heart and doesn't leave room for things of a diverse nature. Thus when the soul is in very lively exercise of the love of God, there will not be very strong actings or bodily appetites at the same time. Even men's ordinary meat and drink at such times is often very much forgotten. Thus the saints are said to "mortify" the members of their bodies in Colossians 3:5.

2. The change of the body consists of the change of the acts and behavior of the body. Sometimes a remarkable change occurs in the outward actions and deportment of the man. He has the air of Christian sobriety and solidity, humility, and meekness instead of that light, vain, carnal, and grand air that he had before.

But the acts of the body that I have shown regard to, as that wherein the change of the body mainly consist is in the new improvement the soul makes of the members of the body after conversion. The soul employs the body in a new manner, in a new work, and service. This is the change of the body that the Scriptures have main respect to, as is manifest by Romans 6:11–13.

When they are converted, men donate their bodies to a new service, to the service of God. In this sense they are said to proffer their bodies a "living sacrifice" to God: "I beseech you . . . by the mercies of God, that ye present your bodies a living sacrifice" (Rom. 12:1).

So a man before conversion was said to have an evil eye. Lustful men are said to have an eyeful of adultery but as they improve their eyes to fuel their lusts. So wicked men are said to have wicked hands and wicked tongues as they improve their tongues and hands in wickedness. So their throat is said to be an open sepulcher, their feet swift to shed blood or to go to do other wickedness.

But when they are converted, they have new tongues; their tongues are changed. Instead of backbiting, profanity, unclean or idle and malicious tattling, they now praise God. In their tongues is the law of kindness. They have new hands, clean hands. Their hands be not employed to such impure purposes as they were before but to holy purposes: to serve God, to minister to the necessities of the needy and the like.

So they have new eyes, that instead of being employed to seek the objects of their lusts are employed in reading God's holy Word and beholding the wondrous works of God. They have new ears, that instead of listening to vain talk, to loud slanderous songs, or back-bitings of others, are now attentive to things of great importance and excellency.

They have new feet, that instead of walking after worldly things do now follow after God, follow the Lamb, carry them where they may be under best advantages to do and to get good. These things are brought to pass by true conversion.

APPLICATION

Use of instruction. Hence we may learn that is a very unscriptural, lustful, and dangerous notion for any to entertain. That a man may be converted and live no better than he did before. That there must indeed be an inward change but that there is no need of any external change. Men may find out such a conversion in their own imaginations, but they don't learn it from the Scriptures. The Scriptures are a stranger to any other conversion but that which is of the whole man, wherein they are sanctified throughout in soul, body, and spirit.

If we look at many of the professors of religion and form our doctrine of conversion from what we see in them, we shall indeed be in danger of coming into such a principle that there may be a true conversion without any change of the body or any alteration in their outward behavior. But if we look off from them and look only in the Scriptures and search them, then we shall find no such thing, no conversion that is true and genuine but only that which consists in renewing the whole man, putting off the old man with his deeds and putting on the new man.

But the foundation of many false and dangerous principles that men interfere is that the way they take is not to bring men to the rule and to try them by that but to bring the rule to men and to form their notions of the rule by what they see in such as make their best of the case.

Use of examination. If it be so that in a true conversion men's bodies are changed as well as their souls, this should put such as hope they are converted in examining themselves, whether their bodies have passed under such a change as has been spoken of. In order to know that your change be genuine, you should ensure that it be universal, for a partial change is no true change.

Inquire wherein your body was corrupt before your supposed conversion. What appetites of body you chiefly prevailed and inquire whether there be any considerable alteration in that respect since your body was brought under. Do you keep it in subjection? Have you crucified the flesh with the affections and lusts? Are your governing appetites those new appetites that you received when you received your change? Does sin still reign in your mortal body? Are you still obeying it in the lusts thereof? And consider after what manner you used to employ the members of your body—your eyes, ears, tongues, and hands—in the service of sin before what you call your conversion. Then inquire how has it been since. Have you new bodies in that respect? Whereas before your conversion you used to use your ears in listening to your neighbors reproach taking delight in hearing others run down and your tongues talking against neighbors, inveighing, backbiting, venting your malice. Is there any remarkable alteration now? Have you circumcised ears and new tongues? Have you new hands whereas before worked wickedness? In scraping together all you could for yourself, is that an alteration? Are you more ready now to distribute and communicate with a liberal hand to show mercy? Or do you otherwise much more employ your hands in the service of God and your fellow creatures than you used to do?

When you have considered all things—how it was before and how it has been since and how it is now—must not your own conscience say that there is nothing considerable and remarkable of an alteration in your outward behavior in any wise worthy of being called a new body?

Use of exhortation. Put off the old man with his deeds and put on the new man. Crucify the flesh, crucify the old body, and put on a new body. I direct this exhortation both to those who never have been truly converted and so never have done it and also to those who are converted and have done it already in some measure. They had need to be exhorted to do it much more than ever yet they have done. The apostle Paul exhorts the Christian Ephesians that he had charity for those who had been savingly taught of God. Notwithstanding still to put off the old man and put on the new as you may see in Ephesians 4:22–24: "Be exhorted therefore to mortify your bodily appetites and keep under your bodies and bring them into subjection by the mercies of God, to subject your bodies a living sacrifice and whereas you have yielded your members, be exhorted to love God with new tongues and hands and in all your external behavior." Here behold the following things:

1. This will be the only way to prevent your bodies being a dour person to your soul here. Those who are kept in subjection to their bodies are in miserable slavery. They are prisoners more wretched than those who are shut up in a loathsome dungeon.

2. This will be the only way to prevent your bodies being a weight to sink you down into hell forever. The body in its unrenewed state with its corrupt appetites and lusts is a dead weight to the soul. Its lusts, its exerting itself in a manner becoming a rational creature debases the soul, pulls it down from its proper objects, and makes man like a beast. All the while the soul dwells in such a body, it sinks it lower and lower into a most guilty and miserable state. Every soul that goes out of such a body infallibly goes out of this prison into the prison of hell. It sinks down into everlasting perdition and the blackness of darkness forever.

(3) This will be the only way to save your body from being tormented forever in hell. For not only the souls of wicked men but all their bodies are in a sense corrupt, so they shall be cast into hell. Matthew 10:28 says, "Fear not them which kill the body, but are not able to kill the soul: but rather fear him which is able to destroy both soul and body in hell." Such as were unconverted in this life shall burn and fry to all eternity in a dreadful furnace of fire after the resurrection, from the crown of the head to the soles of the feet, within and without in every part full of pain and strong flames of fire of punishment and fierceness of heat. Christ teaches us that the way to have our bodies saved from the fire is to mortify its corrupt members and deny the inordinate appetites of it and to forsake the wicked use of the members of our bodies (Matt. 5:29–30).

4. By this means your bodies which have been the hold of foul spirits of soul and a cage will become the temples of God. The bodies of the saints are sanctified, and they are sanctified to this end—that they may be fitted for so holy a ghost as the Holy Ghost, that God himself may dwell in them as the tabernacle and temple of God were first cleansed and sanctified before God visibly entered into them. The more your body is sanctified, the more the appetites of it are subdued, the more its members are employed in the service of God, and the more will you have of God dwelling in you (1 Cor. 6:19–20).

5. This is a sure way to have Christ to take care for the needs of your body while you live in this world for those bodies that are sanctified do become the members of Christ. First Corinthians 6:15 says, "Know ye not that your bodies are the members of Christ?" He doubtless will take care to supply the needs of his own members. Yea, he has promised in 1 Timothy 4:8 that "godliness is profitable unto all things."

6. If your body be thus removed, it will be a kind of a reformation of the body. The body that is deserted to the service of sin is now in a state of death. 'Tis dead while alive. First Timothy 5:6 says, "She that

liveth in pleasure is dead while she liveth." But when both soul and body are sanctified, they are brought into a state of life whereby they are risen with Christ. They are now made partakers with Christ in the reformation of his body. Colossians 2:12 says, "Ye are risen with him." It will be a certain sign and a kind of a pledge of your more eternal and glorious reformation hereafter. When your body that is now sanctified shall be glorified and shall be made like unto Christ's glorious body and may be in time improved by you in service of God and used to holy purposes. The members of it being made instruments of righteousness unto holiness, it shall then be raised a spiritual body in incorruption, power, and glory to be a fit improvement of God's service. Being very fit for the use and improvement of our holy soul, it shall shine forth as the sun in the kingdom of your Father.

19

⟿ ⟾

Jesus Christ Is the Great Mediator and Head of Union in Whom All Elect Creatures in Heaven and Earth Are United to God and to One Another

> For there is one God, and one mediator between God and men,
> the man Christ Jesus.
>
> *1 TIMOTHY 2:5*

Edwards did not date this particular sermon from 1 Timothy. But the editors at Yale noted on the original manuscript that Edwards's handwriting is probably too late to be prior to 1733. Perhaps it should be dated in the middle 1730s.

Edwards is not so much concerned in this sermon to describe what a mediator does but why Christ was the most fit person to be a mediator between God and men.

Christ is the most fit person because he is the middle person between the Father and the Holy Ghost, and so is the most fit of any persons of the Godhead to be the middle person between the Father and sinners. His role is to procure the Holy Spirit for man and to

311

bestow it upon him. Christ is also the most fit person because he is both God and man. He has the nature of both and so undertakes for each and reconciles both.

The sermon manuscript is a typical duodecimal booklet, consisting of thirty leaves with a little evidence of damage. In the body of the sermon, there is considerable evidence of deletions, additions, and corrections in Edwards's own hand but nothing on the scale of a major rework of the sermon as a whole. The length of the application is unusual in that it consists of only five pages.

Those words are to enforce the exhortation the apostle Paul had given the Christians to pray for all men and particularly for their heathenish rulers: "I exhort therefore, that, first of all, supplications, prayers, intercessions, and giving of thanks, be made for all men; for kings, and for all that are in authority; that we may lead a quiet and peaceable life in all godliness and honesty" (1 Tim. 2:1–2). And then in the four next verses follows the enforcement of this exhortation which is taken from the extensiveness of the mercy of God through Christ. It extends to all sorts, Jews and Gentiles, and therefore the apostle would have them pray to go and seek his mercy for all. For this is good and acceptable in the sight of God.

The apostle declares to the Christians for them to pray for the heathen and particularly for their heathen rulers—that they would be acceptable in the sight of their God and Savior because God had been so good to them and had manifested such wonderful mercy in them. He sought that all men should be saved and come to the knowledge of the truth, and then adds a twofold argument to receive the truth of what he had said and to enforce the duty that he had urged. The first is that there is one God. Though the heathen world seemed to be parceled out to many gods, one nation by their profession especially belonging to one God and others another, yet all were united under the dominion and providence of one God in whom all lived and moved and had their being. This was a great argument for eventual union and love, seeing all were indeed united under one God. They should be united in heart and affection and all should seek the favor of that God for each other.

This was an argument why the Christians should pray to their own God for the heathen. The Christians made no prayers to any other God. If this God had not the disposal of the heathen, it would be in vain for them to pray to him for them. Not he but other gods would have the care of them. Thus men should not be wont to make supplication to one prince for mercy towards the subjects of another prince, but every king is to be sought to for his own subjects. Hence the heathen of different nations that worshiped different gods don't use to pray one for another who looked on their places as under the care of different gods. But the apostle would not have it thus amongst Christians who worshiped him who was indeed the God of the whole earth.

And not only was the dominion and providence of this God over all but his goodness. He did good to all, giving fruit in season, causing his sun to shine and did specially in those days of the gospel appear ready to be the God of the Gentiles as well as the Jews. This might convince them that such prayers would be acceptable to him.

The other argument used here is that there is one mediator between God and man, which was an additional enforcement of duties and offices of love towards the heathen. It showed the union to be yet stricter and would be a powerful motive to Christians. For this man Christ Jesus was dear to them. If he was ready to be the mediator of the heathen as well as their mediator, this would be a great injustice to their prayers for them. It would be a great encouragement to them to pray for them. Though all had been under one God, yet if Christ had not stood ready to act as a mediator for the heathen, there could be no encouragement for Christians to pray for them—because God hears no prayers through this mediator and shows mercy on none but for his sake.

This is an argument of the truth of what the apostle had said in verse 3—that it was acceptable to God that they should pray for them, though they were now abominable, wicked idolaters. The Christians know that it was an acceptable thing to God to show mercy to the chief of sinners through this mediator.

The apostle here mentions the manhood of Christ. There is one mediator, the man Christ Jesus. Not that he would exclude the Godhead but because there is connected in this an argument of the truth of what be here offered—that Christ was ready to act as mediator not only for the Jews but for mankind. He was man and had united himself to the human nature. He stood nearly related to that whole race of beings who had that nature and was ready to do the part of a mediator to eternity who were equally partakers of that nature with the Jews.

DOCTRINE

Christ is mediator between God and man. Here I shall not stand particularly to explain the notion of a mediator. It may be sufficient to say in one word that a mediator is one who interposes as another person between parties at variance or difference, to reconcile them or unite them and would directly proceed in speaking to this doctrine.

Jesus Christ is the great mediator and head of union in whom all elect creatures in heaven and earth are converted to God and to one another. God had a design before the foundation of the world of gathering all things to himself. Since all things are of him and through him, so he intended they should be to him and also of uniting all chosen creatures one to another in one society in perfect union, one unto another. When he made the world, it was with this purpose. When he made heaven and made the angels in it, it was with this design. When he made this lower world and made man in it, it was with this design. His Son was the person pitched upon and chosen of God, by whom and in whom this great event should be brought about. He was to be the head of the union, that all might be united in him and by him to himself. Therefore, God created all things by Jesus Christ (Eph. 3:9–11).

The elect creatures in this affair are to be considered as two. When it was God's design to unite those two in one, a third person was required to intervene as the medium of the reunion. Christ is that medium or third person. So elect creatures themselves with respect one to another in this affair are to be looked upon as in themselves diverse and separate. Therefore, when God intended to unite, a third was required to be a common head and medium of union amongst them, that they might all be united in this person as head of union in whom they are united one to another.

Therefore, in handling this doctrine, I would show how Christ is the great medium and head of union in whom God united his elect creatures both of heaven and earth to himself, and that he is the head of union in which God unites them one to another.

Christ is the great mediator by whom God and man who are alienated and enemies one to another are reunited.

1. Christ is the most fit person to be the mediator between God and man because he is the middle person between the Father and the Holy Ghost. In being the middle person between the Father and the Holy Spirit, he is the most fit of any of the persons of the Godhead to be the middle person between the Father and sinners in order to their holiness and happiness. For in acting the part of a middle person between the Father and sinners in spiritual concerns, he acts the part of a middle person between the Father and the Holy Spirit in them. He

promises the Holy Ghost of the Father and bestows it on them and therein acts intermediately between the Father of whom the Holy Spirit is obtained and the Holy Spirit that is obtained for sinners and bestowed on them. John 15:26 says, "When the Comforter is come, whom I will send unto you from the Father, even the Spirit of truth."

What Christ does for men in the office of a mediator between God and men is to procure the Holy Ghost for man and bestow it upon him, and the whole may be summed up in that. Christ as mediator purchases holiness and spiritual happiness for men. But the sum of all holiness and spiritual happiness consists in the bestowment and indwelling and influence and fruits of the Holy Ghost in the heart. In this souls have holiness in this world. This is the way they have perfect holiness and happiness bestowed upon them in another world. The Holy Ghost is the sum of all spiritual good things. That which is called "good things" in one Gospel is called the "Holy Spirit" in another. Matthew 7:11 says, "How much more shall your Father . . . give good things to them?" Luke 11:13 says, "How much more shall your heavenly Father give the Holy Spirit?"

This was the great blessing purchased by the mediator for sinners, but the price is intermediate between the person of whom the purchase is paid and the thing purchased. 'Tis the means of it, and therefore it was proper that Christ who is the buyer and the price by whom the Holy Spirit is purchased for sinners of the Father should be the middle person between the Holy Ghost and the Father.

Again, Christ acts as a middle person between the Father and Holy Ghost not only in purchasing the Holy Ghost of the Father for them but in conferring the Holy Ghost from the Father upon them. And the mediator between God and man acts as a middle person between the Father and the Holy Spirit not only in transacting with them from the Father but also in transacting with the Father from them as when their faith and their love, their desires and prayers, and praises and their obedience is offered to God through this mediator. These were carried by him to God and presented through his blood to the Father. For that faith and that love and those prayers and praises were the acting of the Holy Spirit on them. So the mediator, acting as a middle person between their believing, loving, praying, and obedient hearts to God, acts as a middle person between the Holy Spirit and God. Their faith and love are the breathings of the Holy Spirit.

This seems to be the first and highest reason why the Son of God was at first pitched upon as a proper person to be a mediator between God rather than any other person of the Trinity—because he was the middle person between the Father and the Holy Spirit. It was not proper that the Father should be the person of the mediator because he was the first person in the Trinity. He properly sustained the dignity and righteousness of the Godhead. He was the person of whom the purchase was to be made and likewise where and to whom the mediator was to act. And it was not proper it should be the Holy Ghost, because he was the benefit that was to be purchased by the mediator for sinners and be bestowed by him on sinners to dwell in their hearts and there to act forth and love and offer prayer, praise, and obedience through the mediator. Therefore, Christ as the Son of God was the only fit person to be pitched upon.

2. A secondary reason why he is a fit person to be a mediator between God and man is that he is both God and man. So he is not only a middle person between the Father and the Holy Spirit but also a middle person between God and man—those whom he was to be a mediator between.

However, the end of his incarnation whereby he was God and man was that he might become fit. The business of a mediator's being is as a middle person to make peace between two parties who are alienated and to reconcile them one to another. This way we see that a mediator should be nearly aligned to both parties. So is Jesus Christ. He is the

Son of God and the son of man. He is both God and man. He is God's Son and our brother.

3. Christ, because he has the nature of both God and man, has experience of the circumstances of both. The glory, majesty, and happiness of the one and the infirmity, meanness, diligence, and misery and by imputation the guilt and so the condemnation and suffering the punishment of the other. He has not only the nature of man, but he is in many respects become subject to the circumstances that man is in as sinful man—the weak, the evil, the disgraceful and calamitous circumstances that sin brought him into—being made in the form of sinful flesh and so becoming subject to the infirmities and temptations and sufferings that man is subject to by sin. Christ yet is higher than the heavens and so has also experience of the glory and blessedness of God. So that experience of the circumstances of both, this the apostle speaks of as what qualifies Christ for the office of a mediator between God and man.

Hebrews 2:17–18 says, "Wherefore in all things it behoved him to be made like unto his brethren, that he might be a merciful and faithful high priest in things pertaining to God, to make reconciliation for the sins of the people. For in that he himself hath suffered being tempted, he is able to succour them that are tempted." Hebrews 4:15 says, "For we have not an high priest which cannot be touched with the feeling of our infirmities." It was required in order to his being both God and man, that he should be the subject of our calamities. That he might know, on the one hand, how to pity man who suffers or is exposed to those calamities, as on the other hand it was required that he should be possessed of the glory and majesty of God that he might know how to value that majesty and glory and to be careful and tender of them and essentially engaged to see to it that they were well secured and magnified.

Now I will observe wherein Christ acts the part of a mediator between God and man in order to a reconciliation and union between them.

1. He undertakes for each with the other. He undertakes for sinful man with God and was surety for him. He undertakes that the law shall be answered and God's majesty vindicated and glorified with respect to man and that the law as it respects him shall be answered, fulfilled, and satisfied. Yea, he so undertakes for sinners that he assumes them to himself and puts himself before the Father in the sinner's stead that whatever justice had to demand of the sinner it may demand it of him. He takes the sinner's debt upon himself, becomes bond for him so that justice no longer looks to the sinner who believed in him for a discharge of the debt but to Christ.

And so on the other hand, he undertakes for God with man in order to their being converted to him and in order to their being induced and encouraged to come to him and love him and trust confidently and rest completely in him. He undertakes with sinful man for God's acceptance favor towards them if they will repent and return. 'Tis by faith in him as we see he says in John 14:21, "He that loveth me shall be loved of my Father." He undertakes that the Father shall hear and answer their prayers. He becomes as it were surety for God to be that purchased by him. John 14:13 says, "Whatsoever ye shall ask in my name, that will I do, that the Father may be glorified in the Son."

He engages for the continuance of God's presence with them and of his favor towards them and for supplies of his grace necessary to uphold them and to preserve them and to keep them from finally parting. John 14:16 says, "I will pray the Father, and he shall give you another Comforter, that he may abide with you for ever." Verse 23 says, "If a man love me, he will keep my words: and my Father will love him, and we will come unto him, and make our abode with him."

Christ doesn't only declare that God will give us needed grace, but he himself undertakes to see it done. He promises that he will bestow it from the Father. John 15:26 refers to "the Comforter . . . whom I will send unto you from the Father." It was necessary that someone should not only undertake for man with God but also that he should undertake for God with man for the continuance of his preserving, sanctifying grace in order for the sinner's being fully reconciled to God and brought fully and quietly to rest in him as his God. Otherwise, the sinner, being conscious of his own weakness and sinfulness, would have no quiet rest in God for fear of the union being broken between God and him and for fearing of incurring God's displeasure and wrath. So his fearing would be that enemy forever which man in his fallen state is in himself and is a thousand times liable to as he was under the first covenant.

2. Christ mediates between these two parties by standing in the stead of both as the representative of each to the other. In his priestly office he puts himself in our stead and appears as our representative before the Father. But in his kingly office he appears in the Father's stead and as the Father's representative to man. For that authority of rule and government of the world that Christ has as God-man and our mediator is a delegated authority, authority that the Father has given him. He receives his kingdom of the Father to govern it for him as his vice-regent. Matthew 28:18 says, "All power is given unto me in heaven." Luke 22:29 says, "I appoint unto you a kingdom." Psalm 2:6 says, "I set my king."

So Christ is an appointed judge to judge the world in the Father's name. He will come to judge the world with the Father's authority committed to him, and therefore 'tis said that he will come "in the glory of his Father" (Matt. 16:27). He is in a capacity to undertake and answer for each to the other. He is in a capacity to answer for us to the

Father because he has put himself in our stead as our priest in that office.

He does and suffers what we should have done and suffered. He is in a capacity to undertake for his Father with us because the Father has put him in his stead as King. God has committed to him his judgment and his governance of the world. So he is in a capacity to answer for God to us by doing and ordering and hastening what we need from God. As our priest, he undertakes for us in things that are expected for us as subjects because he has put himself into our subjection. He appears in the form of a servant for us. He undertakes for God in that which is desired and hoped for of him as king. The Father has put him into his kingdom and dominion and has committed all authority and power to him. He is in a capacity to undertake for the Father with us because he can say, "All things that the Father hath are mine" (John 16:15).

3. He takes away the curse of the enmity of each against the other by his blood. He thereby takes away that on our part which was the partition with and the cause of God's enmity towards us—our sin. And by the same he takes away that which was the partition wall on God's part that was the occasion of our enmity toward him—the law of commandment, particularly the sensible threatenings and awful curse of that law. Romans 6:14 says, "For sin shall not have dominion over you: for ye are not under the law, but under grace." He takes the law and covenant of works which condemned us and so rendered God the object of our loathing, fear, and hatred out of the way as to its condemning power.

4. He has offered the strongest inducement to look, to receive, and to be united in heart with the other, by offering up himself a sacrifice. He by this act has offered to God the strongest inducement to receive man through a most glorious act of righteousness and obedience in Christ to the Father. By the same act he has offered the strongest

inducement to men to receive God and love him. The strongest argument to win his love and his so doing was the most glorious and most winning manifestation of the mercy and love of God that ever was.

5. He goes from one to the other. He in the first place came down from God to man and dwelt in this world and then ascends to God again to obtain salvation. At the last day judgment will come down from God hither again. He will appear the second time, having actually obtained salvation to bestow it (Heb. 9:28). And then he will ascend to God again with his disciples. His first coming is from God, and his last return is to God. He is the Alpha and Omega in this affair.

6. He pleads and manages the cause of each with the other. He pleads the cause of God with us as prophet, and he pleads our cause with God as priest. He is an advocate for each with the other. He is an advocate and pleads for us with God in his intercession in heaven. He is the Father's advocate and pleads for God with men in his Word and by his Spirit. The Spirit that Christ sends is therefore called the advocate. He brings to each what is needed by the other. He brings the Word of God to man as prophet, makes instructions and counsels. John 3:34 says, "He whom God hath sent speaketh the words of God." John 8:26 says, "He that sent me is true; and I speak to the world those things which I have heard of him." John 8:28 says, "As my Father hath taught me, I speak these things."

On the other hand, he carries our words to God and in our prayers, confessions, and praises as priest in his intercession. He is the priest who stands before the throne with the golden censer and much incense to offer with the prayers of all the saints.

7. And lastly, Christ brings them to each other and actually unites them. This he does by various things and designs which consist in the highest confirmation of union at the end of the world. First, he came into the world. Then, inasmuch as he was a divine person, he brought down divinity with him to us. So he brought God down to man, and

then he ascended to God. Inasmuch as he was in the human nature, he carried up humanity with him to God. He from heaven sends down the Holy Spirit whereby he brings God to dwell in the hearts of men. He so influences them to give up their hearts to him and so draws them to him and brings God to dwell with those saints on earth in their conversion. He brings their souls to dwell with God in heaven at their death. Again he will come down from heaven in person and will bring divinity with him a second time and then will ascend and carry men up to God in heaven.

At his first descent Christ brought divinity down to us under a veil. At his second coming he brings divinity to men in its glory without a veil. At his first ascension after his own resurrection, he carried up ourselves with him to God. At his second ascension after the general resurrection, he will carry up our persons with him. He at death brought the souls of the saints to God in heaven whereby a part of the creatures gloriously united to God at the end of the world. He will bring them in both body and soul to heaven and will bring all the church together to that highest, ultimate, and consummate union with God. This will be the last steps by which he will bring the actual union between God and man to a final completion and whereby he will finish the work of a mediator between God and man, having then fully gathered to God all things on earth.

Christ is the head of the angels. This the Spirit expressed in Colossians 2:9–10: "For in him dwelleth all the fulness of the Godhead bodily. And ye are complete in him, which is the head of all principality and power." So Christ be not properly a mediator between God and angels because the notion of a mediator is as a middle person to reconcile natures at variance. Yet he as the head of the angels is a middle person between God and them. He is their head as God-man and he is not their head for nothing but 'tis for that unspeakable benefit. He is our head of communication through which God communicates himself to the angels, as is evident by the manner of expression in the Scriptures just used: "In him dwelleth all the fulness of the Godhead." He is also the head of the angels to fill them—the head of communication from God to them through whom they receive their fullness from God. This is also implied in Ephesians 4:10: "He that descended is the same also that ascended up far above all heavens, that he might fill all things."

The angels and saints in heaven are become society, and Christ is the common head of all—the head of their fullness in whom the whole society is full of light and glory and blessedness. The Lamb is the light of the new Jerusalem to enlighten all the inhabitants of it, both saints and angels. But I shall not any longer insist on this, because it does not so much concern us as Christ's being the head of our union to God.

The consideration of the other thing proposed—Christ's being the great head of union by which elect creatures are united one to another—must be reserved to another occasion.

I shall conclude with a few words of improvement of what has been said of Christ being a mediator and head of union between God and sinful man which I had no need to enlarge upon. In our last public lecture you had an excellent discourse on this subject from the minister that was occasionally amongst us.

APPLICATION

1. Hence we may see the certain truth of the doctrine of the perseverance of the saints. For if Christ be the head of union between us and God, it is a sure evidence that this union is everlasting, for he is one who can't fall as our first head did. If the head lives and remains united to God, so shall the members. John 14:19 says, "Because I live, ye shall live also." The spiritual life of the saints never can cease, because Christ is the head and fountain of this life, who liveth, and is

"alive for evermore" (Rev. 1:13). That life is "hid with Christ" who is with God in heaven (Col. 3:3).

Seeing Jesus Christ—the great Son of God who is the same yesterday, today, and forever—has undertaken to effect and establish and complete the union, it will be forever. You have heard how Christ as mediator between God and man has undertaken for both. He has not only undertaken for God with man, but it has been shown both from the reason the thing and plain Scripture that Christ has undertaken also for God with the saints to give to them the continuance of his favor and presence. This was necessary in order to a complete and perpetuate reconciliation. Therefore, if those who have believed in Christ ever fail of the continuance of God's grace and favor, it will be because he who has undertaken on the behalf of God with their souls, which would be blasphemy to suppose.

2. This may convince us what is the proper condition of the covenant of grace—union of heart with Jesus Christ, seeing that the great end of the covenant of grace is to gather fallen men and unite them to God under Christ as the head of union. And it is seeing that Christ came into the world and did all that he did and suffered all that he suffered for that end that he might thereby be the head of union with God to fallen man. This naturally leads us to conceive that the great thing represented in order to a parting of the benefits of Christ must be a closing with Christ as our union of the heart with him. For certainly 'tis by such a union that Christ becomes our head. The head of the natural body becomes a head to such and such members by virtue of the union of those members. 'Tis a head to such members and not others because such members are committed to it and others are not.

And being that Christ is in himself united to God, so that he and the Father are one, there is nothing else needed in order to his being a head of union to God but only that we should be in him and should have closed with him. So the faith that is so often spoken of in the Scriptures as the great condition of the covenant of grace is without doubt our hearty accepting of Christ as our mediator and our whole souls falling in or a closing with him as our head and Redeemer and way to the Father.

Let me here exhort all in their hearts to close with their glorious head of reconciliation and union of sinful men with God. We are wholly far off from God, being without Christ, and so are strangers. We are far off. There is a great breach between God and man. Heaven and earth that were one originally created are separate by sin. All who are out of Christ are enemies to God and God is an enemy to them. There is no peace between them; the wrath of God abides. They are separated from the salvation of God, and they have an omnipotent, infinitely powerful enemy.

Consider your misery out of Christ and consider that he is the only head of union for poor sinners in whom they can be reconciled to God. First Timothy 2:5 says, "There is one God, and one mediator between God and men, the man Christ Jesus." He is the only way to a reunion with God: "I am the way, the truth, and the life: no man cometh unto the Father, but by me" (John 14:6). And behold the meekness and suitableness of this to be a middle person between God and man to restore peace and union. Christ is the middle person between the Father and the Holy Ghost, and one who partakes of the nature and circumstances of both. Through his almighty and eternal vengeance, Christ procures and accomplishes the union between God and poor, sinful, miserable worms—those who are naturally enemies to God and liable to utter perdition.

20

—◦✈◎ ◎✈◦—

'Tis Impossible That God Should Be Under Any Temptation to Do Anything That Is Evil

Let no man say when he is tempted, I am tempted of God: for God cannot be tempted with evil, neither tempteth he any man.

JAMES 1:13

Edwards titles this sermon as a lecture, a message that he presented in April 1733. The original manuscript has suffered some damage. Where words are impossible to determine accurately, it has been so noted in the transcription, together with the numbers of words that are missing.

Edwards begins by drawing the biblical distinction between trying and tempting. He gives biblical examples that, in one sense, God does often tempt men, but he never entices or tempts anyone to evil. In fact, says Edwards, it is impossible that God should be under any temptation to do anything that is evil.

The sermon manuscript is a typical duodecimal booklet, consisting of twenty-three leaves with evidence of some damage to the original, together with some evidence of deletions and corrections.

In our text, James 1:13, the apostle James had promised blessedness to the man who endures temptation by reason of that glorious reward, that crown of life, which such should receive when tried of Christ. He promised it to all who sincerely love him and whose love will bear temptation.

In this verse he adds a caution that no man when tempted should charge God as the author of his temptation. He also gives a reason—because such a charge would be false and injurious to God, who tempteth not any man.

Tempting is used in two senses in Scripture. Sometimes it only signifies trying, and in this sense God does often tempt men. Genesis 22:1 says, "And it came to pass after these things, that God did tempt Abraham." That is, he tried him. He tried his faith and obedience, and so God doth often tempt and try men in the things that he exercises them with. But *tempting* in the text (James 1:13) is to be understood in another sense, meaning an enticing to evil. This appears to be the meaning of the apostle by the following verse, but every man is tempted when he is drawn away of his own lust and enticed. So that by tempting him, the apostle means drawing or enticing, and in this sense God does not tempt any men with evil.

We may observe the evidence of this—that God himself cannot be tempted with evil and cannot be moved or inclined to any evil. If it be impossible that he should be moved to it himself, certainly he never would move and incline others to it.

DOCTRINE

'Tis impossible that God should be under any temptation to do anything that is evil. The enmity in the heart of man against God appears in this among other things, that men are ready to find fault with God and call in question his justice, truth, and goodness. Men are liable to such thoughts as these: "We hear that God is an infinitely holy and righteous God, but how do I know that 'tis so? How do I know but that he is an unjust and wicked being? How do I know but that he is a being of a cruel disposition and delights in the misery of his creatures? God declares himself to be a holy God and a good God, but how do I know that he speaks true? How do I know but that he deceives the world and that he makes as if he hated sin and as if he were infinitely merciful and gracious but is in the meantime really of a cruel disposition?"

The wickedness of the heart of men disposes them to such thoughts. Especially are they liable to these thoughts upon some occasions as when God's dealings with them cross to them or when they are in fear that they will see great suffering by his disposition. And Satan is ready at hand to promote such thoughts. He watches all opportunities to cast in such suggestions and raise such thoughts in the mind and, when they are raised, to push them forward and carry them as far as possible.

I would therefore now endeavor to make it manifest to reason that what we are told in the Word of God of God's being just and righteous, a God of truth and without iniquity, is true, by showing that 'tis impossible that God should be under any temptation to do anything that is evil. If God deals unjustly with any of his creatures or does anything that is evil, he must be moved to it by something within itself or without himself. He must be influenced by something, by some aim or other. He must aim at some end in so doing. But here I would endeavor to show that 'tis impossible that there should be anything to move or influence God to do anything that is evil. 'Tis impossible that he should under any manner of temptation to it [ms. damage: one word missing] that may appear thus.

If God can be under any temptation to do any evil thing, it must be one of these two ways: From a view of obtaining something by it, self-interest must be his temptation, or because he delights to do evil for evil's sake.

If God can be under any temptation to do evil, it must be from one of these two ways. It must be either because he has a view of obtaining something by it or without a view of obtaining anything by it and that is to do evil only for the sake of doing evil and because he delights in unrighteousness for unrighteousness' sake.

But I will endeavor to show that 'tis impossible that God should be under any temptation to do anything that is evil either of these ways.

1. 'Tis impossible that God should be tempted to do any ill thing by any view of his own interest. This will appear by two things:

'Tis impossible because 'tis impossible that God should be in want of anything or be capable of having his happiness added to. He who has already an all-fullness in himself and is infinitely happy, 'tis impossible that he should desire to be more happy. So that is no such thing as more happy than infinitely happy. There can be no addition to that which is infinite. That which has no bounds, the bounds of it can't be exceeded. But if it be impossible that God should desire to be more happy, then it's impossible for him to be tempted with a view to his own interest, for that is to suppose that he has a view to an addition to his own happiness when at the same time he desires no addition or is capable of it.

Men are liable to temptation because they have an inward craving of happiness. They are tempted by presenting some object to allure him [ms. damage: two words missing]. But he that is self-sufficient is not liable to any such temptation, nor can he be tempted with [ms. damage: two words missing] anything that he should have any such prospect.

Men are tempted to do evil from a view at some profit or pleasure. A view at having something added to by it, but 'tis impossible that he who is intimately happy and blessed should have any such temptation to do any evil or corrupt thing. But then if it be inquired how it appears that God hath such a fullness in himself that he can't be added to.

It appears by this that he can't receive any addition from any other because all others have all from him. It appears that God has all fullness in himself because the whole creation has all from him. He is the fountain of the good that is received and enjoyed in the whole creation. Every creature has all that he has from God. This is most evident because everyone has their very being wholly of God. God created the world; he brought it out of nothing. Therefore, God gave the world all that it has. It received all from God because 'til it received from God what it did, it was nothing. What has been received of God has brought the world from nothing; therefore, take away what it received of him and there will remain nothing again. So 'tis most evident that all creation in the whole universe has all from God.

And therefore surely 'tis impossible that God should be added to by anything. God can't have his being, his happiness added to. [ms. damage: two words missing] those who are first absolutely [ms. damage: two words missing] receive from him all that they have. The creature can't give to God any more than it has, but the creature has nothing but what it has from God. But God can't be dependent on the creature for what the creature has from him. God has it already and had it before the creature had a being, or else how could God give it to the creature?

Therefore, it is said that God can receive no addition from or by the creature or by anything in the creature. If the creature be happy, that makes no addition to God. If the creature be miserable, that makes no addition to God. Therefore, God can be under no temptation to wrong his creatures or to do unjustly by them from any expectation of getting anything by them.

It is impossible that God should be under any temptation to do wrong from self-interest, for Christ can do what he will because he is almighty. 'Tis impossible that a being who is infinitely powerful should be under any temptation to do an ill thing from a view to self-interest. If we should suppose that God is capable of having his interest added to, yet if he be almighty or infinitely powerful, 'tis impossible that he should be under temptation to do any ill to add to it because he can add to it as well as without doing evil or with it.

Let us suppose that there is something that God would [ms. damage: two words missing] obtain. Yet he can't be under any temptation to do anything to obtain. Being infinitely powerful, he can obtain or will without or with a being that is almighty can do what he will and therefore can obtain what good he will and can do with infinite ease. He need not be put upon any indirect method for the obtaining it. He can't be under that temptation to do wrong that he could not gain that self-interest that he desired without doing wrong. Nor could he be under that temptation that he can gain more easily by doing wrong than without. For nothing can be otherwise than easy to him who is infinitely powerful. For if it be not easy, if it be hard and laborious and difficult, that must be for want of his strength. But there can be no want of strength in him who is infinitely strong.

Let us suppose that any man had that power that he could at any time attain what riches he would with infinite ease with only speaking a word or turning a thought without wronging any man. It would be impossible that this man should be under any temptation to wrong his neighbors from a view to riches. So if he could with infinite ease attain what please he would, or advance himself to what [ms. damage: two words missing] he would without doing any wrong, it would be impossible for that man to be under any temptation to do from a view to his own happiness or pleasure. If such an one should do evil, it must be because he delights in evil for evil's sake.

So 'tis impossible that God who is almighty and can do what he will and can do what he will with infinite ease should be under any temptation to wrong his creatures for self-interest. 'Tis from weakness that any being is liable to any temptation. 'Tis impossible that this temptation should take hold of an infinitely strong being.

But then it may be inquired, How do I know that God is so strong? You have a demonstration of it every day before your eyes in the work of creation. You need not go to the Scriptures for a proof of it. It will appear evident to any considering person that he who created and governs the world must be almighty.

It shows infinite power to create anything. All the finite power united can't create out of nothing one grain of sand. But if this be a demonstration of almighty power, how much more is the creation of the whole earth and seas, of birds, beasts, and fishes, of men, especially the soul of man? And not only this earth and the fullness of it but how much more this whole universe—sun, moon, and stars? And what a mighty strength does it manifest to give those heavenly bodies their motions. And not only the creation but the government of the world shows that God is almighty. It shows an infinite strength to manage all the motions of sun, moon, and stars, and all the changes and revolutions of the universe day and night and without ceasing one moment, and yet without weariness.

If God were not infinitely strong, he would be weary of this. But if he were weary, he would not continue that without ceasing for sure, or fix thousands together. Isaiah 40:28 says, "Hast thou not known? hast thou not heard, that the everlasting God, the LORD, the Creator of the ends of the earth, fainteth not, neither is weary?"

This demonstrates that God can't be under any such temptations as man. When men are tempted to evil 'tis always from some self-interest. The whole of the corruption of nature may be resolved into an inordinate self-love. Therefore, in all the evil that men do 'tis self that governs him. He has some view at some self-interest in it, after some profit or honor or pleasure of his own. But to illustrate this argument, let it be considered in whatever temptation any being is subject to. The temptation must work better upon hope or fear if neither fear of any evil draws nor any hope of any good draws. It is impossible that anyone should be under any temptation.

There are but these two ways that temptation can work. But impossible that any temptation should work either of these ways on God. He who needs nothing and is already so happy that nothing should be added to him can't be tempted by hope of anything, for he has all things already. And he who is almighty can't be driven to any evil by any fear, for what has an almighty being to be afraid of? He who is infinite in power can't be in any danger.

Thus we have shown that God can't be under any temptation to do evil from self-interest.

2. God can't be tempted with evil from any delight in doing evil for evil's sake. Many reasons might be given of this, but I would confine myself at this time to arguments that are purely rational. I will endeavor to show the impossibility of God's delighting in evil from reason independent of the assertions of the Scriptures concerning it and may appear by putting together the following two things:

'Tis impossible that any should delight in evil and lust what is excellent that is not blinded and mistaken as to the nature of those things. It is impossible that any should set a value upon things directly contrary to his true nature unless it be through ignorance or errant about the nature of those things.

'Tis impossible that anyone should delight in that which is in itself evil and hateful, that at the same time sees its hatefulness. If a being loves and delights in a thing that is really hateful, it must be that he doesn't see its hatefulness. If he is fully sensible of his hatefulness, 'tis impossible that he should love it. If he loves it, 'tis because it appears to him not hateful but lovely and eligible.

On the other hand, 'tis impossible that anyone should hate that which is excellent that sees and is sensible of its excellency. He who sees an excellency and amiableness in justice and holiness, 'tis impossible but that he should love it. He will either love or hate it as it appears to him lovely or hateful.

Therefore, if God takes delight in evil for its own sake, he must be ignorant or mistaken about the nature of good and evil, being ignorant of the excellency of the one and the hatefulness of the other and mistaking that which is indeed hateful to be lovely and that which is lovely to be hateful.

'Tis impossible that God should be thus ignorant and mistaken about the nature of good and evil. God is infinitely wise. He who is infinitely wise cannot be mistaken. Neither is there anything that he can be ignorant of. If God be infinitely wise, he must know all truth and must know it all fully and perfectly. And that which is indeed excellent God must perfectly know it to be excellent. He must clearly see all the excellency that is in it, for if there be anything that he doesn't fully understand then he is not infinite but imperfectly wise.

But here if any should ask, How do I know that God is infinite in understanding? I have proved already that he must of necessity be infinite in power and if he is infinite in one attribute, he must be in another. To allow God to have some perfections infinite and others but finite will involve us in great absurdities. If God has any one attribute infinite, that shows that his being is infinite. For 'tis impossible there should be an infinite attribute in a finite being. If God's being is infinite, then it will follow that all his others are infinite, for the attributes must be coextended with the being of which it is an attribute. This is an absurdity—that he has infinite power without being capable of knowing how powerful his power is to the millionth part.

But then God's infinite Word as well as power appears in the work of creation and providence. For if God created all things, then he knows everything that he created—every grain of sand, every particle of matter, every little atom in the whole universe—and consequently, must know all those things. All those things must be centered in his understanding with their whole state and all their circumstances. For God did not create anything ignorantly, not knowing what he did. But if God's understanding comprehends a different knowledge of every single atom in the whole universe, vast doth that show his understanding to be.

And then in order to uphold and govern the world, God must know all the things that he governs. He must have an actual view of them in his mind. This God hath constantly without any reasonable attention and thus argue his understanding to be infinitely capacious. If it were not infinite, a constantly viewing and beholding the working of the whole world would at last cause need for attention. Constantly to live in actual view, any one thing will tire our understanding and we shall be soon tired in endeavoring to constantly and without intermission to view many things at once. But God hath now for many thousands of years, together constantly day and night, beheld and managed and governed the whole universe.

'Tis impossible that God should be ignorant of the excellency of good and hatefulness of evil, because many of his creatures have the knowledge of it. What an absurdity it is to suppose that some of God's creatures have got further in their knowledge and understanding than God himself who gave them a being. That they should know that true excellency of God and hatefulness of evil and herein exceed him who created their souls out of nothing and gave them their faculties of understanding. Psalm 94:9 says, "He that planted the ear, shall he not hear? he that formed the eye, shall he not see?" It would be strange indeed if he should not see as far as the eye that is of his own forming. He that teacheth man knowledge, shall not he know?

APPLICATION

1. Hence we may trust God out of sight. Men are apt to be suspicious of God when he is out of their sight. They will trust him as far as they can see him and no further. Men can believe that God's Word is true in those things that they see the truth of. They can believe that he is just when they see him and can comprehend the justice of what he does. But when once God is out of their sight, they will trust him no further but begin to doubt of his truth and righteousness. This shows the mean opinion and unworthy thoughts that men secretly entertain of God in their hearts.

They won't trust God so far as they will a man whose honesty and probity they are well persuaded of. If men have had acquaintance with another man and have ever seen in him the greatest tokens and evidences of his being a man of the highest principles, men dare trust such an one out of sight. They will believe what such an one asserts for truth of his own knowledge, though it seems very strange. If some of his actions appear strange and they can't hitherto see through them, yet they will trust to their former knowledge of him as a man of tried and strict honesty and faithfulness. They can believe that he is so still, though they don't as yet understand the grounds and reasons of some of his behaviors. Thus men will trust a man who is a poor, infirm, changeable, sinful creature liable to be carried away with temptation, further than they will trust a being infinitely great and holy and infinitely above all possibility of being tempted with evil.

But if we are convinced of the truth of this doctrine, we shall not be apt to be suspicious of God in anything that he says or does, howmuchsoever happened in our sight or comprehension.

If this doctrine be true, we may totally depend upon the truth of God's Word, though the things declared are beyond our sight or understanding. God in his Word tells us of many things that are out of sight to us. He tells us of spiritual things, things that can't be seen by a bodily eye. He tells us in his Word of an incredible world, of a heaven of eternal blessedness and glory. He tells us that there is Christ. He tells us many things of the state of the inhabitants of that world. He promises that all those who are sincerely godly when they die shall go to that glorious state and be there forever with Christ and the full enjoyment.

This world is out of sight to us. We have the account of it relying only upon the mention of it in God's Word, but we may safely trust him. What he says is certainly true, and there is indeed such a world of blessedness. He will certainly fulfill his promise of transporting the souls of the godly to that blessed state when they die. We need not be afraid to trust the mention of it, for 'tis impossible that God should be under any temptation to lie. Titus 1:2 says, "In hope of eternal life, which God, that cannot lie." So God in his Word tells us of another opposite state—a hell of darkness and dreadful misery that the wicked shall go to when they die. This also is out of sight. We have God's word for it, but we never saw it, nor did ever any wicked soul come from hell to tell us.

But there is no reason for us to suspect whether it be so or no. There is no room for any wicked men to think within him, "It may be I shall not find it true when I come to die, or may God only say it to fright us but never intends to inflict this misery, for 'tis impossible that God should be under any temptation to deceive men with such a fiction."

Though we don't see it, yet we may certainly depend upon this: Every wicked man's soul as soon as it parts from the body goes down to that world of misery to dwell with devils and other damned spirits forever. We may depend upon the truth of all God's promises and threats and that not one word will ever fall to the ground, however strange and remote and hid from our sight and difficult to conceive the things promised or threatened are for the present. God cannot lie, and he cannot be under any temptation to lie with promises or threats. For God in his Word tells us many things that are beyond the comprehension of our understanding—three persons. God became man.

'Tis distinct that God in declaring these things is out of sight to us in these doctrines—doctrines that we cannot comprehend. Yet we may surely depend upon it that they are true because he hath said so.

If this doctrine be true, then we may depend upon it that God is just and true in those dispensations of his that we cannot understand. There are many methods of dealing with his creatures and particular dispensations of his providences that we can't fully understand or see the reason of. There are his absolute decrees of whatsoever comes to pass, his electing some from all eternity to everlasting life and leaving others to perish eternally. God acts as absolute sovereign over the souls of men with respect to their eternal damnation—his having mercy on whom he will have mercy, his hardening whom he will, and his imparting Adam's sin to all his posterity. These things are what we cannot fully comprehend or see the reasons of, but yet we may depend upon it, for God is altogether just and righteous.

Men are often ready to find fault with God because he charges them so heavily for their unbelief. They can't believe of themselves and are ready to debate with God about the extremity and eternity of hell's torments and to look upon as hard and cruel that God should so make a creature so miserable for his sins committed only for a few days here in the world or even only for original sin. God is in a measure out of sight to us in those things. We don't see now as we shall see. But we may surely conclude that these dispensations of God are perfectly just and holy from all we have heard under this doctrine.

And so whatever we meet with in the course of God's common providence, though we can't see the reasons of many of God's dealings with us, why he so afflicts us, hides his face from us, can't see how 'tis consistent with his promises, yet however dark and unintelligible

God's ways are to us, this ought evermore to tell us that God is perfectly and constantly just and true in all his ways and works and is doubtless faithful to his plan. Numbers 23:19 says, "God is not a man, that he should lie." We shall greatly distrust God and think most unworthy thoughts of him if we can never trust him but when he is within sight. 'Tis fit that we should have such trials, that God sometimes should in his Word and in his dispositions be beyond our comprehension, for a trial of our esteem of God and whether or no we can trust him where we can't see him.

2. Let us give God the glory of his righteousness and truth if there be so great evidence of his being perfectly and unalterably righteous and true. Let us ascribe the glory of it to him. Let us do it in the following ways:

By submitting to his will. Whatsoever his declared will be, whether it be declared by his Word or by his providence, let us entirely submit to it, being confident that it is surely most just and holy and that there is nothing amiss in it. Let us submit to God in all his established methods of dealing with his creatures. Let us willingly acknowledge God's sovereignty and own that we are the clay and he the potter.

And quietly submit to whatsoever God is pleased to lay upon us in the course of his providence. Let us imitate the psalmist who says in Psalm 39:9, "I was dumb, I opened not my mouth; because thou didst it."

By putting our trust in him. This would be a suitable acknowledgment of God's unalterable righteousness and faithfulness, that he cannot do any other than deal justly by us and do as he hath promised in his holy Word.

By praising of him. 'Tis that wherein God is exalted above all other beings that he is above all possibility of being tempted to do evil. Men in innocency, a nobler being, and men endeavored with great wisdom, but he was liable. The glorious angels of heaven are created of an extraordinarily exalted nature bright with heavenly wisdom, being of a mighty strength, a flame of fire activity. Spotlessly holy and pure but yet they were not above a natural possibility of temptation to evil, as the fall of many of them prove (Isa. 14:12–15; Jude 6). It is God alone who is essentially and unalterably just and true. It becomes us, therefore, to praise him upon this account. The angels praise him for it day and night, crying, "Holy, holy, holy." It becomes us to join them herein as we hope to join them in this work to all eternity.

21

⭆ ⭄

That God Is the Father of Lights

Every good gift and every perfect gift is from above, and cometh
down from the Father of lights, with whom is no variableness,
neither shadow of change.

JAMES 1:17

Edwards begins this undated sermon of thanksgiving by stating
that the title, "Father of Lights," speaks of the fact that God is
compared to the sun, in that every good gift comes as much from God,
as light comes from the sun. As the sun sheds abroad its light, enlightens the world, and fills it with his benign influence, so God diffuses
abroad his blessings and gracious influences, but he remains the true
Fountain of Light.

Edwards includes an interesting illustration of how he had read of
a Protestant in Spain who was kept imprisoned in a dungeon for three
years. During that entire time he never saw the sun. When he was
brought out to be executed and saw the sun, he publicly proclaimed at
the sight of such light how any person could worship anything other
than its Creator.

The sermon manuscript is a typical duodecimal booklet, consisting of twenty-four leaves with little or no evidence of damage or
corrections.

Notice particularly that expression, "the Father of Lights." The apostle James is writing to the believing Jews who were scattered abroad amongst the Gentiles. In James 1:5, he exhorts them, "If any man lack wisdom, let him ask of God, that giveth to all men liberally, and upbraideth not." In verses 6–7, he tells in what manner we must ask what we want of God. It seems to be with an eye to this exhortation to prayer that he here puts them in mind that every good thing comes from God. By a good gift and a perfect is meant every gift that is for our real good and advantage.

There are many things that men are glad of that be not for their benefit. They are glad of means and opportunities to satisfy their lusts, but these are not good and perfect gifts. But everything that is for our real benefit is from above. Not only spiritual blessings but our bread that we eat is from above as well as the manna that the children of Israel ate in the wilderness. Our common and daily mercies come down from God as really as if it were immediately rained down in an indescribable manner out of heaven.

It comes down from the Father of Lights. It is spoken as comparing God to the sun. Every good gift comes as much from God as light comes from the sun or the sun in the firmament sheds abroad his light and enlightens the world and fills it with his benign influence. God diffuses abroad his blessings and gracious influences and is in a more glorious sense the Fountain of Light than the sun is. But the apostle takes notice of one thing, particularly wherein this spiritual Fountain of Light differs from the sun, the corporeal fountain of light. In him is no variableness nor shadow of turning. The sun is a variable fountain of light.

As to us, sometimes the sun is shining and sometimes it doth not shine. The sun rises and sets and is subject to variable revolutions. But God is as a sun always fixed in the hemisphere that shines without interruption. When it is said that he is without shadow of turning, the meaning is without shadow by turning. The sun by turning round in the heavens leaves us in the dark shadows of the night. But God is a sun without such turning, as are attended with shadows. He is light without shadows, nothing but light: "God is light, and in him is no darkness at all" (1 John 1:5).

It is said that he is the Father of Lights. It is a Hebrew way of expression. It was common in the Hebrew language, when they would set forth the excellency of a thing, to speak of it in the plural number. So when it said the "Father of Lights" and not the Fathers of light, the meaning is the author of glorious light or it may signify that God is the fountain of all sorts of lights. There are various kind of lights. God is the fountain of them all, as we shall show by and by under this doctrine.

DOCTRINE

God is the Father of Lights. Here we shall explain more generally what is meant by his being the Father of Lights and show particularly what lights he is the Father or author of.

1. When it is said that God is the Father of Lights, it signifies that he is essentially and of himself a very glorious being. Light or brightness signifies glory. The glory of the sun and of the moon and stars is their light or brightness. The sun is the most glorious being that we behold in the material world because of its great brightness. Therefore, the sun is used commonly amongst the heathen to be worshiped as God. But God is exceedingly more glorious. The light which Paul beheld was above the brightness of the sun. The brightness of God's glory is so great and so excellent that we can't conceive of it. God arrayeth himself "with light as with a garment" (Ps. 104:2). When God used to appear under the Old Testament, he used to appear as all arrayed in light to signify his glory. We read that in the wilderness from

time to time the glory of the Lord appeared (Num. 14:10). A great brightness appeared that signified God's glory.

God is arrayed with an infinite brightness, a brightness that doesn't create pain as the light of the sun pains the eyes to behold it, but rather fills with excess of joy and delight. Indeed, no man can see God and live, because the sight of such glory would overpower nature, but 'tis because the joy and pleasure in beholding would be too strong for a frail nature. God has this glory essentially and of himself. He is independently and necessarily glorious. The sun is glorious, but it derives that glory from another. But God is glorious in and of himself, so he is the Father of glory.

2. God is a communicative being. Light is communicative or rather a communication from the luminary. The sun communicates itself to the world by light. It sheds abroad and diffuses around its light or brightness and fills the world with its beneficial influences, enlightens and enlivens and comforts the universe. God is like the sun in this respect; he is abundantly communicative. He is a fountain of goodness, continuously scattering abroad his kindness and diffusing of his bounty plentifully and abundantly as the sun diffuses his rays. As the light of the sun fills the world, so does God's goodness. God's goodness is most extensive and universal, reaches to all sorts of creatures. He opens his bountiful hand and satisfies the desires of every living thing. He provides for angels and men and the beasts of the earth and fouls of the air and fishes of the sea and for insects. As the sun shines continually, so God's goodness is continual. His mercy endureth forever.

Yea, God communicates himself more continually than the sun. The sun turns from us and leaves a shadow, but God is without a shadow of turning. God has in himself an infinite fullness and sufficiency, and his fullness is continually overflowing. He is an infinite fountain perpetually sending out pure streams. God's communicativeness is of two things, of excellency and of happiness. God is an incomprehensible fountain of both. He communicates excellency to the creature. He beautifies and adorns the world as the sun adorns the world with his rays. All the perfection and all the excellency that is to be discovered among men or angels or any other creature is a communication of this fountain, as rays are communicated from the sun. All creatures receive their excellency from God, as the moon and planets have their light from the sun. So God communicates happiness, being infinitely happy in himself. He rejoices and blesses all others. The rays that stream forth from this sun are streams of God's pleasure and happiness. God is a fountain of happiness, and he is the only fountain of happiness.

Now I propose to show particularly what lights God is the Father of.

1. He is the Father of Jesus Christ, the brightness of his glory and the Light of the world. Jesus Christ is the eternal communication of God's essence. The creation of the world and the communication of God's goodness to the creatures is not the first communication of God. But there is an eternal and essential communication which is the Son of God to whom God effectually communicates all his essence and all his excellency and all his happiness. He is an eternal and infinite effulgence of the Godhead by which God always shone before the foundation of the world with an infinite glory. 'Tis a comparison often made use of by divines to represent the Father and the Son in the Trinity—that the Father is as the sun in the firmament, and Christ as the rays or the lights that proceeds from him. Since Christ is the essential brightness and glory of God, so he is the Light of the world. He is the Sun of Righteousness, the bright and morning star. This is the light that lighteth every man that cometh into the world. 'Tis he who makes manifest the Father, who reveals to us the divine nature and

makes known the mind and will of God and discovers the heavenly world. "Whatsoever doth make manifest is light" (Eph. 5:13).

2. God is the Father of material light, that light which we behold with our bodily eyes. Light is one of the most wonderful things, if not indeed the most excellent and marvelous thing we behold in the material world. It is indeed a wonderful work enough to convince any atheist of the being, power, and wisdom of God. God is the Father of this beautiful and admirable creature, the light. He said in the first creation, "Let there be light: and there was light" (Gen. 1:3). Before that the world was overwhelmed in perfect darkness, but God spoke the word and the light shined forth.

It was God who created the luminaries of heaven. It was he who gave the sun his light that detailed his orb in golden beams, that arrayed him in beautiful garments as a bridegroom. 'Tis he who makes the stars to glisten and to adorn the spheres. He maketh Orion and the chambers of the south. God made the light at first, and he upholds it. If God should withhold his influence, the sun would go out. Like a candle, his light would immediately die away, and the stars would cease their shining, and the world would be left in its primitive darkness and obscurity. The sun, moon, and stars are but God's servants to obey his commands and to do his will. So God is the author of this outward glory. The glory of the sun and heavenly bodies is a faint reflection or rather a shadow of his glory.

3. God is the author of all outward good. Outward prosperity is often in Scripture called light and calamity is called darkness. God gives us all our outward good things. Men are ready to think that they are to be attributed only to second causes, or to their own skill, strength, and care, but they are all the gifts of God. They are his proper and mere bounty as much every whit as the "bread and flesh" that ravens brought to Elijah morning and evening (1 Kings 17:6). If you say that you procure bread to eat by your own labor in tilling the fields,

then I ask, "Who gave you strength to labor, or a field to 'til or the field strength to bring forth upon your tillage?"

So that how many sound causes sown are made up of as means, yet it must be granted that these second causes are caused and ordered and derive their efficiency from the first cause, and though we should suppose that second causes act merely naturally and in a necessary chain of causes and effects, as for instance in rain. If rain comes by mere natural causes, God made them natural causes and gave them such nature as to produce such effects and ordered them so they should produce their effect at such a time by that nature. So that all those good things that men attribute to themselves, or to their fellow creatures, or to natural causes, or to good fortune are indeed the mere gifts of God.

God is the author of our good things in a sense that he is not of our evil things. Though the evil that we meet with is brought upon us by God's providence, yet we procure it ourselves. 'Tis our due, we deserve it, 'tis wages that are due to us. So we ought rather to look on ourselves as the author of it, rather than God. But as to our good things, they are not our due, so God and not we ourselves is the author of them.

4. God is the Father of the light of spiritual knowledge. The soul in its natural state is as the air in the night, all filled with darkness. The mind is ignorant and blind. When God converts a soul, the day does break in their hearts and the shadows flee away: "Until the day dawn, and the day star arise in your hearts" (2 Pet. 1:19). Or rather it is with the natural man as it was in the first creation when darkness filled the world 'til God said, "Let there be light: and there was light" (Gen. 1:3). Second Corinthians 4:6 says, "For God, who commanded the light to shine out of darkness, hath shined in our hearts, to give the light of the knowledge of the glory of God in the face of Jesus Christ." In this text we are told wherein this spiritual light consists—in "the knowledge of

the glory of God in the face of Jesus Christ." The natural man is wholly ignorant of these things. He sees no glory of God and no divine excellency or beauty in the face of Jesus. But 'tis God himself and he only who gives this light. It is he who shines into the heart and causes his own rays to illuminate the mind. He sends forth his own Spirit and teaches and instructs the soul in spiritual and divine things. He causes us to see the certainty and the excellency of the truths revealed in the gospel. He opens a glorious prospect of before unseen and unknown truths and glories. The light that shines into their heart discovers to them heavenly things. It does open heaven, in that it discovers God and Jesus Christ and their glory, majesty, love, and grace which are the main things of heaven.

5. God is the Father of the light of true comfort and joy. Sorrow and grief and distress are often in Scripture called darkness, and comfort is compared to light. God is the only author of this part of light. Therefore, he is called the "God of all comfort" (2 Cor. 1:3).

There is no true comfort to be found anywhere else but in God. There are a great many other things that men hope to find comfort in. They seek it in riches. They seek it in luxury and in sensual pleasures, but 'tis not to be found in any of these things. God is that spring from whence issues the pure stream of comfort where the thirsty may satisfy their longing souls and the weary may find rest. This fountain is an ocean without shores or bottom, enough to satisfy the most capacious and enlarged desires. When God shines into the heart, he makes a difference in it like the difference there is in the atmosphere when all darkened with clouds and disturbed with storms and tempests and when the sun brightly shines in a calm and clear day. Or like the difference there is between the dead of winter and the spring when the trees and the fields look green and are adorned with flowers and the voice of the singing of birds is come.

"The voice of the turtle is heard in our land" (Song 2:12). The fig tree putteth forth her green figs and the vines with the tender grape give a good smell as the sun makes such a difference in the face of the earth. Such likewise is the difference that God, the Father of Lights, makes in the soul when he lets in the light of comfort.

6. God is the author of the light of glory, of that light that enlightens heaven that shines in that world of light where there is no night, nor darkness, nor shadow. Heaven is filled with a glorious light in comparison of which the light of this is as darkness: "Having the glory of God: and her light was like unto a stone most precious, even like a jasper stone, clear as crystal" (Rev. 21:11). The glory of God is that light that is like a stone most precious that is an exceeding clear and pleasant light. God is the sun that shines in heaven; they have no other sun: "And there shall be no night there; and they shall need no candle, neither light of the sun, for the Lord God giveth them light" (Rev. 22:5).

The light that will be given to the souls of the glorified saints will be a most clear manifestation of God's majesty and beauty. They shall see God as he is. That perfect holiness which they themselves shall have shall make they themselves shine like the sun forever and ever. Being changed into the same image, they shall also shine forth in the kingdom of their Father when they behold the shining of God's glory. But this light of their holiness will be only as the reflection of God's light, and lastly there will be the light of perfect happiness. God gives the light of comfort here, but there he gives the light of perfect joy and pleasure forever more.

And besides those, there will doubtless after the resurrection be a light of glory to be seen with bodily eyes. This probably will be the light that shines forth from Christ's glorious body, a visible glory far exceeding that which appeared in his body and countenance at his transfiguration. The bodies of the saints also will then probably shine with a glorious brightness, but only with a derived and communicated light, so that God is still the Father of Lights. He is the Father of that innumerable company of angels and saints which then will shine as so many lights.

APPLICATION

1. Let us improve this doctrine to admire and love God. The doctrine represents God to us as an exceeding glorious being. Let us admire and magnify him who clothes himself with light as a garment. Who is not clothed with gold and silver and gems that appear glorious for their shining, but is clothed with light itself with earth and essential glory. See how the glory of God is represented: "And he that sat was to look upon like a jasper and a sardine stone: and there was a rainbow round about the throne, in sight like unto an emerald" (Rev. 4:3). He was surrounded with a transcendent and most delightsome glory. Let us therefore love and extol him who is a fountain of such glory.

God is to be loved by us also in that he not only possesses this glory in himself, but is so abundantly communicative. He pours forth his goodness as plentifully as the sun pours forth his light. The whole world is beautified and supplied by his diffusive communication. He shines down upon all those who are not his enemies, as the sun in May shines down upon the flowers and refreshes and receives them and causes them to send forth a pleasant fragrance. Consider how glorious he must needs be who created the visible light that we behold, who decks the globe of the sun in his rays and commanded it to shine. We are so used to the light of the sun that we don't consider what a testimony it is of the glory of its Father. If we had hitherto been kept in a dark dungeon and were brought out to behold the light of the sun, how it would fill us with admiration to behold it.

I remember I have read of a Protestant in Spain who was three years kept in a dungeon and never saw the sun. And when he was brought out to be put to death and saw the sun, he was greatly affected at the light and expressed his admiration. He wondered how any could worship any other but the Maker of that glorious creature. And indeed this one work of God—the sun—is a greater testimony of the being and glory of God than a thousand miracles. Solomon takes notice that light is sweet and that it is a pleasant thing to behold the sun. But if it be pleasant to behold the glory of the sun, is not the glory of him who made the sun much more pleasant and admirable?

Therefore, when we behold the sun let us consider that there we behold the shadow of God's glory. In the morning when you awake and behold the light, consider that you behold a fresh manifestation of the lovely glory of God. When you see the sun lifting up its head over the mountains, consider the brightness of the Sun of Righteousness. And if outward light be such a testimony of the excellency of the Father of it, much more is spiritual light the light of spiritual knowledge and of spiritual comfort.

This light is far more excellent. The light of the sun only discovers to us this world, helps us to see one another and to behold the fields, and trees and clouds, and other material objects. But spiritual light discovers to us the Creator of all these things, and the Redeemer of our soul and helps to see heaven as Moses saw Canaan from the top of Pisgah. Let us therefore love and admire the author and fountain of this light and love him who is the diffusive fountain of all true comfort, of spiritual peace and delight. You who have experienced this, you know how sweet it is. Shall not so pleasant a gift that came down as the warm beams of the sun make you love the author of it?

But above all does the light of glory afford an argument for the love and praise of the Father of that light. We have but a very faint conception of that light. We know but little of it. All the comparisons that we can make use of will not suffice to set it forth. But yet that little that we do know of it, or may know of it, may suffice to show us reason of exceedingly admiring and delighting in God. For God is the sun of heaven. If the sun of this lower world be so glorious, how glorious must the sun of that supreme world be that is the metropolis and highest palace of this universe. But God is that sun from whom came streams of light as rivers of pleasure forever more. Whose light is like a stream most gloriously clear as crystal. Whose light fills the eyes of angels and their hearts brimful of delight unspeakable. Wherefore admire and love and see that you magnify the Father of Lights. Love this most lovely object and fear this supreme majesty. Love him and delight in him. Rejoice with joy that is full of glory.

2. Let those who are in darkness come to God for light. Those who are in the darkness of affliction, you have heard that God is the author of all true comfort. Therefore, now you know where to go when sorrows and afflictions surround you. You may at any time go to a healing spring that affords such sweet water as is an effectual remedy against all grief and sorrow. You need not live in darkness while there is such a sun that shines.

Whatever your grief and sorrow is, God has sufficient consolation for you. He is able to make persons rejoice in fiery flames and to keep them so that so much as their hair shall not be singed in Nebuchadnezzar's furnace (Dan. 3:27).

If a man is afflicted in his outward goods with losses and poverty, God is able in such a case to make a man richer than the kings of the earth with or without earthly riches. If we are afflicted in body by grievous pain or languishing sickness, God is able to give us inward health and so renew our inward man as our outward man decays so that the comfort of this spiritual health shall be far greater than the affliction of bodily illness. If we are afflicted by the malice and ill will of man, God is able to make us see that he is our friend and to give us more joy in that than those who are enemies are able to give us sorrow. If we have lost near and dear relations, God is able more than a thousand times to make it up in the enjoyment of himself. If we have trouble of conscience for our sins and are followed with fear of wrath, God is able to give us that peace which passes all understanding. If we groan under spiritual desertions and God hides his face from us if we come unto him, he is ready to take away the evil, that we may again behold his smiles and see the light of his countenance.

In any temporal affliction God can easily comfort us either by remaining the cause of our sorrow, or by giving us that spiritual comfort that shall make us forget our sorrow. In spiritual affliction we need nothing also but that God should lift up the light of his countenance in order to the removal of it. God is a God who comforts those who are cast down.

3. Let those who are in the darkness of spiritual blindness and ignorance come to God for light. James 1:5 says, "If any of you lack wisdom, let him ask of God, that giveth to all men liberally, and upbraideth not, and it shall be given him." You lack wisdom and you want it exceedingly. Come to this Father of Lights for it. Come by Jesus Christ, and it shall be given.

How doubtful a thing it is to dwell in total darkness as you have done ever since you were born. What a doleful world it would be for us if the sun should finally set and rise no more upon us. We should not only be deprived of the light of the sun, but of the moon and stars, also of the light of candles and all other light, and be cast in absolute darkness. So that we could not see one another, could not see the ground, or our houses, or anything at all. You may easily conceive how doleful this would be.

It was one of the greatest plagues of Egypt to be in such darkness for three days (Exod. 10:21–22). How dreadful to be in such darkness for one's lifetime. How miserable are you who have dwelt in darkness and more dreadful darkness ever since you were born. If you say you be not sensible that your case is so doleful, yet that is no evidence that it is not indeed. He who has been blind ever since he was born is not sensible of his misery because he doesn't know what light is, and he knows not how much he loses in being without it. But you may be rationally convinced that it must be very doleful to be spiritually blind, much more than to be outwardly so, for he who is blind as to his bodily eyes is miserable because he can't see the things that concern this life and his temporal interests.

But he who is spiritually blind is blind in things that are of infinitely greater concern. It is exceeding dangerous to dwell in such darkness. He who walks without a guide in natural darkness is in danger of stumbling or falling and wounding himself. But he who walks in spiritual darkness is in continual danger of stumbling upon the dark mountains of death and of being led astray by the devil and of falling into the pit of hell.

That you may be induced earnestly to seek light of the Father of Lights, consider how excellent and pleasant a thing light is. Natural, corporeal light is the most beautiful thing that we behold in the visible world. How much more excellent is spiritual light. This divine light is capable to fill your soul with the most substantial, satisfying joys. If you have it in your soul, it is of that nature that it will change you into the same image, make you partake of that light in yourself and cause you also to shine.

Consider the beneficialness of this spiritual life. 'Tis of use not only to instruct us in the most important and excellent truth and to lead and conduct us in the way of wisdom and prudence, and to our own happiness, but it gives life to the soul as the rays of the sun doesn't only give light but also quickens and enlivens things, causes the trees to grow and bring forth the grass, and causes things to blossom and bear fruit, so their spiritual light enlivens the soul and therefore is called the "light of life" (John 8:12). Wherefore, remain no longer in darkness, but come to God, the author and fountain of marvelous light.

22

Nothing Else Is Required
of Us in Order to Our
Having an Interest in Christ,
but That We Should Find It
in Our Hearts to Be Willing
That Christ Should Be Ours
and We His

Behold, I stand at the door, and knock: if any man hear my voice, and
open the door, I will come in to him, and will sup with him,
and he with me.

REVELATION 3:20

W e conclude this wonderful collection of Edwards's sermons
with a lengthy example of a message he preached from the final
book of the Bible—a sermon taken from Christ's Word to the
Laodicean church. What Edwards draws out in a masterly way is
the wonder of what Christ says to this group of his people. Though he
can speak no good of them, yet he offers good to them, in that he again
offers himself to them.

What is significant in Edwards's treatment of the passage is that he
seems to make no reference to the fact that this text was taken from

Christ's message to a church, and not unbelievers. And as many other preachers have done, the text has been used as the basis for a direct challenge from Christ to sinners to open their hearts to him as Lord and Savior.

The sermon manuscript is a typical, though lengthy, duodecimal booklet. In fact, this is the longest sermon in this volume, consisting of sixty leaves. There is some evidence of water damage to the original, together with some evidence of changes Edwards made to the text.

This is part of what Christ says to the church of the Laodiceans. This is not one of the seven churches that Christ finds so much fault with as with that of some sins he found with most of the other churches. Christ tells them he has somewhat against them. But yet it may be observed that there is not one of all of them except that of Laodicea but that he speaks some good of. The church of Ephesus is much commended for their labor and patience and not for turning to false apostles. The church of Smyrna for their tribulation and poverty and being prudentially rich. The church of Pergamos is also commended that they hold fast to Christ's name and have not denied their first love. The church of Thyatira is commended for their charity and service and faith and patience. The church of Philadelphia is also greatly commended for their good works and having kept Christ's word. And the church of Sardis, though Christ finds much fault with them, is told they had a name, that they lived but were dead. Yet he tells them that there were a few names even in Sardis who had not defiled their garments.

But of this church at Laodicea, Christ says no good at all. He tells them that he knows their work, that they are neither cold nor hot, and he threatens to spew them out of his mouth. He charges them with pride and selfishness, that they said they were rich and increased.

But though Christ speaks no good of them, yet he offers good to them. He takes occasion after he had set forth their sinfulness and misery to make gracious offers of mercy and invitation to come to him for those things they needed to make them better. Thus we find none of the seven churches so much changed and as highly charged. Yet neither do we find the gracious offers of grace so fully made to anyone as to those of Laodicea. This is agreeable to what Christ says—that they who are rich have most need of a Savior and that he comes to call sinners to repent (Matt. 9:12–13). He finds them poor, but he doesn't smite them for that. He would have them come to him that he might make them rich. He finds them naked, but he doesn't destroy them for that. He invites them to come to him that they may be clothed. He finds them blind but doesn't leave them.

Christ tells them that they are poor and have nothing. Yet he advises them to buy gold of him to make them rich. But if they are so poor, what shall they buy this gold with? Is it not strange that a beggar who has nothing so much as to buy a bit of bread with should be advised to buy a great estate that he may be rich? But we find an answer in Isaiah 55:1: "He that hath no money; come ye, buy, and eat; yea, come, buy wine." And Christ explains himself in the verse of the text that presently follows, "Behold." He signified that when he advises them to buy he expects no more than only that they should accept the free offer that he makes, that they should open the door and let him in, that he may come and bestow these things upon them that they need and feed their needy and famishing souls. Christ, in these words found in our text (Rev. 3:20), represents the freeness of his grace to sinners in three things:

1. In the thing here offered, union and communion with him: "I will come in to him, and will sup with him, and he with me."

2. Consider the condition of the offer: "If any man hear my voice, and open the door." To hear Christ's voice spiritually is to receive it and spiritually to understand it and to have the will bowed and inclined to it. To open the door is to be willing to receive him as he offers himself. When any who knocks at our door seeks entertainment of us, opening the door is a sign that we admit and receive him and are willing to entertain him.

3. Observe the gracious manner in which Christ makes this offer: "Behold, I stand at the door and knock." This signifies more to us than if Christ merely said, "Behold, I make you an offer." It signifies the very gracious and condescending manner of the offer. If a king should make an offer of some present to a subject, it would not manifest such a word of grace and condescension as if he came himself in person and knocked on the subject's door to bring him the offer of the benefit in such a manner. It holds forth to us that Christ not only makes the offer but that he seeks and desires the person's acceptance of it and that he is earnest and importunate that they would accept it and works upon them to accept it.

He not only condescends to knock at our door, but he stands at the door, knocking and waiting for admittance as loathe to go away with a denial which is agreeable to that in Song of Solomon 5:2: "It is the voice of my beloved that knocketh, saying, Open to me, my sister, my love, my dove, my undefiled: for my head is filled with dew."

DOCTRINE

Nothing else is required of us in order to our having an interest in Christ but that we should find it in our hearts to be willing that Christ should be ours and we his. Christ's knocking at the door implies his offer is himself to us, to be ours. He knocks and waits at our door for us to admit him and receive him, that we may take him into our souls to be our own, to abide with us and to be for us and to be possessed by him, as he offers himself to be enjoyed by us, to come in to sup with us and we with him.

His knocking at our door implies his seeking. We should also give ourselves to him to be his, for we are to observe that door that he knocks at is the door of our hearts. He seeks to be admitted into the heart to take possession of that, that we may let him come in to dwell there as the owner of the house and claiming entrance or possession. He would have the heart given wholly to him, empty of all other inhabitants. Embracing of him in the arms of our heart and accepting him as ours and casting ourselves into the arms of his grace and love, signifying ourselves up to him to be his.

Our opening the door implies accepting Christ as he offers himself. If a man comes to our house as a stranger and knocks at our door as a guest for a night and we know it, then an opening of the door to him implies that we accept him as a transient guest. But if we know that a person knocks at our door seeking to be admitted to dwell with us as a friend and companion, then opening the door implies an admitting and entertaining of him as such. And if in a time of war a captain or general of an army, a junior officer in his name, came and knocked at our door, our opening our door to him would imply our accepting him as our master and yielding up ourselves to his power.

So opening the door to Christ signifies our accepting him in the reality in which he comes to us. He comes to us as a Savior and suitor, so our opening the door implies our accepting him to be ours. And again, he comes in the reality of a Lord and King. So our opening the door to him implies our being willing to be his, a giving ourselves up to him as 'tis sometimes the manner at the first inauguration of a king or chief magistrate. He comes from some place to the gates of the city, which being shut he demands entrance. The chief officers of the city open the gates to him. This action signifies a giving up the city to his authority and government. This is what is signified by our opening the door to Christ—being willing that Christ should be ours and we his. This is all that is required of us in order to our having an interest in Christ.

Many seem to think the terms of salvation hard and difficult as though God had not dealt well with us in fixing the terms of salvation. But 'tis only required in order to our having Christ's favor that we should find in our hearts to be willing that he should be ours and ourselves to be his.

To clear up the doctrine, I would show how we must find in our hearts to be with that and that nothing else is required of us in order to our having an interest in Christ.

1. We must find it in our hearts to be willing that Christ should be ours. Christ in the Gospels offers himself to us to be ours. He is ready and willing to be wholly ours with all that he is and has. As much as we are capable of having of him our own and so to be most for our happiness and what is required of us is that we should be indeed willing that he should be ours. Receiving Christ, which is the same thing as accepting of him for ours, is mentioned in Scripture as the thing that entitles us to salvation: "But as many as received him, to them gave he power to become the sons of God, even to them that believe on his name" (John 1:12).

'Tis here spoken of as what is the nature of faith. We must obviously consider again Colossians 2:5–6, "Beholding you and the steadfastness of your faith as you have therefore received Christ Jesus the Lord so walk ye in him." Faith is spoken of in Scripture as being the opposite to rejecting and disallowing of Christ. So it is in John 12:46–48, "Whosoever believeth on me should not abide in darkness. And if any man hear my words, and believe not, I judge him not . . . . He that rejecteth me . . . hath one that judgeth him." Not believing and rejecting are spoken of as the same thing. Therefore, believing is the same as accepting: "Unto you therefore which believe he is precious:

but unto them which be disobedient, the stone which the builders disallowed, the same is made the head of the corner" (1 Pet. 2:7). The believing and disallowing are in opposition one to another. Not believing and disallowing are the same thing.

'Tis required that we find in our hearts to be willing that Christ would stand and be ours as a Savior. 'Tis as such that he offers himself. We must be willing that Christ should be ours in that. Observe that he is always represented in the Scriptures as a mediator and in that work which he came into the world. We must find it in our hearts to be with that Christ who was concerned to save us. We must find a real willingness to be saved in that way—by the blood and righteousness of Christ. That must be the way that we choose.

We must find it in our hearts to be willing that Christ should free us from our sins and not only from punishment of sin. Christ appears in that station and office—a Savior from sin: "He shall save his people from their sins" (Matt. 1:21). This doubtless includes his saving a soul from sin itself and not only the fruits of it.

We must find it within our hearts to be willing that Christ should become our way to God and therefore must be willing to be brought into union with God. If we aren't willing to come to God at all, we can't be willing that Christ should be our way to God. We must be willing that Christ should be our way not only to the favor of God but to a conformity to him.

We must be willing that Christ should be our way to happiness, not a carnal happiness, but a spiritual happiness, to the happiness that consists in holiness. In order to this, we must be willing to have such a happiness. If we aren't willing to have it, we can't be willing that Christ should be our way to it.

We must be willing that Christ should be our portion. Christ doesn't offer his benefits separate from his person. Herein the union of believers with Christ is like a marriage union as when a man offers himself to a woman in marriage. He doesn't offer his estate separately from his person, but he offers her himself with all that he has together. So Christ offers himself with his benefits. There are many who would gladly have some of the benefits of Christ, but they have no love to the person of Christ. They see no form or comeliness in him, no beauty. We must be willing that Christ should be ours in all the qualifications and excellence of his person, not only in his love and mercy but in his holiness.

Holiness is the beauty of the divine nature. We must be willing to have the beauty of Christ to be ours. There are two ways that the holiness of Christ may be ours—by being ours to behold and enjoy and ours to have communicated to us for us to be partakers of.

Unbelievers aren't willing that the holiness of Christ should be theirs either of those ways. They have no desire that the holiness of Christ should be theirs for them to enjoy and be crying in beholding of it. They have no sense of any happiness in any such thing as beholding the glorious beauty of Christ.

Neither are they willing that the holiness of Christ should be theirs by being communicated to them. They don't desire that Christ should make them partakers of his holiness. They don't love holiness, but on the contrary their hearts are wedded to sin. It does not suffice that we be only willing to have Christ to force a turn, but as our whole portion. We should receive Christ as the spouse and husband, our souls passing by all others, choosing him above all the world. Choosing him in that near relation to be our nearest friend and companion to the exclusion of all others. Giving that consent to receive him that offers himself, to have him only, with a rejection of all others. Thus we must be willing that Christ should be ours.

We must also find it in our hearts to be willing to be Christ's. We must willingly and cheerfully and of free choice give up ourselves to

Christ. Thus the apostle Paul says of the Macedonians that they "gave their own selves to the Lord" (2 Cor. 8:5).

Some are willing that Christ should in some respects be theirs, but they are not willing to be his. We must receive Christ after such a manner as therein to give ourselves. By that act whereby the soul closes with Christ, it doth both these things—it accepts of Christ and gives up itself. In this transaction between Christ and the soul, there is a mutual giving and receiving. The soul entirely embraces Christ and at the same time entirely gives up itself to Christ. From this and other resemblances between the union with Christ and marrying a relation, 'tis very often in Scripture compared to that picture frequently than to anything else.

The act of closing with Christ is compared to the consent of the bride in taking the bridegroom and giving herself to him in the marriage covenant: "I have espoused you to one husband" (2 Cor. 11:2). Romans 7:4 says, "Wherefore, my brethren, ye also are become dead to the law by the body of Christ; that ye should be married to another, even to him who is raised from the dead."

I would show first to what purpose we should be willing to be Christ's and, secondly, in what manner.

We must be willing to his persuasion. We should be willing to be subject to his disposing will, to be disposed of for his ends. We should be willing that Christ should be our master, that he should have an absolute right to us.

We should be willing to give up ourselves to him, disclaiming all rights in ourselves, consenting that all the propriety of us should be vested in him. Anything is said to be a man's own and in his possession when he has it to dispose of his own ends. We should be willing that Christ should thus own us. We should be willing to renounce our selfish ends and not to be for ourselves but to be for Christ, to be for his ends and purposes.

We should be willing to give ourselves up to the designs of his glory. To be so disposed of in the world and to be in such circumstances as Christ shall see most for his honor. We should be comfortable that we are not our own but out of right belong to Christ and that we are subject to his will and not our own. We should consent to it and choose it and have pleasure in it that it should be so.

We should be willing to be Christ's disciples. We should be willing to be subject to his instructions, to learn of him, to give up our minds to him, to be instructed to resign up our reason to him, and to be guided by his teachings. We should willingly put ourselves into the school of Christ. We should be wholly subject to his justice, as a little is to the influence of a great, to learn all the doctrine that he teaches, being convinced of his Word and truth and not to sit up one week in opposition to his word.

We should be willing to be his servants. We should give up our wills to be subject to the commands of Christ, willingly donating ourselves to his work to seek his glory and promote his kingdom. To have all our powers and faculties tempered for him. To labor and lay out ourselves in his service, we should choose this. We should prefer such a life and be cheerful in it, accounting it the happiest life, not esteeming it any bondage but as delight. We should come to Christ and take his yoke upon us (Matt. 11:29). We should willingly take all the difficulties of his soul upon ourselves.

We should be willing that our souls should be the spouse of Christ. That our affections shall be appropriated to him, willing to give up our hearts to Christ's possession that he should reign in our lives.

We should be willing to be Christ's friends and companions to dwell with him, to be separated from all the world in order to fellowship and commune with him, to spend an eternity in this. Unbelievers are not willing that themselves should be the spouse of Christ. They aren't willing to yield their hearts to him. They don't desire to have their souls separated from all other loves, for communion with and concourse with him but 'tis the spirit of believers. Revelation 14:4 says, "These are they which follow the Lamb whithersoever he goeth."

I have shown to what purposes we should be willing to be Christ's. I proceed now to the second matter—to show in what manner believers are willing to be Christ's. That may be described in three things: They are willing to be wholly Christ's, to be only Christ's, and to be forever Christ's.

They are willing to be wholly Christ's. They aren't only willing to give part of themselves to Christ, receiving a part to themselves and giving a part to some other lord. But they are willing that Christ should have all. They are willing that their souls should be Christ's. They are willing that all 'tis theirs should be his—that their understanding should be his and that their wills and affections should also be his. They are willing also that their bodies should be Christ's. They present their bodies a "living sacrifice" (Rom. 12:1). They are willing that their hearts should be Christ's. They are also willing that their lives should be his, that their outward actions and practice should be his. They are willing to live to him as long as they do live. They would have Christ, have the whole of their lives, for they see that he is worthy. Therefore, they are willing that Christ should have themselves and all that they have.

Herein hypocrites fail. They never are brought to be willing to give themselves wholly to Christ. They may be willing to give him their bodies, their outside in some measure, but they aren't willing that their heart should be his. They may be willing to be partly Christ's, but they won't give themselves to Christ without reserve. They keep back a part for themselves and for the world and reserve a part for their lusts.

They won't give their lives wholly to Christ. They may seem to live to Christ for a while, but they won't complete, neither will they persevere in living to Christ to the end of their lives. They let Christ have only some parts of their lives. They will seem to come to Christ at some seasons when they can do it without hurting the flesh as to prejudicing their outward interest. But no longer they are by no means willing that their whole lives should be Christ's.

They are willing to be only Christ's. They want to be Christ's and no other's. They desire that he should be the sole proprietor of them. They are not only willing that Christ should own them in subordination or in partnership with other lords, but they are willing that Christ should have the supreme right to them—that he should have a right above themselves and any creature.

They are willing that their souls should be the spouse of Christ without entertaining any other lover. They are willing to be the servants of Christ and his only—not to serve him sometimes and their lusts sometimes. Not to be partly the servants of Christ and partly the servants of mammon but to have Christ to rule over them alone, to have him for them only as Lord and King. Isaiah 26:13 says, "Other lords beside thee have had dominion over us: but . . . ."

They are willing to be Christ's forever. They are willing to be his as long as they are in this world and not only so but to all eternity. They are willing that Christ should have their thoughts, have the possession of them, that he should forever possess their hearts. They desire no other than that all their powers and faculties should forever be employed in serving and glorifying him. They are willing to have their souls united to Christ, and they desire that this order may forever continue. They desire to spend their eternity no other way than for Christ and in communion and fellowship with him.

2. I have shown how we must find it in our hearts to be willing that Christ should be ours and we his. I come now to the second thing under the doctrine—that this is all that is required of us in order to our having an interest in Christ. As soon as ever a man is brought to be willing that Christ should be his and he should be Christ's, Christ

immediately takes possession of him as his own and gives himself to him to be his. Thenceforward there is a most near relation between Christ and him. Christ becomes his Savior and Redeemer and his portion and all that is in Christ his. His power is his to be employed to conquer his enemies. His wisdom, his dying love is his, and all his grace is his. All the great and wonderful things that Christ has done and suffered—they are his. He is entitled to the benefit of them. The divine and human nature of Christ are both his. The righteousness of Christ, it is all his. He puts it thenceforward on and wears it as a robe. His nakedness and depravity are forever gone, and he becomes beautiful in the eyes of God, saints, and angels.

The precious blood of Christ is his to cleanse him from his sin. The resurrection and exaltation of Christ is his. He has a title, the benefit of it. Christ's intercession in heaven is his. The Holy Spirit of Christ is his to sanctify him, to dwell in him to be a principle of life in his soul to quicken, to comfort, and to glorify him. Christ and all Christ has is his. Christ has life, and because Christ lives he shall live also. Christ has heaven. He is the owner of heaven, and so it is his. Christ will prepare a place there for him. Christ is the heir of the whole world, and so this is all his in Christ Jesus. All things are his as soon as ever he is brought to be willing that Christ should be his and he Christ's. He by Christ thenceforward stands in good terms with God the Father.

When once a soul is made entirely willing, it becomes the spouse of Christ. It is married to Christ. Neither time nor eternity shall dissolve the bond of union. Such a soul shall be for Christ, and Christ will be for it. The time will come when that soul shall be prepared as a bride adorned for her husband and shall shine forth in a glory fit for the bride, the Lamb's wife. Such an one shall dwell with Christ in the nearest union and fullest enjoyment, world without end.

There is no righteousness required. God the Father requires no righteousness of man to make him willing to give them an interest in

Christ. Christ requires no righteousness of us to make him willing to accept us and take us into union with himself. 'Tis not expected or required of us that we should offer any sacrifice, or do any great thing to purchase to ourselves design and happiness of an interest in Christ. There is no money or price expected of us; Christ requires only our consent. He asks our heart be willing that he should be ours and we his. Christ doesn't insist upon or expect any good or loveliness in us to work upon him and overcome his affections and incline himself to them into union with them.

If we will but give our consent to have Christ for ours and to be Christ's, Christ won't wait for anything further. He will at once accept us, though we never have done any one thing that has any good in it besides that in our whole lives. There is not required anything of us to make any atonement for our past sins. If we once consider it in our hearts to be willing, all our past sins shall be no hindrance. The blood of Christ shall cleanse them away, and the robe of the righteousness of Christ shall cover them. If we will but give our consent to this, Christ doesn't desire that we should suffer anything to satisfy justice. He doesn't desire that we should continue one moment longer under remorse and terrors of conscience. We may set our hearts at rest and enjoy peace as soon we will if we will but consent to this.

If we can find it in our hearts to be willing for this, Christ will accept us without any expectation of our doing anything to pay him for it afterwards. Christ doesn't expect that we should ever pay him for an interest in him and a title to his benefits. We never can recompense him for it. Neither can we recompense God the Father for giving us an interest nor can we recompense Christ for accepting.

Christ doesn't stand in any need of us. He is far above all need of the creature. He has enough, and it is impossible that we should add anything to him. Our love and our service and our praises to all eternity will never obtain Christ, nor does he at all expect it. No, there is no other condition required of us but only that we should truly find it in our hearts. I would here mention two or three additional evidences.

This is naturally significant by the expression, "coming to Christ." The condition of having an interest is often in Scripture represented to be only coming to Christ: "Come unto me, all ye that labor" (Matt. 11:28). "And him that cometh to me I will in no wise cast out" (John 6:37). "Ho, every one that thirsteth" (Isa. 55:1). "If any man thirst, let him come" (John 7:37). "Whosoever will, let him take the water of life freely" (Rev. 22:17). "He that believeth on me shall never thirst" (John 6:35). This coming to Christ signifies nothing else but a coming, a closing of heart, an action uniting of himself. But wherein does that union consist but only in a mutual relation and propriety whereby Christ is ours and we his. 'Tis he who truly comes to Christ who comes in his inclination and will. Christ comes to us and offers to be ours. He is the person who truly comes to him who meets him and is willing to be his.

This appears from the nature of the covenant of grace. The matter of the covenant of grace is often in Scripture represented by these words, "I will be your God, and ye shall be my people" (Jer. 7:23). This is the covenant that we are to agree to. We are to consent that God should be our God and that Christ should be our Savior and our portion and should agree that we will be his people. Which is the same that I have said—that we should be willing that Christ should be ours and we his.

It appears from the form of the covenant of grace whereby it is a covenant of grace and different from the covenant of works. 'Tis from hence that it is called a covenant of grace, that nothing is required, no other condition but only our consenting. Herein it differs from the covenant of works. The covenant of works requires that we should work out a righteousness of our own. But the new covenant is called a covenant of grace in contradistinction to that because 'tis offered freely without our working anything, only our being willing to receive Christ and give ourselves.

Being willing is expressly mentioned in Scripture as the condition of an interest in him. "Ye will not come to me" (John 5:40). "How often would I have gathered thy children . . . and ye would not (Matt. 23:37). "Whosoever will," let him come (Rev. 22:17).

APPLICATION

The first use I would make of this doctrine of conviction to convince sinners how justly they may be left to perish forever in that they aren't willing that Christ should be theirs and they his. How justly may they be left without an interest in Christ when an interest in Christ is what they won't have. It is the thing they refuse. How justly may they be left without ever being united to Christ when a union is what they are opposite to. They cannot find it in their hearts to be willing that Christ should be theirs and they his. What can be more remarkable than this—that they have Christ? If they will only give their consent to it, Christ shall be theirs.

If they can but find it in their hearts to be willing that it should be so with them. But they bolt the door against Christ and refuse to arise and open to him and then complain how hardly they are dealt with, that he doesn't come in and help and save them. If they would open the door, he would come in and save them. He would come in and make them happy.

He stands at your door day and night, telling of you, "Go," and urging you to open the door that he may come in and sup. He has stood 'til his head is wet, and he stands there yet. What can be more reasonable than such an offer as this, that because you have provoked God and deserved hell, yet you may have a Savior and may have all his benefits if you can but find it in your heart to be willing that this Savior should be yours? How justly that you may be left to perish, seeing that you won't give your consent to this. You won't have eternal life when offered. When life and death are set before you, you choose death (Prov. 8:36).

Is it any wonder that God does not force salvation upon you, whether you will or no? How unreasonable would it be to expect this? How unsuitable would it be and disagreeable for God to save and carry men into heaven when they are all the while opposing and resisting and struggling to go to hell? This would be to cast "pearls before swine," who trample them under foot and then turn again and rout him who offers them (Matt. 7:6).

But here I am aware that persons as soon as ever they hear this will be ready with their objections. Therefore, I will answer these objections before I proceed any further.

Some may object and say that they be not convinced, that they be not willing that Christ should be theirs and they his. Why should they be charged with being unwilling for this when they won't give all that they have in the world that they might have it? That is what they are seeking. That is what they have prayed for and worked for hundreds of times—that Christ might be theirs and they his. I would therefore here say a few things to convince sinners that 'tis not in their hearts to be willing that Christ should be theirs.

Consider how it is possible that you should easily be led to accept Christ and give yourself up to him. When you question whether there be a Christ, when you are utterly ignorant and at a loss whether the whole story about him be not a fable, you don't know whether there ever was any such man in the world or no, or if there was, whether he was any more than a man. And you don't know whether he ever rose from the dead. You don't know whether when he died there was an end of him and whether there be any such person now in the universe. Now how is it possible that while this is the case with you, you can with any manner of depravity be said to receive Christ for your salvation and your portion and give yourself up to him to be his possession and his servants? Is there any such thing as a person truly giving himself up to an imaginary person who he at the same time is altogether ignorant of and doubts whether he has any being or not reason to suppose any such thing?

Consider how it is possible that you can receive Christ as a Savior from that which you be not sensible you have deserved. Consider whether it be proper to say that you are willing to have Christ as your Savior from your guilt and desert of hell, when at the same time you be not sensible that you have deserved hell. What do you receive Christ as a Savior from, if not from guilt? And what guilt is it if it be not a being guilty of death? A guilt that deserves hell. Christ did not come to save us from any other guilt. He came to save men from hell, from eternal misery, to free them from their guilt that they have deserved. If you do not deserve hell, you have no occasion for Christ. If you be not sensible that you have deserved hell, you be not sensible that you have any occasion for him. Surely we should not need Christ to save us from eternal misery if we had not deserved eternal misery.

How can you truly and properly say that you are willing to receive Christ as your Savior from eternal misery, when at the same time you be not sensible that is any occasion for such a Savior and don't know why you might not have been free from eternal misery without him as well as with him? Is there anything as willingly receiving and accepting of a needless Savior?

If you say that though you be not sensible that you have deserved eternal misery, yet you are afraid you must have. You are afraid that God will bring it upon you whether there be any justice in it or no. So you would be glad to have Christ for a Savior from it. And to this I would say it so offers you a Savior from a punishment you have not deserved, then the very offer is an injury to you. It contains in it a charge of this—that you be not guilty of it but that guilt by which you have deserved hell there the very offer of a sacrifice to accept for their guilt carries in it a false charge. It implies that you have such guilt. Can you be truly said willingly to receive such an offer?

Consider how it is possible that you should be willing to have Christ as a Savior from your sins, at the same time that you be not willing to part with your sins. If you are saved from your sins, you must part with them. If you are saved from your sins, this will be parting with them. 'Tis a downright contradiction to say that a man is saved from that. He is not separated from but that still remains with him. Therefore, if you be not willing to part with your sins, why do you say that you are willing to have Christ for your Savior? If you be not willing to have Christ for a Savior from sin, you be not willing that he should be yours in the reality in which he offers himself.

'Tis to be found there are many now in this congregation who live in some secret or open indulgence of their lusts which they will not part with, notwithstanding all that ever has ever been said to them to part with them. They never would part with those sins, nor are they yet brought to it. It is questionable whether they ever will. Yet if they be asked whether they be willing that Christ should be theirs, they think they will be as ready to answer in the affirmative as any other. They think they would by no means be without Christ. They would not fear all the world, for if Christ be not theirs and they his, they must go to hell. And there is no natural man has any other sort of willingness that Christ should be his. They may as truly be said to be willing that Christ should be theirs as natural man. Yet how plain is it that they are not willing that Christ be their governor, because they be not willing to part with that lust that Christ came to save men from.

There is no natural man whatsoever who has a real, thorough willingness finally and for ever to part with all his lusts and therefore be not be willing to be saved from them. Natural men may sometimes flatter themselves that they are made thoroughly willing, yet they deceive themselves. In a time of trial they lay fast hold again of those sins that they seemed to part with. They abstain from them for a while, yet there is no final parting. They will not persevere in abstinence but will return to their sins again at last.

This may convince you that you are mistaken when you say you are willing that Christ should be yours and that you give all that you have in the world that it were so. The thing that you are so willing for is not to be obliged to burn in hell forever. But there is a difference between that and being willing that Christ should be yours and you his.

Consider how it is possible that you should be willing to have him for your portion, that you see no loveliness or excellency in him. Every man desires happiness for his portion. 'Tis impossible to persuade any man to take up with anything for his portion that is not happiness. Therefore, 'tis impossible that any man should be willing to have Christ for his portion who does not see that happiness is on him. How can any man see happiness in Christ who sees no beauty or excellency in him?

Every man desires something for his portion that he loves. 'Tis possible any man should be willingly taken with that for his portion that he has no love to. But how can any man love that in which he sees no loveliness? How can any man be willing to have that for his portion that he takes no delight in? How can you take delight in Christ when you see no excellency or beauty in him?

Consider also how is it possible that you should be willing to give yourself up to be wholly Christ's if you have no love to him. Your having no love to Christ shows both you be not willing to have him for yours and also that you be not willing to be his. It also shows that you be not willing to be his and also that you be not willing to be Christ's.

We have shown that they who are truly willing to be Christ's are willing to be eternally his and only his and forever his. To give themselves up utterly and finally to be his possession, to be his disciples, to be his servants and give their hearts, their souls, and their bodies—all that they have and are. Now how is it possible a man should find it in his heart to be truly willing and all this towards a person whom he does not love?

Was there ever such a thing heard of as a person's being willing wholly to give up himself, to donate himself entirely, absolutely, and finally to one whom he had no love to and whom he did not see worthy of his esteem and affection? In order to a person's being thus willing to see another's, 'tis not only necessary that he should love him and esteem, but he does not do it unless he esteems him above all and loves him with a supreme love more than anything else whatsoever.

How is it possible that you should be willing to give yourself to Christ when you be not willing to give him your heart? If a man does not give his heart to another, he surely can be said to be truly unwilling to give himself to him because the heart governs the man. The man is and does as his heart influences and dictates. So if you are willing to be Christ's, why don't you give your lives and practice to Christ? If a man is willing to be Christ's, he will be willing to leave the world. He will be willing that Christ should have his life and actions. He will be willing to act for him and to live to him. But if you are willing that Christ should have your lives and practice, then how comes it to pass that you don't live to him? How comes it to pass that you never did one act out of sincere respect to his glory in your life? It must be because you but desire the glory of Christ. If you desired Christ's glory, you could seek it and act for it. But if you don't desire the glory of Christ, 'tis impossible that you should be willing wholly to devote yourself to it. How can a man devote himself to that which he doesn't desire?

These things may convince sinners that they are not willing that Christ should be theirs and they his. But here I foresee another objection—that if it be that we be not willing to receive Christ, yet we but make ourselves willing. But I will give an answer to this objection by laying down two solutions that I think are most self-evident.

1. 'Tis no excuse that persons can't receive Christ of themselves unless they would do it if they could. This is exceedingly evident and I think needs no proof. It is the same thing as to the blame that lies upon them whether they can do it or cannot. For let it be which it will, it is the same to them as if they could they would not.

2. If they would do it if they could, it is no excuse to them, unless they would from a good principle. Would-ing is no better than no would-ing at all unless it is a good would-ing from a good principle. He who would receive Christ if he could—unless he would from some good sense of his duty to Christ and love to that duty—what is his would-ing good for?

Reason teaches that that would-ing to receive Christ that carries is in no degree of respect to Christ but only from self-love. It has no moral goodness in it because self-love is not a moral principle, being common alike to both good and bad. And if there be no goodness in such would-ing, then 'tis no better than none. If it be no better than none, then it does not excuse men any more than if there were none.

Having therefore now answered these objections, I may return once again and argue with sinners how justly they may be left to perish forever when they won't comply with the terms of salvation that God has, though they be only to be willing that Christ should be theirs. Here I would mention two things further to manifest it.

1. How can you reasonably expect to have what is Christ's without Christ himself? How can you expect that you shall ever have the benefits of Christ if you won't have Christ himself? That is what wicked men would feign have. They would have some of the benefits of Christ, but they won't have Christ himself. They would have the gift, but they hate the giver. If they could have the benefit separated from the person, they would. They would feign have the benefit, but they have no

love to the person of Christ. But how unreasonable it is to expect that God will honor your wicked disposition in your breast against an infinitely lovely person and separate the benefits of Christ from Christ himself. How just will it be that you should go without Christ if you won't receive Christ himself?

2. How unreasonable to expect that Christ should make the soul of man happy any otherwise than as his own. If men won't so be willing to be Christ's, how can they expect that he should make them happy? If they will give themselves up to him, he promises to beautify and adorn and glorify and fill them with blessedness unspeakable. But if they refuse this, how justly may they be left destitute and miserable to seek help as they can find? If they won't give themselves up to Christ, how may Christ justly let them go seek happiness where they can find it?

Christ knocks at their door and says, "If any man hear my voice, and open the door, I will come in to him, and will sup with him, and he with me" (Rev. 3:20). But if they will not open the door, 'tis unreasonable in them to expect that Christ should sup.

A second use may be exhibited. I may now declare to you from Christ that if your heart yields to this, you shall have an interest in Christ. All your sins shall be pardoned, and God will be your God. Christ will be your Savior, and heaven with all its glory shall be yours. This is all that Christ waits for. He has stood at your door knocking for this. He has made the offers of an interest in him to most of you many hundreds of times.

You who have been in great exercise of mind about the condition of your soul and have gone about with a restless and heavy heart and have been terrified with a sense of God's wrath and a sense of your danger of hell and been ready oftentimes to be different, here has been the stick all this while. You can't find it in you to be heartily willing. If you had, the difficulty would be all over. All your distress and terror would have been needless. You would never have been in the enjoyment of peace and rest.

It may be you have distressed your own mind and have been ready to find fault with God and a notion that it was some great thing that was required, some being hard terms. But I can assure you from the Word it is nothing but this, nothing but that you should be willing.

I would now put it to each one whether or no you find it in your heart to be truly willing to have Christ for your Savior to save you from sin and hell and to be your portion. And whether you find in yourself a real willingness to be Christ's, that he should have the sole possession of your heart, to be his disciple, his servant, and give up yourself to him. To be wholly Christ's, to give your heart to him and your life to him. To be Christ's and his only, and to be his forevermore. If you are of Christ, you feel this within yourself. I do now pronounce unto you in the name of Jesus Christ that Christ is yours. He freely gives himself to you. He gives you his blood to make atonement for your sins and his righteousness to clothe you. He gives you himself with all that he has. Your sins are pardoned, and God is your Father and heaven is your portion.

You may rejoice in Christ as your own Redeemer. You may say, glorying in it as the spouse did in Song of Solomon 2:16: "My beloved is mine, and I am his," and as the psalmist did in Psalm 116:7, "Return unto thy rest, O my soul; for the LORD hath dealt bountifully with thee."

But if not, if you cannot find this in your heart, go away and blame yourself. Condemn yourself, cry out of your own obstinate, perverse heart that has such an enmity to Christ as your own good.

I now offer some motives to enforce this exhortation: motives to the whole of the duty spoken of in the doctrine and motives to influence you to be willing that Christ should be yours and you to be willing to be Christ's. First, consider some motives to the whole of the duty spoken of in the doctrine—to be willing to come to Christ.

That Christ Should Be Ours and We His

1. Consider that Christ has nothing to move him than to woo us and to make suit to us for this but his grace towards us. We can't be profitable to him. If we receive and accept him, what is he the better for being ours? Will he be an outcast because we don't receive him? Is he a poor, needy person who stands in necessity of prayer and relief from us? What will he be profited if we are willing to?

What addition shall we make to him that will be the greater, or more remarkable will be the reason for it? Have we anything to give him to add to his riches? Will he be the happier? Does he stand in need of the love of a worm to make him happy?

If we are willing to be his and bestow ourselves upon him, what a miserable present will it be. What will the King of glory be profited by it? It will be no more than he has a right to already. We shall not add to his propriety by giving ourselves to him. We shall but give no consent to that right that he has already.

No, it was only grace that influenced in this matter. 'Tis only respect to our good that makes the Lord of both worlds thus become our suitor. He knows how miserable we shall be if he is not ours and we his. He knows how happy such a union will be to us and how needful it is—that so great a person should be willing to be ours, that he should offer himself to us in so near and intimate a union. How wonderful that he should be willing to accept us to be his in so honorable a relation to him and that he should thus condescend to come and knock and call and importune and wait upon us and though so many denials from us and be so many affronts and so much ill-usage before he leaves us. How wonderful is this grace. How wonderful that the great King who is God over all blessed forevermore should thus seek to espouse a poor, despicable worm. That he that is the bright light of the highest heaven should thus seek to unite himself to all of earth.

He sees no beauty in sinners to claim his heart that makes him so importunate. It is only his free and infinite grace that pities us in our misery and seeks our happiness. The consideration of the wonderful grace of Christ one would think should move hearts and draw it to a compliance to the notion that he makes to us.

2. Consider that the happiness of men consists in union and friendship with some other being. 'Tis purposed to the creature only to be fully happy in the enjoyment of himself. The creature has not enough in himself to fill his own desires, and the heart seeks some other being to be happy in. Man is a creature who cannot be happy but in union and friendship. If he alone is united to none as his friend, he is desolate. Now when shall we ever have a better offer? When shall we have the offer of a more glorious friendship to be united to a more excellent person than the Son of God? A life of love to Christ and communion with Christ is the most happy life of all. First Peter 1:8 says, "Whom having not seen, ye love."

I proceed to offer some consideration to influence you to be willing that Christ should be yours.

1. I would ask under what more winning character Christ can offer himself to you than as your Savior? He offers himself not only as a deliverer from some small or inconsiderable evil but as a Savior from destruction and from the most dreadful destruction. If the destruction that he affords himself as a Savior from were only some temporal destruction—especially some very painful death, to rescue us out of the hands of some cruel enemy who was going to torture us to death—so gracious an offer might well win our hearts. But the destruction that he offers himself as a Savior from is not any temporal but an eternal destruction that infinitely exceeds all temporal calamities. The enemy whom he offers to save us from is no ordinary sort of enemy or an enemy of an ordinary degree of strength and cruelty. He is the prince of darkness, that old serpent, the devil and Satan.

And Christ does not only offer himself to save us from destruction but to bring us to glory. Not only to save us from death but to bestow eternal life upon us. He offers himself as the mediator of eternal happiness. Now under what more winning character could he offer himself to us than as a Savior and a Redeemer? He offers to save us from such destruction and to bring us to such happiness.

2. In what more winning manner could Christ offer to be our Redeemer than to redeem us by his own blood? When a person not only saves another from destruction but is at a heartbeat of difficulty to save him and lays out himself. This will hinder such a person more than if he saved without any expense or trouble. The person delivered is more obliged to his Savior that he was willing to be at so much trouble and difficulty to help him. But Christ was not only at a great deal of trouble; it cost him his life. Thus he offers himself to us to be our Savior—by his own blood. He gives his blood as the price of our redemption. He gives his own life to save ours. Now how could Christ have offered himself to be our Redeemer in a more condescending manner than this, especially when we consider how much he suffered in his death? How cruel, painful, and dreadful his death was.

3. To influence you to be willing that Christ should be yours, consider that he is the greatest and best portion that ever you have had or ever will have the offer of. Jesus Christ is in Scripture called God's "unspeakable gift" (2 Cor. 9:15). Therefore, when he is offered to you for your portion, it is an unspeakable offer. It is a portion of unspeakable value and excellency. If the qualities of gold will render a lump of lifeless matter so precious in the eyes and esteem of men, how precious may the infinite divine excellencies of Jesus Christ render him in our eyes. With a fine and durable contexture and as beautiful color of gold and pearls render them so highly esteemed and shall not the infinite majesty, wisdom, holiness, grace, and love of Christ Jesus the Son of God render him infinitely more precious to us. How well may he who has those excellencies be accounted a pearl of great price, a stone elect and precious.

In Christ being offered to you, all those divine perfections of his are offered to your enjoyment. And Christ's being offered to you involved full enjoyment of the great and unspeakable love of Christ that is also offered to you. In the offer of this portion, there is offered to you the portion of angels. Yea, it is in a sense true that herein is offered to you the portion of God himself.

For God's happiness, God's infinite delight is in the enjoyment of the person who is offered to you for your portion. And in Christ's being offered to you, all his benefits are offered to you. The forgiveness of sin, the favor of the privileges of children, the conferring of the image of God, communion with God, and eternal life. In Christ's being offered to you, communion with him is offered in his glory and happiness. Christ has a kingdom appointed him of the Father. Therefore, in Christ's being offered to you a kingdom is offered—a spiritual and heavenly kingdom. In Christ's being offered to you, heaven is offered. Christ is in the possession of exceeding glory at the right hand of God. In offering himself, Christ offers you to be partakers with him in that glory (John 17:22–24).

Now I would offer some consideration to influence you to be willing to be Christ's.

1. Why should men think much to give themselves to Christ who has given himself for men? Christ of his own free accord gave himself for man when he saw man in a miserable and lost condition—when he stood in need of Christ and could not do without him. He spared not himself. He freely gave himself for us. Which is the greatest thing—for us to give ourselves to the Son of God or for the Son of God to give himself for us? Consider the great difference in the following things.

Christ is infinitely greater than we are. Consequently, it must be an infinitely greater thing for him to give himself than for us. He is the Creator, and we are the creatures. He is in the form of God and thought it [not robbery to be equal with God]. We are worms of the dust, dwell in houses of clay, and have our friends in the world. His goings forth are of old from everlasting; we are but of yesterday.

He is the Almighty who hath created all things and upholds all things. We are but poor, feeble dust and ashes. How much a greater thing was it for such an one to give himself for us. To leave the bosom of his Father to come down from heaven and give himself in our nature and offer himself for us—a sacrifice for our sins, a victim to divine justice—than for us to give ourselves to him.

Christ is infinitely deserving that we should give ourselves. He gave himself to us when we deserved nothing of him but to be loathed and abhorred of him. This again shows how much a greater thing it was for Christ to give himself for us than it will be for us to give ourselves to him. Christ in himself has excellency enough to merit that we should devote ourselves to him. He deserves all that he expects or requires of us. He deserves all that we have to give. If we had ten thousand times more, he would be worthy of it. But he gave himself for us when we were infinitely unworthy of it. We deserved his loathing and hatred and wrath that he should be our eternal enemy. He gave himself for us when we were altogether hateful and abominable. Should we then think it much to give ourselves to him, who is infinitely above all others worthy?

Christ only wants what is already his. By giving ourselves to him, we only give him what is already his. He gave himself to us who could claim nothing of him. He has a right to us not only because he is worthy on the account of his excellency, but because we are naturally his property. He is our Creator and possessor. We have our being from him, and therefore are bound to give ourselves to him. In so doing, we do but give him his own. We be not required to give ourselves to Christ as adding anything to his propriety but only acknowledging and recognizing that which he has already when we have given up ourselves to Christ. We may say as David did in 1 Chronicles 29:14, "Of thine own have we given thee." But Christ gave himself for us who had no right to him. It was a free gift; Christ was under no obligation to us. Our right was wrath and eternal death. This is the wages of sin. This again shows how much a greater thing it was for Christ to give himself for us than for us to give ourselves to him.

Christ gave himself for us. If we give ourselves to him it will be after Christ had many calls and invitations. We never had so much as asked it of Christ when he came into the world to offer himself a sacrifice for our sins. We were his enemies and deserved no communion with him. He gave himself for us while we were yet enemies. We never had made any motion towards him. But if we give ourselves to Christ, it will be after he has done great things to win us and influence us thereto after he had first laid down his life to win us. And after many calls and invitations and after he had been living with many men and had often knocked at our door and had waited for us, how often would he have gathered us as a hen (Matt. 23:37).

Christ gave himself to us for our infinite profit. If we give ourselves to him, it won't be for his profit but for our own. Christ had no profit of his own in view by giving himself to save us. He doesn't need our salvation, but he did it for us. Seeing therefore that Christ has given himself to us for our profit, will it be any great thing to give ourselves to him for our own profit?

Christ gave himself for us to be made a curse for us and to suffer wrath for us. If we give ourselves to him, it will be only to be made happy by him. He gave himself for us to be made the object of scorn and contempt. If we give ourselves to him, it will be to be exalted to the highest heaven and dignity, to be made kings and priests and to reign with Christ. Christ gave himself for us to be subject to extreme pain and torment. If we give ourselves to him, it will only be that he may fill us with pleasures and joys unspeakable, to drink at the river of pleasures that flows at God's right hand. He gave himself for us to suffer death for us. If we give ourselves to him, it will be to enjoy life forever. He gave himself for us to have his body torn and tormented. If we give ourselves to him, it will be here our Lord is glorified and shining forth as the sun in the Kingdom of his Father. He gave himself for us to have his soul filled with inexpressible anguish, to be made sorrowful even unto death, to bear the wrath of God. If we give ourselves to him, it will be to be blessed with the eternal enjoyment of the love and complacence of God.

He gave himself for us to be delivered into the hands of Satan to be buffeted by him, to suffer a grievous conflict with him. But if we give ourselves to him, it will be to be delivered from Satan and to have the ministry and society of angels. He gave himself to us to descend into the dark and gloomy grave. If we give ourselves to him, it will be to ascend into the heaven of heavens and into the regions of light and joy.

Considering these things, why should you think it much to give yourself to Jesus Christ or to be unwilling to be his? But a motive to influence you to be willing to give yourselves to Christ is that Christ desires no other than to give himself to you in the same bargain. You have no reason to think it a hard thing that Christ asks of you when he stands at your door and knocks and desires you to open the door and admit him and to give yourself to him. He purposes no other than to give himself to you at the same time and in the same covenant. And surely if you gave yourself to Christ and Christ gave himself to you, you but think that there is any loss in the bargain on your side. You give a poor, sinful worm and receive the Lord of heaven and earth, the intimate fountain of glory and blessedness.

2. Consider that you must lose yourself by giving yourself to Christ. You are not to lack respect as though you throw yourself away. But on the contrary, you will find yourself by it. You are lost forever if you don't give yourself to him. You are already lost while you are

separated from Christ as a lost sheep. 'Tis the only way that you can have your own being any advantage to give yourself to Christ. Thereby you will find your true happiness. You will both gain yourself and gain Christ by the bargain. 'Tis not as a bargain that man makes one with another whereby they give one thing in exchange for another. The thing that they give they part with. They part with the benefit of it for the benefit of the thing they exchange it for. But in this transaction with Christ, the thing that you give you gain by giving, and you also gain the thing that you receive. You gain both by the bargain.

3. Consider Christ doesn't ask it of you to give yourself to him but in the most honorable relation. He doesn't ask you to give yourself to him as his slave, to give yourself up to him as a captive, but to give your soul to him as his spouse. To be united to him in the most honorable relation, to dwell with him as a friend and as a partner forever of his honor, glory, and blessedness. Being his may well be made of joy and prosperity to you. "My beloved is mine, and I am his" (Song 2:16).